The Devil's Triangle:
Ben Bickerstaff, Northeast Texans, and the War of Reconstruction

By
James M. Smallwood
Kenneth W. Howell
and
Carol C. Taylor

University of North Texas Press, Denton, Texas

©2007 James M. Smallwood, Kenneth W. Howell, and Carol Taylor

All rights reserved.
Printed in the United States of America.

10 9 8 7 6 5 4 3 2 1

Permissions:
University of North Texas Press
1155 Union Circle #311336
Denton, TX 76203-5017

The paper used in this book meets the minimum requirements of the American National Standard for Permanence of Paper for Printed Library Materials, z39.48.1984. Binding materials have been chosen for durability.

Library of Congress Cataloging-in-Publication Data is available from the Library of Congress

ISBN: 978-1-57441-772-2 (pbk. : alk. paper)
978-1-57441-782-1 (ebook)

The electronic edition of this book was made possible by the support of the Vick Family Foundation.

Originally published by Best of East Texas Publishers, Lufkin, Texas

For
Pete Coley and Billie Coley King
And
The Texas history Mafia:
Chuck, Pat, Donaly, Bill, Henry, Patrick, Frank-David, Linda, Mary Jo, and Harold
And
Everybody else, too

Some people said that Benjamin Bickerstaff was quite handsome despite his short stature. This image of Bickerstaff is an artist (Mike Pinney) rendering of the only known image of Bickerstaff. To learn more about the artist see www.mcpinney.com. Courtesy of Kenneth W. Howell.

Contents

Dedication		3
Preface		7
Acknowledgments		8
Introduction	The Devil Holds High Carnival in Texas	9
Chapter 1	The Makings of a Killer	19
Chapter 2	The World Turned Upside Down	32
Chapter 3	Initiating a Reign of Terror	48
Chapter 4	Living in Pandemonium Itself	60
Chapter 5	Every Loyal Man in the State May Fall, May-July, 1868	72
Chapter 6	The New Rebellion, August, 1868	88
Chapter 7	The Devil be Damned, September, 1868	99
Chapter 8	In a State Worse than War, October-December 1868	112
Chapter 9	Send All of Them to Hell, January-February, 1869	131
Chapter 10	Killing the Bravest Man in the South, March-April, 1869	143
AfterWord		160
End Notes		163
Appendices:		
Appendix 1	Major General George A. Custer's congressional testimony about affairs in Eastern Texas	191
Appendix 2	Mrs. L. E. Potts written testimony about affairs in Northeast Texas	201
Appendix 3	Report on Violence delivered to the Texas Constitutional Convention of 1868-1869	206
Appendix 4	Charles Rand's report on the death of Ben Griffin	215
Appendix 5	General J. J. Reynolds orders to Captain Adna Chaffee	216
Bibliography		217
Index		230

Preface

The "Devil's Triangle" was an area where guerrilla fighters operated in Northeast Texas during Reconstruction, an era that amounted to the continuation of the Civil War. Those guerrillas were legion, but three stand out: Benjamin Bickerstaff, Cullen Montgomery Baker, and Bob Lee--all three being Confederate veterans. During the war, those men lived with violence and destruction, and they brought that violence and destruction to Northeast Texas when they returned home. They refused to accept the judgement of the war. They caused death and chaos wherever they went. While their major interest was plunder, such men wrapped themselves in the Confederate flag, voiced support for the Lost Cause, and gained much support from former Confederates.

In Reconstruction Texas, most Rebels belonged to the Democratic Party, the same party that a majority of them supported before the war. It was the party of slavery. It was the party of the Civil War. In the post-war days, many party leaders informally endorsed the chaotic actions of guerrillas such as Bickerstaff because the party benefitted. Many Democrats realized that such raiders undermined the Reconstruction process and, along with terrorist groups like the Ku Klux Klan, ensured that the Reconstruction process would fail. That failure guaranteed that the ex-Confederates would ultimately control the state.

So, then, this book is about death. This book is about violent men like Bickerstaff from Northeast Texas who made the streets, the towns, the rivers, and the countryside run red with blood as they targeted, robbed, and killed so many other men--and women. Those men helped ensure that ex-Confederates would ultimately control Texas. This is their story. They all lived in the "Devil's Triangle."

James M. Smallwood
Kenneth Wayne Howell
Carol C. Taylor

May 2007

Acknowledgments

The authors incurred many debts in writing this volume. Our friend Archie MacDonald read and critiqued the entire manuscript and made numerous suggestions that improved our work.

Joel D. Kitchens, Reference Librarian of Texas A&M Libraries, provided assistance as we searched for government documents and other primary sources. Nicole English and Lisa Ragsdale, interlibrary loan librarians at the W. Walworth Harrison Public Library in Greenville, Texas--who helped the authors collect a number of primary sources such as newspapers on microfilm and various secondary sources--have our thanks. John Sellers of Sulphur Springs shared his research pertaining to Seaborne Bickerstaff's Masonic membership.

Charles and Pat Spurlin provided help in the form of a morale boost, as always. Chuck read and critiqued various chapters of the manuscript. Both Chuck and Pat researched in Austin at the Texas State Library and the University of Texas Center for American History, looking for Benjamin Bickerstaff and his connections with the various Northeast Texas units of the Ku Klux Klan and other terrorist groups. Donaly Brice (of El Paso fame), a supervising archivist at the Texas State Library, gave valuable assistance in running down the sources that the library has to offer. Others who helped include Bill Stein, of the Nesbitt Library in Columbus, and Henry and Linda Wolff of Victoria. Sharon Barnes and Elizabeth Corte of the Regional History Center of Victoria College/University of Houston at Victoria Library provided much assistance when we researched in the Barry Crouch Papers housed at the Center.

We appreciate our publishers Bob and Doris Bowman, who have included our work in their "Best of East Texas" series. Both Bob and Doris went over the manuscript to ferret out errors. Doris was the hands-on editor who turned our manuscript into a book.

While we had the assistance of all the friends mentioned above, as always, the authors take responsibility for any errors found within this volume.

Introduction:
The Devil Holds High Carnival in Texas

Just before sundown on April 5, 1869, desperadoes Benjamin Bickerstaff and Josiah Thompson, both wanted for murder, roared into sleepy little Alvarado, the oldest town in Johnson County, Texas. Military and civilian authorities in Northeast Texas had driven Bickerstaff and Thompson out of East Texas; whereupon, they transferred operations to Johnson County. As the two men rode into town, they observed merchants closing their shops and saw people quickly darting off the main street, finding shelter behind closed doors and in dark alleys. Believing that their arrival had frightened the locals, the two killers gained a false sense of security. Bickerstaff and Thompson "gave vent to a lusty laugh" and raised their hats to salute the town. According to one source, Bickerstaff boomed out: "Rats to your holes, damn you all!"[1]

After drawing their pistols, Bickerstaff and his companion stopped their horses in front of one of the town's mercantile stores, apparently intent on killing the two owners because they had complained to state and federal authorities that Bickerstaff and Thompson were responsible for the lawlessness in their region, and they requested federal troops be sent to restore law and order to Johnson County.[2]

Intending to foil the renegades' plans, gutsy merchants and other men poured from their hiding places, all well armed. Before the desperadoes could dismount, the townsmen began delivering lead in massive doses. In the general mayhem, they shot Bickerstaff off his horse. Though receiving a shotgun blast to the face, Bickerstaff lifted himself on one elbow and randomly fired his handgun with little effect while swearing that he would never be taken alive. Just then, a ball disabled Bickerstaff's right hand, his shooting hand, so he shifted his sixgun to his left. The change ruined his aim; all his shots went wild. Recognizing the gunman's difficulties, several men rushed him, subdued him, and confiscated his weapons.

Mortally wounded, Bickerstaff noticed the lifeless body of Thompson laying nearby. The townsmen's initial shots had knocked the man out of his saddle, dead before he hit the ground. Amazingly, Bickerstaff clung to life for about two hours, all the while cursing Thompson for dying so quickly and for being no help at all. In a final defiant boast, Ben snarled at the vigilantes, "You have killed as brave a man as there is in the South."[3]

There, on the streets of Alvarado, one of the most notorious of all the Reconstruction desperadoes met his end, but not before he had tormented and murdered countless numbers of Texas' freedpeople and their white Unionist allies. His was a long story that began after the Civil War, a story that pitted former Rebels against native Unionists. The stakes were high and involved the question of who would control Texas after the war.

Earlier, for a brief time, the Unionists had high hopes. After the fall of the Confederacy, most Unionists in Northeast Texas wanted to cooperate with federal authorities and bring positive change to Texas. They believed cooperation was the only way to escape punitive action by the national government, punitive actions that could include treason trials and a lenghy military occupation of the state. On July 17, 1865, a group met in Paris,

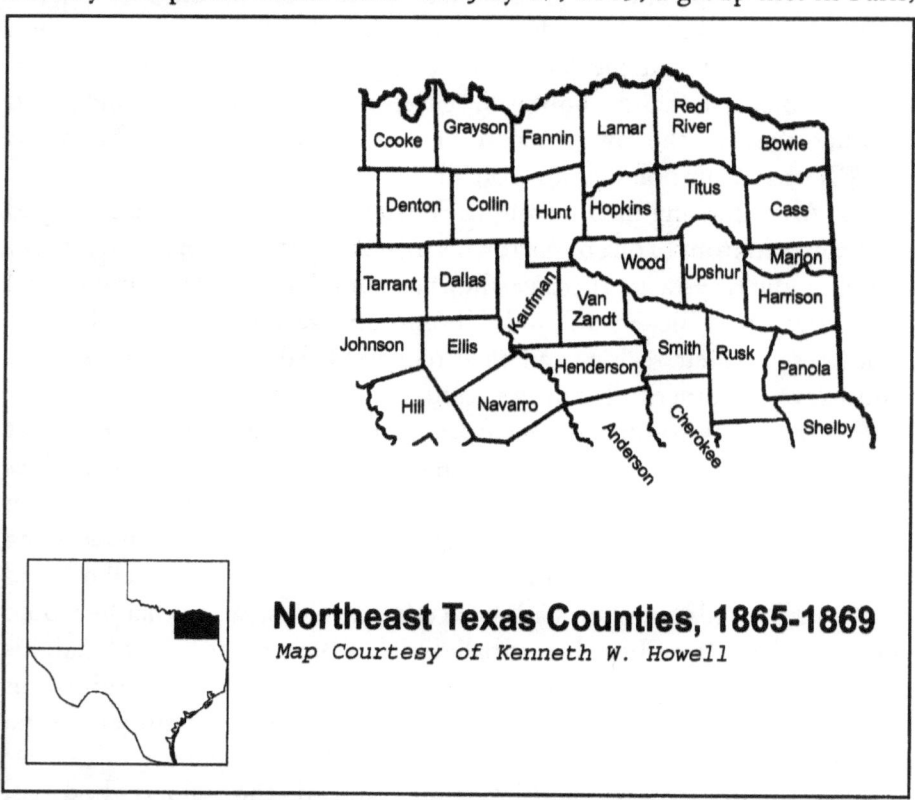

Northeast Texas Counties, 1865-1869
Map Courtesy of Kenneth W. Howell

East-Northeast Texas where violence was endemic during Reconstruction. Courtesy of Kenneth W. Howell

Lamar County, Texas; swore loyalty to the national government; and vowed their willingness to follow the law. Many Northeast counties sent delegates to the meeting. Represented were Lamar, Fannin, Hunt, Titus, Red River, Hopkins, Collin, and Grayson. The delegates elected W. B. Gray of Titus as their president, T. G. Wright of Red River vice president, and E. L. Dohoney of Lamar secretary. Rising to speak, Gray stressed the importance of cooperating with the president and congress. He told the Unionists that such cooperation might obviate the need for coercive congressional legislation. A realist, Gray counseled obedience and submission for the good of Northeast Texas.[4]

Rice Maxey of Lamar County moved that Gray support a Resolutions Committee to draft a document to explain their views and that copies of such a statement be forwarded to the president and congress. Maxey said that the delegates should distribute copies to newspapers and to the public-at-large. Gray made Maxey the chairman of the Resolutions Committee. Other committee members included R. H. Taylor and Sam G. Galbraith of Fannin County; William M. Ewing, L. A. Lollar, and Joseph Smith of Hopkins County; Hardin Hart and M. H. Wright of Hunt County; Henry Jones of Titus County; and W. H. Johnson, G. W. Wright, and E. W. Miner of Lamar County. The document the committee produced accepted military rule until the provisional governor was satisfied that the people had given "evidence of their loyal dispositions to the Government of the United States, and a willingness to yield obedience to the Constitution and laws there of."[5]

That such a Unionist document came out of Northeast Texas was not surprising, for a majority of the citizens of many counties in the region had voted against secession in 1861. During the secessionist drive, there was even talk in Northeast Texas of seceding from Texas and remaining loyal to the Union. But the Unionists' dreams of a peaceful reconciliation with the North proved just that--only dreams.

The plan of those Northeast Unionists was the best hope for an alternate history, one that would have led to a constructive rather than destructive Reconstruction, but forces at work at the end of the war dashed their hopes. During Reconstruction, Texas became a dark and bloody ground, home to both Klan-like terrorist groups and outlaw gangs--both supported by the pro-Confederate Democratic Party so long as the malefactors fought for the goals of the party. Even before the meeting in Paris, Texas had spun out-of-control.

Following General Robert E. Lee's surrender to General Ulysses S. Grant at Appomattox Courthouse in Virginia on April 9, 1865, the local and state governments in Texas collapsed, leaving vast regions of the Lone Star State in total chaos. Armed bands of Southern soldiers, deserters, and common criminals swarmed throughout East-Northeast Texas. In Tyler, Smith County, for example, lawlessness became commonplace at the end of the Civil War. The town had been home to various Confederate installations, including a post commissary, a wartime prison, an armory, a pharmaceutical laboratory, and a quartermaster's warehouse. Women forced their way into the laboratory, taking whatever they wished, and desperate people with hungry families tried but failed to break into the commissary.[6]

Smith County men tried to steal the horses on the post, but the commanding officer held them off. Local Confederates blew up the armory rather than let panicky men, who could not be trusted, secure arms and ammunition. When the smoke cleared, where the armory used to be was a hole in the ground big enough to hold a modern battleship. Many area women were afraid to leave their homes for fear of robbers. Some did so, but most went armed and rode in groups of three or more for collective defense. Worse developments were averted when a company of Union troopers

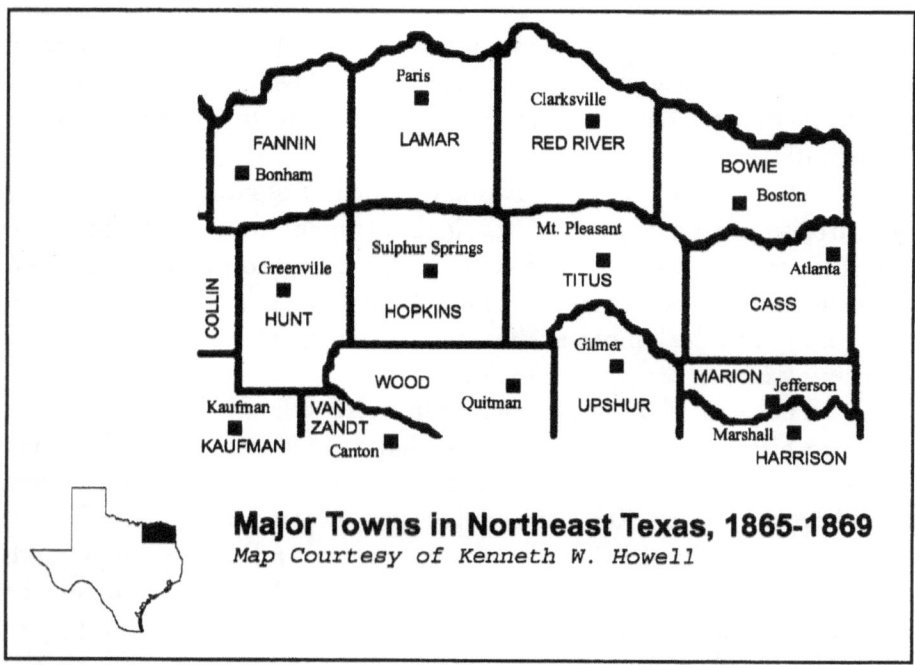

Northeast Texas and its major towns. Courtesy of Kenneth W. Howell.

temporarily stopped in Tyler and helped to reorganize town and county governments.[7] But even as the Federals tried to restore order, Kate Stone, a transplanted Louisiana aristocrat temporarily living in Tyler, reported that there had been "four or five men shot or hanged within a few miles of us [in Tyler] in a week."[8]

On June 11, 1865, unknown parties looted the state treasury in Austin, and officials could neither protect the treasury nor restore order. The robbers made their move in the middle of the night and disappeared before anyone could react. All across East-Northeast Texas mobs of men and women looted Confederate commissaries, stealing anything of value. Men swarmed over supply depots, looting them for arms and ammunition. Some robbed private homes, threatening the owners with death if they resisted.[9] Such violence did not end for years, and it preceded Congressional "Radical" Reconstruction which did not begin until 1867. The early violence remained ongoing even though Confederates still controlled what little government that remained in Texas. This early turmoil had little to do with politics, but future conflicts did center on the political events taking place in the state and nation.[10]

On June 19, 1865, General Gordon Granger landed at Galveston with 1,800 men and was hailed by area Unionists. He intended to take control of Texas and end the lawlessness that the end of the war had spawned. From Wayne County, New York, Granger (1822-1876) was a West Point graduate who fought with distinction in the Mexican-American War. During the Civil War, he fought in such engagements as the Battle of Wilson's Creek and the Battle of Chickamauga, where his important counter-attack saved the day for the Federals.

Granger became the first commander of the Department of Texas during Reconstruction. He applied President Abraham Lincoln's Emancipation Proclamation to the state when he landed at Galveston and announced that the slaves were free (Celebrated as "Juneteenth," the moment of liberation was special to the black community. "Juneteenth" is still celebrated but has outgrown Texas, spreading throughout the South and even into some Northern states).

Next, Granger paroled all men who had served the Confederate Army or Navy and declared all laws passed by the Confederate Legislature void. He had little time to implement policies and directives because he commanded the District of Texas only from June 19 to August 6, 1865, before being transferred. He later commanded the Department of New Mexico from 1871 until his death in 1876.[11]

From the moment he reached Galveston, Granger's command was a difficult one. Since troops at his disposal did not even have the strength of two full regiments, he could only send small detachments into the interior. He stationed them in Tyler, Marshall, Austin, and San Antonio. Like commanders later stationed in the state, Granger never had enough troops to adequately police Texas, a fact that doomed would-be Reconstruction reformers like the Unionists of Northeast Texas. Although Union forces in Texas increased to 51,000 in 1865, in part because of the threat posed by Emperor Maximilian in Mexico, the number of soldiers in the state had fallen drastically by the end of 1866 to a mere 3,000, with most of them serving on the Indian frontier.[12]

Violence, much of it racial in origin, continued unabated and pushed Reconstruction policies along a path bound for failure. By the summer of 1865, whites were beating and killing black Texans by the score. Most of the freedpeople became victims of crimes because of their new status in society. They became victims of irrational racial hatred simply because they were free. In many cases the perpetrators were young men, mostly Confederate veterans. One Union officer called them "half-grown rowdies." They hated Yankees and the outcome of the war. In their frustration they targeted freedpeople and white Unionists, the very groups most unable to defend themselves. One historian listed reasons why Anglos killed freedmen:

> [F]reedman did not remove hat when he passed him [a white man]; Negro would not allow himself to be whipped; freedman would not allow his wife to be whipped by a white man; he [a freedman] was carrying a letter to a Freedmen's Bureau official; [one murderer killed] Negroes just to see them kick; [one white killed] because he wanted to thin out niggers a little; [freedman] did not hand over his money quick enough; [freedman] would not give up his whiskey flask.[13]

More than racial hatred was at work in 1865. By the end of the cotton harvest in late summer of 1865, economic motivation likely explained the rising outbreaks of violence. High prices on cotton led many planters and yeoman farmers to borrow heavily to renew their cotton production. They were too successful.

Surplus developed that drove prices down to approximately 50 percent of peak prices earlier in the summer. Many planters and farmers passed the loss to their sharecroppers. Early Freedmen's Bureau figures suggested that 90 percent of the employers simply refused to pay their workers either in cash or as a percentage of the crops. Many employers drove blacks off their land and claimed that the laborers had "run off" and therefore had broken their labor contracts. Employers who had a tougher time dealing with their workers paid outlaw gangs to get rid of the problem, gangs led by such men as Ben Bickerstaff.[14]

One might wonder why whites felt that they could, with impunity, whip, torture, or kill freedpeople. After all, the South had lost the Civil War. Explanations are not that complex, and one need only look to Presidential Reconstruction to find answers. Near the end of the war, many white Texans--and other white Southerners--wondered why God had deserted them. They became afraid of Northern revenge. Some Southerners, including Texans, who supported the Confederacy, believed they would be punished for treason. Some chose self-exile. They left the country, some going to Mexico; some to Brazil, where slavery was legal until 1888; and some to various European countries.[15]

Their fears and escapes were premature. Under Abraham Lincoln and Andrew Johnson, the national government's policy did not include pursuing charges of treason against former Confederates. The Lincoln and Johnson administrations formulated a most lenient policy toward the Southern people. Lincoln's prescription for renewing the Union was called the "Ten Percent Plan." It required little of the defeated South. Lincoln was willing to restore the Confederate states to the Union when just 10 percent of the number who had voted in the election of 1860 swore allegiance to the United States--that, and the ratification of the Thirteenth Amendment which abolished slavery.

After John Wilkes Booth assassinated Lincoln, the new president, Johnson, also pursued a lenient policy although he had little sympathy for the Southern aristocracy and insisted that they personally petition him for a pardon. Both Lincoln and Johnson decided that race relations were to be best managed at the state level, so the presidential plans included few, if any, safeguards for the new freedpeople.[16]

Former Confederates, including those in leadership positions in Texas, may have interpreted the "lenient" plans of Lincoln and Johnson as weakness. They breathed easier, now. Some believed that they could find a way to restore old Dixie. (See Appendix I). In Texas, some newspaper editors even predicted that it might be possible to save slavery or to bring forth a new institution, one that would enable whites to control black labor. The editors were correct, and the answer was sharecropping. That economic institution entrapped most poor blacks and poor whites in a state of permanent poverty that lasted well into the twentieth century.[17]

By 1866, white Texans had discovered more ways to control the freedpeople. Dominated by former Confederates, the Texas legislature passed "Black Codes" which were similar in nature to the Old South's Slave Codes. The Black Codes gave whites control over most aspects of black life, including labor and civil rights, as well as control of black children. The Codes made it clear that many white Texans had not given up on the Civil War. Violence was another indicator. The former Rebels continued to fight in the new guise of guerrilla warfare where partisans had both a military and a political role.

From 1865 to 1874, seventy-seven Texas counties gave birth to terrorist groups that went by many names--the Ku Klux Klan, the Knights of the White Camellia, the Knights of the Rising Sun, the Red Hand, the Ku Klux Rangers, and so on. The formation of several terrorist groups, particularly in Limestone and Freestone counties, preceded the founding of the historic Ku Klux Klan in Tennessee in 1866. By whatever name, these organizations had the same goals: to enforce the doctrine of white supremacy and to help former Confederates "redeem" Texas through the Democratic Party. Many of the terrorist groups became informal, paramilitary arms of the party.[18]

Outlaw gangs were also legion and did much damage. Some used the Democratic Party and were, in turn, used by it. Many criminal gangs wrapped themselves in the Confederate flag and proclaimed loyalty to the Lost Cause. Former Confederate Democrats tended to look the "other way" as long as such gangs only targeted freedpeople, native Unionists, and Union soldiers. In Northeast Texas alone, gangs coalesced around such desperadoes as Benjamin Bickerstaff, Cullen Montgomery Baker, Bob Lee, Elisha Guest, Ben Griffith, Henry Farrar, John "Pomp" Duty, "Indian Bill" English, George English, John Marshall, Tom Emmitt, and others. Every single one of these men claimed to be fighting for the Lost Cause. The spunky Bob Lee was once heard to say that he would fight the Yankees "from the thickets and canebrakes of Texas for a hundred years if necessary."[19]

Terrorist Klan groups and many--but not all--outlaw bands had common characteristics. The major goal of such groups was to thwart the Reconstruction process because it threatened the *status quo antebellum*. Rampant racism was a major factor because the majority of whites intended that the blacks should have no rights and still show much deference in matters involving whites. Such people were willing to use persuasion, intimidation, and violence when necessary to achieve their goal. They were most willing to kill if that is what it took to defeat the proposed reforms that Reconstruction was meant to bring about. The groups objected greatly to the federal government's decision to abolish slavery. Dixie's brand of bondage--and the strident demand that the national government protect its expansion--was a major cause of the Civil War. Then, the Union defeated Dixie, and slavery was no more.[20]

That Reconstruction in Texas and the wider South was simply war in a new guise came to the attention of a number of people in the Lone Star State. Many Unionist newspaper editors reported on the runaway violence in Texas. After touring East-Northeast Texas in 1869, a correspondent of the *Cincinnati Commercial*, who had a certain gift for hyperbole, wrote:

> You cannot pick up a paper in East Texas without reading of murder, assassinations, and robbery . . . and yet not a fourth part of the truth has been told; not one act in ten is reported. Go where you will, and you will hear of fresh murders and violence . . . The civil authority is powerless—the military insufficient in number, while hell has transferred its capital from Pandemonium to Jefferson, and the devil is holding high carnival in Gilmer, Tyler, Canton, Quitman, Boston, Marshall and other places in Texas.[21]

General Philip Sheridan, who commanded the Fifth Military District from 1866 to 1867, was not as eloquent as the correspondent, but he allegedly muttered that if he owned both hell and Texas, he would rent out Texas and live in hell. Other contemporary observers and later historians have held that Texas was among the most lawless, the most violent of the Southern states during Reconstruction. In 1869, Governor Edmund J. Davis said that all the turmoil amounted to a "slow" Civil War, while District Judge A. B. Norton wrote--referring to widespread violence in Northeast Texas--that if the ongoing violence was not a war, he wondered just what would constitute war. Texas became the murder capital of the United States. For two years in a row, 1868 and 1869, the state led the nation in the number of homicides despite its relatively small population. And it was far ahead of Louisiana, the runner-up.[22]

Professional armies find it difficult to effectively wage a war against terrorists. Professional armies are trained to fight other professional armies and depend on military logic, on strategy and tactics, but guerrillas and terrorists played by no rules of engagement, and their tactics varied with each new situation. Able to strike quickly and then disappear, they frustrated military commanders who were trying to restore order. Similar to the Plains Indians that caused havoc in West Texas, terrorist groups and outlaw gangs in the interior used hit-and-run tactics to defeat Union forces stationed in their region of the state. Even when law enforcers identified criminals, it seemed easy for such people to commit devilry in one locale and then vanish into the state's vast landscape. Even the state's jails factored into the equation. Most were not worth the name "jail" and were most porous. Untold numbers of felons escaped the rickety places.

During their "War of Reconstruction" most settled areas of Texas experienced widespread disturbances, but the Northeast region became the most violent, perhaps because the area had strongholds of Unionist sentiments that many former Confederates would not tolerate. As well, authorities always lacked the manpower needed to deal with the terrorist groups and the various outlaw bands like the one led by Benjamin Bickerstaff. His ruthless activities were an important part of the larger story of violence in the Reconstruction South. His story tells what happened "on the ground" during Reconstruction. Study of his life represents a new "window on the past," one that reveals what happened to real people in the local areas that made up the larger region of East-Northeast Texas.

Although scholars have given some attention to important desparadoes such as Cullen Montgomery Baker and Bob Lee, no in-depth study of Bickerstaff exists.[23] The work presented here seeks to remedy that historical oversight while also putting his murderous career into the larger context of violence throughout the entire Northeast Texas region and generally into the larger context of violence in the Reconstruction South. The authors hope to demonstrate that Reconstruction in Texas has been viewed from a slightly skewed perspective. In 1865, the Civil War did not end; rather, it continued until the "Redeemers" regained control of state government in 1874. The same is true for all the states of the Confederacy, the only difference being the exact dates when the various states were "redeemed."

The South won this second phase of the Civil War. Though Congress established the political and constitutional foundations necessary for reconstructing the Southern states between 1865 and 1877, the real Reconstruction of the South did not occur until the modern Civil Rights movement of circa the 1940s through the 1960s. Even now, the Reconstruction remains incomplete. Bickerstaff did his part to make it so.

1 The Makings of a Killer

Born on or around August 17, 1839, Benjamin "Ben" Bickerstaff was one of three children of Seaborne and Francis Mayfield Bickerstaff, the former born in 1811, the latter in 1812. Ben's older brother, James B. "Black" Bickerstaff, was born while the family lived in Jackson County, Alabama. The Bickerstaffs soon moved to Monroe County, Mississippi, where Ben and his younger sister, Amanda, came along. Seaborne supported his family working as a carpenter and manufacturer, and he spent some time working on small steamers traveling up and down the Tombigbee River. The Bickerstaffs lived in the rural countryside.

The nearest town of any size was Cotton Gin Port, located about seven miles west of the present-day town of Amory. The Bickerstaffs did not stay in Mississippi long. Like many other Southerners of his generation, Seaborne dreamed of going to Texas where land was cheap and economic opportunity seemed limitless. Early in the 1840s, the family packed their possessions in a covered wagon and began the long trek toward their new home in Texas.[1]

The Bickerstaff family became pioneers on the northern frontier of the fledgling republic, an area known as the Red River District, a vague geographic area that encompassed thirty-nine present Texas counties. For a brief period, Seaborne served as captain of an aging river steamer, the *Victress*. The old boat ran freight up and down the Red River between Pine Bluffs and the Great Raft, a massive logjam that backed up the river and made it possible for shallow-draft vessels to operate but prevented the steamers from traveling the river's entire length. While captain of the

Victress, Seaborne undoubtedly met many leading planters and yeoman farmers in the Northeast Texas region. Likely such men convinced Seaborne to leave the river behind and to occupy land that he anticipated expanding into a small plantation.[2]

The Republic of Texas awarded the Bickerstaff family more than 1,500 acres. On part of the land, they established a 320-acre farm on the

The grave of pioneer Seborn Bickerstaff, the father of outlaw Ben Bickerstaff, lies in Gray Rock Cemetery. Courtesy of Bob Bowman.

Cherokee Trail which was located approximately a mile from the town of Gray Rock--now spelled Grayrock--in what became Franklin County in 1875 but was then part of Titus County. Seaborne and Frances built a two-story log cabin complete with a "dog trot" through the middle of the first floor and a kitchen shack attached to the back of the cabin. To supplement his income, Seaborne continued to work as a master carpenter until the mid-1850s when he inherited more land from two older brothers. Throughout the 1840s and 1850s, Seaborne and his family prospered. After acquiring a good reputation in the Gray Rock community, he became a Mason in 1857. As further evidence of his status in Titus County, he was elected as a constable in the late 1850s. By 1860 Seaborne had added a fourteen-year-old female mulatto slave to the household to assist Frances with her domestic chores. A young man also lived with the family and worked at carpentry as Seaborne's apprentice.[3]

The land that the Bickerstaffs settled was bountiful. Organized by the Texas legislature in 1846 and settled mostly by Southern whites and blacks, Titus County, once the home of the Caddo Indians, became part of the cotton culture of the Old South. The area had a growing season that averaged 233 days a year, while the annual average rainfall was forty-six inches. The region was excellent farm country, and the Bickerstaffs made the most of it. They planted cotton, the county's chief cash crop; corn, the major food crop; sweet and Irish potatoes; turnips; squash; tomatoes; onions; and other eatables. Pioneer farmers in Titus County produced 66,000 bushels of corn and 202 bales of cotton in 1850--the numbers rising to 326,385 bushels and 5,129 bales by 1860. Like the Bickerstaffs, most farmers also had chickens for meat and eggs and small herds of livestock. By 1860, county farmers held 13,183 head of beef cattle, 5,278 dairy cows, 7,147 sheep, and 22,075 ever-present pigs--pork being the mainstay of Old Dixie. Seaborne and his sons fished and hunted to bring variety to the dinner table. Like other pioneers, the Bickerstaffs strove for self-sufficiency and solved the problems of existence.[4]

Ben Bickerstaff thus grew up on the family farm. When he was old enough, he participated in all aspects of farm work. Like most young Southern boys of his day, he spent much of his time out-of-doors. He became an excellent horseman and developed proficiency with weapons, skills that later would make him valuable to the Confederacy during the Civil War and the bane of white and black Texas Unionists after that war. Once he matured, Ben Bickerstaff was not a physically imposing man. He had a slight build, standing five feet, six inches tall and weighing approximately 135 pounds. His hair was sandy brown, and his eyes were either gray or blue, depending on the source cited. He had fair skin and a "baby face" that was more refined than rugged. Some people said that he was a handsome man. He often wore suits and bow ties. He had the ability to be a gentleman of good manners who could often manipulate others.[5]

Evidence suggests that he had a formal education, but no records survive to show where or how many years he attended school. Still, as an adult he commanded a large vocabulary, wrote well, and possessed a basic knowledge of mathematics.[6] No one could have guessed that he would become one of the most notorious desperadoes in Reconstruction Texas.

Through the late 1850s to 1861, Seaborne and his sons performed periodic service as members of Titus County's slave patrols in rotation with other men. They visited slave quarters to verify that the chattels obeyed the Slave Codes, especially those that forbade bondsmen to posses liquor or weapons. As tensions mounted between the Northern and Southern states over slavery in the 1850s, the patrols also closely studied the activities of strangers in the county because they might be abolitionists who encouraged slaves to rebel or to flee. By 1860 every supposed crisis in Texas was blamed on the "Northern Conspiracy." There was hushed talk of the "Mystic Red," a supposed abolitionist plot led by ministers of the Methodist Episcopal Church, North, and by John Brown's secret admirers who intended to introduce murder and mayhem into the Lone Star State. White Texans became deathly afraid of potential slave rebellions.[7]

In the summer of 1860 an arson-insurrection panic swept through eastern Texas as well as Tennessee. In Northeast Texas a number of unexplained fires occurred, and many people automatically assumed that abolitionists and cooperating slaves were responsible for setting them. On July 8, apparent acts of arson erupted simultaneously in Dallas, Denton, and Pilot Point, suggesting that a coordinated abolitionist-slave uprising might be in the offing. The next day, a Smith County slave patrol killed a man who was allegedly trying to set fire to downtown Tyler. On July 17, another man tried to torch the same town, but a patrol discovered him. Men in the patrol shot and wounded the man two or three times before he got away. Similar incidents occurred in Black Jack Grove, Hopkins County; Honey Grove, Fannin County; and Milford, Ellis County. Reports of these events led to widespread panic in eastern Texas. Fears escalated with false rumors that fires had erupted in Gainesville, Waxahachie, Jefferson, Belknap, Marshall,

Quitman, Daingerfield, Mt. Vernon, Sulphur Springs, Rusk, and Paris, and throughout most of Kaufman and Navarro counties. These false reports gave citizens the impression that all of East Texas was ablaze.[8]

On August 5, Henderson was seriously damaged when a conflagration swept through the town's business district; that was fact, not rumor. Authorities investigated the incident and estimated damage at $220,000. Those authorities found and hanged one white man, a supposed abolitionist, and a black woman who reportedly helped the man set the fire. Across East-Northeast Texas authorities, or mobs, executed at least thirty-seven whites and approximately eighty blacks.[9]

By the time of the Henderson fire, Titus County authorities had organized more slave patrols, and the Bickerstaff men were almost constantly in the saddle, but in September the arson panic subsided almost as quickly has it had begun. Investigations proved that many of the supposed fires had been only rumors and fires that actually occurred were caused by new phosphorous matches that spontaneously ignited during the hottest summer that the region had ever experienced.

On July 8, the day of the first real blazes, Marshall recorded a temperature of 115 degrees. Nevertheless, many people refused to believe the "scientific" evidence and continued to associate the destruction of towns with northern abolitionists and rebellious slaves. Some people indicted the newly-formed Republican Party which vigorously opposed the expansion of slavery in the western territories of the United States.[10] For the Bickerstaff household in Titus County, the end of the panic meant that the men of the family, like other yeomen farmers in the area, could get back to work.

Ben and his brother became independent yeomen farmers when their father portioned out acreage to them. Titus County tax rolls indicate that by 1859, Seaborne had given 600 acres to Black, whom the rolls also identified as the owner of several beeves and horses. Later, in 1866 Ben appeared on the tax rolls as owner of approximately 600 acres, also having livestock, including cattle and horses. Over the next two years, Ben added more land to his holdings. According to the tax rolls of 1868, he owned a farm of 721 acres. It seems certain that prior to the Civil War, Ben planned to follow his father's example, settling permanently in Titus County and living a quiet, agrarian life. A harsh fate intervened to spoil such a dream.[11]

The routine of the pioneers was interrupted during the 1850s as the question of slavery and its expansion came to dominate the nation's politics. Majorities in the North and South developed different perspectives about the future of the United States, and the presidential election of 1860 was crucial in deciding which section would control the country. Southern Democrats believed that their party had to run on a platform that guaranteed the protection of slavery in all the territories of the United States. At the Democratic National Convention, held in April 1860 in Charleston, South Carolina, pro-slavery Democrats threatened to bolt the convention if the party refused to include a plank endorsing slavery. Such a plank was not forthcoming, and the delegates of seven Lower South states bolted.

Without a quorum, the Democrats were forced to call another convention to convene in Baltimore. Once again, differences over the slavery issue led Southerners to bolt the convention, leaving the party hopelessly divided into Northern and Southern contingents. Southern Democrats later met in their own convention, wrote a platform that was favorable to slavery, and nominated John C. Breckenridge of Kentucky for president. Northern Democrats nominated Senator Stephen A. Douglas of Illinois and wrote a platform based on the idea of "popular sovereignty," a plan that called on the white people living in the territories to decide the fate of slavery in the West. Like most white Southerners, the Bickerstaff men favored Breckenridge.[12]

The Republican Party's chance for electoral victory was greatly enhanced by the sectional divide separating their Democratic opponents. Republicans nominated the gangly Illinois lawyer, Abraham Lincoln, as their presidential candidate. He received his party's nomination because of his moderate position on slavery. Though he stood steadfast against the expansion of slavery in the territories, Lincoln opposed the more radical idea of immediate abolition of the "Peculiar Institution" in the Southern states.

Many Northern voters believed that the Republican candidate's moderate position might prevent a war that increasingly seemed inevitable.[13] Southerners like the Bickerstaffs were otherwise minded. They believed Lincoln was a "Black" Republican who intended to pursue policies that would lead to the emancipation of Southern chattels.

The dynamics of the election took another turn when a fourth candidate emerged. Unionists, primarily from the Upper South, were unsatisfied with the platforms of either the Southern Democrats or Republicans. They formed a political organization that devoted itself to the principles of the Constitution and the Union. Their platform did not directly address divisive issues such as slavery in the territories but instead focused on preserving the Union. Though Texas' Sam Houston was a strong front runner for the party's nominee for president, instead the delegates nominated John Bell of Tennessee.[14]

Since white Southerners comprised the majority, as one would expect, Titus County's voters, the Bickerstaffs included, went with the Southern candidate John C. Breckinridge who promised to protect and to expand slavery. To the dismay of Titus County voters, as well as white Southerners in general, Abraham Lincoln won the election. When Texans learned of the Republican victory, the same irrational fears associated with the mysterious fires earlier in 1860 surfaced again.

Despite Lincoln's proclamation that he opposed the expansion of slavery in the territories but did not intend to interfere with the institution where it already existed, Texans and other Southerners insisted that his election would place slavery on the road to extinction, a view that was probably correct. Leading Southern politicians began to discuss seriously--as they had done many times before--the possibility of seceding from the Union and creating a new republic that would protect their "way of life," a phrase that meant the protection of slavery.[15]

As early as October 1860, when it became apparent that Lincoln would become president, secessionists in Texas began to plan the withdrawal of their state from the Union. When South Carolina seceded from the Union in December 1860 and five more states of the Lower South followed, the secessionists' cause gained strength in Texas. Despite public pressure for that cause, the movement could not move forward without the cooperation of Governor Sam Houston, a Unionist. In Texas, the governor retained the power to call the legislature into special session, and only the legislature had the power to call a convention. Houston refused to call the legislature into special session, hoping that the passion for secession would wane.

Houston opposed secession and told Texans that leaving the Union would lead to war and a Northern victory. Northern industries would shift to a war footing and supply the Union military with everything needed for a prolonged war. The Union Navy would blockade the Southern coasts, would capture New Orleans, and would eventually take control of the entire Mississippi River and divide the South while Union armies would overwhelm the Confederacy by fighting a war of attrition. Finally, "Old Sam" correctly predicted that what Southerners were most anxious to protect--slavery--would not survive a Northern victory.[16]

Houston's political stance inflamed the secessionists in the state, leading Oran M. Roberts, chief justice of the Texas Supreme Court, and other prominent leaders to take extra-legal steps to achieve secession. In early December, they called on Texans to hold elections on January 8, 1861, to select delegates to a secession convention scheduled to convene in Austin on January 28. The public responded to the call by electing representatives to attend the convention.[17]

Hoping to thwart secessionists' plans, Houston called the legislature into special session in mid-January with the hope that it would declare the scheduled meeting illegal and delay the breakaway movement in Texas. Instead, the legislators validated the actions of the secessionists, allowed the convention use of the House chamber, and adjourned. Some of the legislators questioned the legitimacy of the convention and requested that the final decision on dissolving the Union be placed before the people of Texas in a statewide referendum.

Because secessionists blocked Unionists' participation in the local elections held earlier in the month, the majority of those who assembled at the convention supported a break with the Union. On February 1, the delegates voted 166 to 8 to approve an ordinance of secession. Honoring the legislature's request for a referendum, the delegates announced that a vote on withdrawal would be held on February 23.[18]

Voters in Titus County were an exception regarding the selection of their delegate to the convention. They chose Unionist Joshua F. Johnson as one of their county's representatives, thereby showing that they were divided in their opinions. Johnson voted "no" on the secession question and then was one of the Unionists who submitted an "Address to the People of Texas," a document urging voters to stay with the Union and to vote against on the secession referendum.

Johnson then watched helplessly as the men of Titus County voted to leave the Union, 411 to 285. Statewide, voters supported the referendum by a huge majority. The vote undoubtedly pleased the Bickerstaffs. Like the county majority, they were caught up in the fervor of the times and hoped to become members of the slaveholding planter class.[19]

The Bickerstaff men fought for the Confederacy during the Civil War. Ben, Black, and their father were called "red hot Southerners." Some men from Titus County, including Ben and Black, organized the "Gray Rock Dragoons," later known as the Titus County Guards, a unit that joined the First Division of the Texas Militia. Ben was twenty-one years old when he enlisted. The men rode to Camp Reeves in Grayson County for instructions on the rudiments of war. The Confederate Army absorbed their unit, making it part of Company I of the 11th Cavalry Regiment, 8th Cavalry Brigade, on October 2, 1861. Colonel William C. Young of Grayson County, a former state senator, commanded the regiment.[20]

When Colonel Young assumed command of the 11th Cavalry, he had already become a noted defender of the North Texas frontier. In May 1861 he raised a regiment of North Texans and led them across the Red River into Indian Territory. By mid-May, his troops had taken possession of Fort Washita, Fort Arbuckle, and Fort Cobb, fortifications that Federal troops had abandoned at the start of the war. Military strategists believed the forts vital to the defense of North Texas from potential Indian raiders.[21]

Afterwards, Young returned to Sherman, Texas, where he established his headquarters and assumed the duties of major general of the Northern Division of Texas. Later, when rumors surfaced that some tribes were aligning themselves with United States troops, Young raised the 11th Texas Cavalry for service in the territory.[22]

Ben Bickerstaff's company was comprised mostly of men who came from Titus and Bowie counties. Both James and Ben entered the war as privates who earned $12 per month for their service. Eventually, the command promoted Ben to sergeant, his highest rank. His brother became the regimental butcher in July 1863. The Bickerstaffs' first company commander was Captain John P. Hill. A Virginian, Hill settled in Titus County in the 1850s and began practicing law.[23]

As Young's regiment prepared for service, warfare between Confederate forces and a contingent of Native Americans erupted in Indian Territory. The Creek Chief Opothleyahola (usually called "Yahola"), the leader of approximately 7,000 warriors, tried to remain neutral in the early phase of the Civil War. Area Confederates and their Indian allies under the command of Colonel Douglas H. Cooper, however, did not trust Opothleyahola and considered him a Unionist sympathizer.

Pursued by Confederate forces coming out of Texas and Arkansas, the Creeks fought to a stalemate in the Battle of Round Mountain, east of present-day Tulsa. Afterward, Opothleyahola moved his people northeastward for safety. On December 9, 1861, Cooper's men caught the Creeks just northeast of Tulsa near Bird Creek and attacked them again in the Battle of Chusto-talasah (also referred to as the Battle of Caving Banks). Another stalemate resulted, so Opothleyahola directed his people northnorthwest, hoping to reach Kansas Territory, then held by Union troops.[24]

After receiving supplies, Confederates under Colonel James McIntosh, who had assumed command of the troops in the Indian Territory, pursued the Creeks and fought again at the Battle of Chustenahlah on December 26, 1861, on Battle Creek in present North Central Oklahoma near the Kansas line. Before cornering Opothleyhola at Battle Creek, McIntosh ordered cavalry stationed near Van Buren, Arkansas, to march across the frozen landscape to Fort Gibson.

Colonel Young's 11th Cavalry was among those troops ordered to Fort Gibson. From their location in Arkansas, McIntosh led his men toward Opothleyahola's position, traveling up the right bank of the Verdigris River. Young's cavalry, which included the Bickerstaff brothers, joined McIntosh en route. Once they located Opothleyola's warriors at Chutenahlah, the Confederates overwhelmed them. Captain William Gipson of the Second Arkansas Mounted Rifles, gave the following report of the battle:

> ... On the morning of the 26th December, after marching 10 miles, we came in sight of the encampment of the enemy, between whom and our advance guard an animated fire soon ensued. In obedience to your order I took position in the center, Colonels Greer and Stone's regiment on my right and Colonel Young's regiment and Captain Bennett's company on my left. At the command we charged the enemy, who were positioned at a distance of 200 yards in the timber, and firing upon us from the points of the hill and valley between. After our first fire they fell back among the cliffs of rocks. We then dismounted, again attacked them, and again routed them. We followed up the retreat for 3 miles, shooting and cutting the enemy down all along the route.[25]

Opothleyahola's forces were broken, and the survivors straggled along until they did, indeed, reach Kansas.[26] Colonel Young's men pursued their demoralized enemy, but following a few exchanges of gunfire, the men of the 11th Cavalry broke off their attack and moved into Arkansas to establish winter quarters. As a new private facing his first battle, Ben Bickerstaff acquitted himself well. Young reported that he was "proud to say that both officers and men of my regiment behaved throughout the engagement as [brave] soldiers and Texans."[27]

In the spring of 1862, the 11th Cavalry became part of the

Confederate Army under the command of Major General Earl Van Dorn and participated in the Pea Ridge (Arkansas) campaign, a Confederate effort to regain a foothold in Missouri. The Battle of Pea Ridge raged from March 6 to March 8. Van Dorn's 16,000 men faced Union Brigadier General Samuel Curtis's force of 10,250.

After fighting to a stalemate on the first day, Van Dorn tried to flank the enemy that night but failed. His problems worsened when Union men killed two of his brigadiers, Ben McCulloch and McIntosh, and captured a ranking colonel. After having no success on March 7 and 8, with his men running low on ammunition, Van Dorn abandoned the battle, and the Confederacy lost any hope of regaining control of Missouri.[28]

During the Pea Ridge campaign, the Bickerstaff brothers' 11th Cavalry served admirably. Though temporarily dismounted, Young's men engaged the enemy at Bentonville on March 6 and Pea Ridge the following day. In both battles, the 11th Cavalry charged their counterparts, and during the engagement at Pea Ridge, they took part in the capture of a Federal battery heavily defended by a large contingent of infantry and cavalry troops.

After the battle, the 11th Texas remained dismounted while camped at Des Arc, Arkansas, but had the promise of receiving remounts as soon as possible. Because the 11th had proved its mettle in the face of the enemy, the Confederate high command decided to reassign the 11th Texas to a Texas brigade stationed at Cornith, Mississippi.[29]

Confronted with leaving Texas' Northern frontier inadequately defended, many soldiers in the 11th Cavalry left Confederate service and returned home. The Bickerstaff brothers chose to make the trek east of the Mississippi with the remnants of their regiment. Ben Bickerstaff and his comrades fought in more than 150 engagements. In one important campaign, the 11th Texas Cavalry participated in the invasion of Kentucky that began in August 1862.

Marching in September over a mountain route near Loudon, Tennessee, to Richmond, Kentucky, the men of the 11th Texas encountered Federal troops in the Battle of Richmond. The Rebel victory there opened the road to seize the state, but before they could take advantage of their success, the Confederates lost the Battle of Perryville to Union troops, a loss that forced them to retreat into Tennessee.[30]

Next, the 11th fought at the Battle of Murfreesboro (or Stones River) after the Confederate command reorganized the Army. Union

General William Rosecrans's forces had followed the retreating Rebels as they withdrew from Kentucky. Confederates intended to go into winter quarters at Murfreesboro, but the Federals forced them to fight instead. The battle began on December 31, 1862, when the Rebels attacked the right flank of the Union Army.

Initially successful in driving the flank in, the Southern boys pressed on, but the Yankees finally held near the Nashville Pike. When Union reinforcements coming from the left flank arrived, the battle settled into a lull or a stalemate. The 11th Texas lost a number of privates and its colonel, John C. Burks, during the course of the battle. On January 3, Bickerstaff's regiment retired to Murfreesboro.[31]

During the action, a Union bullet wounded Ben Bickerstaff, and the Southern hotspur needed time to mend. Although details remain sketchy about his recovery, he was soon on limited duty as a "Forage Sergeant."[32] That position led Bickerstaff into the life of a war criminal. According to James Patterson--whose father Bernard was in Bickerstaff's company and who later served as a judge in Lamar County--young Ben's actions almost resulted in his father being lynched.

When stationed in the mountains of Eastern Tennessee and Western North Carolina, and supposedly only "foraging," Ben attacked and robbed Southern civilians. He captured people and burned their feet until they told him where they had hidden money or their other valuables. Sometimes he forced people to stand in scalding water, or he hanged his victims until they were strangling and at last gasp admitted where they had stashed their treasures.[33]

At one point, Patterson and "Dock" Matthews were bringing whiskey from a local distillery to their unit when about forty or fifty armed civilians who believed that Patterson was Bickerstaff confronted them. They decided to hang Patterson on the spot for war crimes. Matthews spoke up for Patterson, saying that he was not Bickerstaff, adding that a nearby farmer whose feet Ben had burned had two daughters who had witnessed the act. The young women could prove that Patterson was innocent.

The vigilantes allowed a runner to go for the witnesses. On their arrival and their inspection of Patterson, the daughters cleared him. His account provides evidence of the vicious activities that Bickerstaff engaged in during the war. Furthermore, it illustrates that he had difficulty in remaining loyal to any single cause greater than satisfying his own interests.[34]

Another incident that involved several men of the 11th Texas

Cavalry occurred on October 26, 1863. Following the Battle of Chickamauga, Confederate forces took possession of a Union hospital at Crawfish Springs. General Joseph Wheeler announced to the hospital surgeons and staff that they were prisoners-of-war and subject to Confederate authority. After Wheeler departed, a group of men from the 11th Texas Cavalry arrived at the hospital. They ordered the surgeons into a line. With pistols drawn, they demanded that the prisoners turn over their overcoats, hats, gloves, sashes, and all side-arms. After taking these items, the Confederate soldiers left.

Though no record exists that ties Bickerstaff directly to this incident, it is highly probable that he was involved, especially considering that his job was to commandeer provisions for the men of the 11th Texas. Given his position as a forage sergeant and his reputation for dealing with Southern civilians, it is certain that he was engaged in numerous episodes similar to the one which unfolded at Crawfish Springs.[35]

Ben Bickerstaff continued to rob civilians and to abuse Union troops until a superior officer learned of his actions. The high command demoted Bickerstaff to private and transferred him to a combat company. Confederate commanders had strict rules protecting citizen and prisoners-of-war against the abuse of their soldiers.

The commanders often told civilians that if any Confederate soldier robbed them, the high command would punish the offender. Likely one of Bickerstaff's victims had enough courage to complain to the military authorities about his abusive behavior.[36] But events proved that being demoted was not the worst thing that happened to him during the Civil War.

2 The World Turned Upside Down

Ben Bickerstaff's world turned upside down on January 29, 1864. While he was on duty that day, Federals captured him near Sevierville, Tennessee. They first moved him to Louisville, Kentucky, but in early February, sent him to Rock Island Barracks in Illinois. Bickerstaff arrived there on February 18. According to an unnamed observer, men such as Bickerstaff were treated better at Rock Island than they were in the Confederate Army. "Confederate generals had but little feeling for the welfare of their men. They were only poorly fed, poorly clothed, and overworked."

Continuing, the writer held that it was only as prisoners that they were well fed on "full rations." Adding that out of 15,000 prisoners only eight died of scurvy, the author concluded that, by contrast, in some Southern military prisons men were starved to death and that Southern commanders had a "want of common humanity."[1]

Others had different views. Like Bickerstaff, J. F. Norman of Sulphur Springs and J. F. Smith of Como, Texas, were imprisoned in Rock Island Barracks. They had experiences there that diverged greatly from the previous observer's report. Captured during the Battle of Missionary Ridge, Norman remembered that the prisoners with him were poorly clad for the winter weather in Illinois, adding that one of the guards even froze to death on Christmas Day.

After mentioning that the prisoners received no food on that day, Norman said that the captives piled all their bedding together and got under the pile to stay warm. He reported that the men suffered through epidemics of smallpox and measles and that "bone scurvy" and pneumonia plagued the inmates.[2]

Also captured at Missionary Ridge, Smith bitterly remembered that prisoners at Rock Island suffered about every disease known to man and that approximately 2,000 prisoners died there. Historians Bob and Doris Bowman added that, of all the afflictions, the most deadly diseases were smallpox, dysentery, and pneumonia. The Bowmans pointed out that four months after Bickerstaff's arrival, the Federals reduced prisoner rations in retaliation for how Confederates treated Union prisoners in the notorious prison-of-war camp in Andersonville, Georgia. The reduction in rations undoubtedly contributed to the failing health of many of the detainees.[3]

Dr. A. M. Clark, surgeon and acting medical inspector of Union prisoners-of-war camps, issued a report in 1863 that apparently corroborated Norman and Smith's accounts. Clark stated that out of 7,260 prisoners, 1,555 were ill. Of those who were sick, 420 suffered from smallpox but had been quarantined. Clark thought that it would "be but a short time before the smallpox will be brought completely under control."[4]

Captain C. A. Reynolds, assistant quartermaster at Rock Island, added that "the water-works and sinks at Rock Island prison barracks [were] found by experience to be inadequate. Heretofore no provision has been made for sewerage or systematic drainage." But, like Clark, Reynolds was optimistic that the problem would soon be solved.[5] No evidence exists that Federal authorities addressed these issues. Given the harsh conditions of the camps, Bickerstaff must have come away from Rock Island with a deeper hatred of the Yankees.

Another incident likely affected the way that Bickerstaff felt toward Union troops in general and African American soldiers in particular. On October 24, 1864, Private Peter Cowherd, Company C, 108th Regiment, U.S. Colored Infantry shot and killed John P. McClanahan, a Confederate prisoner, as he tried to escape. Earlier, guards had dug a ditch surrounding the prison with a line of stakes placed inside the ditch. This ditch, also known as the dead-line, was just inside the walls of the compound.

According to Captain Matthew H. Kollock of the 108th U.S. Colored Infantry, he instructed his men to give warning to any prisoner who approached the row of stakes. If prisoners deliberately passed beyond the ditch toward the outer fence of the compound, Kollock order his men to shoot them with intent to kill. Testifying before a commission that Post Adjunct Lieutenant A. F. Higgs convened to investigate the incident, Private Cowherd stated that he had followed orders.

The private recalled that "When I first saw him [McClanahan] he was lying right by the end of the coal house. Then I went to the far end of my beat and turned round and missed him then, and I looked back and I saw him slipping across the ditch." Cowherd continued, "When I got close enough to the man to be certain, I slipped off my shoes and crept right up over him and stepped right up on the rail and fired at him while he was scratching under the fence."[6]

While the commission found that Private Cowherd acted in accordance with the spirit of the instructions he received while on guard duty and therefore acquitted him in the shooting, Bickerstaff, along with other Confederate prisoners, viewed the private's action as cold-blooded murder, an act that apparently Federal Army officers had condoned.[7]

Additionally, soldiers of the 108th Colored Infantry reportedly stole money from Confederate soldiers. According to Brevet Brigadier General W. Hoffman, "Money sent to prisoners has perhaps been too often kept from them by the dishonesty of those who had [been charged with the duty of] examining their letters."[8] Hoffman added that "Captain Matthew H. Kollock, of the 108th Colored Troops, reported as deserted from the naval service, is unfit to hold a commission in the army."[9]

It seems certain that Bickerstaff's experiences in prison tainted his view of the Federal military, especially African Americans troops, and shaped the man that he would become in the post-war years.

Early in 1865, Bickerstaff's guards scheduled a transfer for him to Point Lookout in Maryland for a prisoner exchange, but he escaped before the transfer took place. There is no parole record and no oath in his Confederate Military Service Record. He did not return to the Confederate Army after escaping. He simply started his trip home, traveling through Missouri, Arkansas, and Louisiana. But in Arkansas--or in territory that the Union held in Louisiana--he had an altercation with an unarmed black man and murdered him. Titus County lore places the murder in the vicinity of Shreveport.

Some sources believe that the unnamed ex-slave may have worked for the Union's military authorities. If Bickerstaff learned of the freedman's position, he had enough motive for a murder because he had developed an irrational hatred for black people. Some brief traditional pro-Confederate sources blamed the black man for "puttin' on airs," but they offered no proof of their assertion. This may have been the first black civilian that Bickerstaff murdered in cold blood.[10]

Most likely, the man was exerting his new rights of freedom, and Bickerstaff could not tolerate it. Witnesses implicated Ben in the killing. Knowing that the authorities would soon be after him, he went into hiding, moving frequently to stay one step ahead of the law.[11] He fell in with fellow Northeast Texan Cullen Montgomery Baker, a young man who later achieved notoriety as a Texas gunman and guerrilla leader, and Ben Griffith, who was a murderer and a spectacular horse thief.[12] How Bickerstaff met them remains a mystery. It is likely that they simply banded together and spent time at a secluded hiding place since all three were wanted men.

When he was still a teenager, Cullen Baker became a murderer and robber who roamed both Northeast Texas and Southwestern Arkansas. Born in June 1835 in Weakly County, Tennessee, the son of John and Elizabeth Baker, he moved with his family to Texas in 1839 and settled in Cass County, where John Baker received 640 acres from the Texas Congress. Adjacent to Titus County where the Bickerstaffs settled, Cass was much like Titus. It was excellent farm country, with about 30 percent of its land suitable for general agriculture.

Like the settlers in Titus, a majority of those who migrated to Cass County were Southerners who developed farms and small plantations in a slavery-driven economy. In 1847 slaves accounted for 31 percent of the population (943 of 2,949). By 1860 bondsmen represented 41 percent (3,475 of 8411).[13]

John Baker became a moderately successful farmer, but his son had little interest in work of any kind. Although he attended school, Cullen learned very little beyond reading, writing, and elementary arithmetic. He became a bully who caused trouble for his teachers and his classmates. On one occasion, he tried to kill another student. In his teenage years, Cullen quit school altogether, preferring to spend his time in saloons, drinking his life away. He tried to change after he married Mary Jane Petty on January 11, 1854, but before the year was out, he had killed his first man, a farmer who had testified in court against him in an assault case. With that murder, Baker made the transition from schoolyard bully to dangerous felon.

The young hotspur, now living life on the dodge, spent much time hiding out on his uncle Thomas Young's farm in Perry County, Arkansas. By the time his wife died on July 2, 1860, Baker had reverted to his old habits of drinking and bullying, and he had killed his second man.[14]

When the Civil War began, Baker decided to join the Confederate Army but would not accept military disciple. He soon became a deserter. Then, inexpiably, he joined the 15th Texas Cavalry on February 22, 1862, at Linden, Arkansas. This time, Baker soldiered longer but became ill in August 1862, and the command released him due to "disability."[15]

Much like Bickerstaff and Baker, Griffith had a misspent Civil War career. Born on July 2, 1840, in Lauderdale County, Mississippi, Benjamin Griffin, was the son of the Jacksonian Democrat Samuel Acass Griffith and Barbara Riddlesperger Griffith. Benjamin was the fourth of seven children. Having a farm family and being part of the planter class, the Griffiths remained in Mississippi until 1858 when they moved to Arkansas. They settled in Sebastian County, located southeast of Fort Smith. By 1860 the family owned 2,000 acres of land and twenty-nine slaves.[16]

When the Civil War came, twenty-one-year-old Ben followed his older brother James. Both enrolled as ninety-day volunteers in the Third Arkansas State Militia, which saw its first action on August 10, 1861, at the Battle of Wilson's Creek. Wounded in the fight, Ben was carried to safety by a family slave who had accompanied the brothers to war. After recovering, Ben Griffith and his brother joined the 17th Arkansas Volunteer Infantry. The unit saw its first action at the Battle of Pea Ridge.

Ben Bickerstaff participated in the same battle. It is possible that the two men met there. Later transferred east of the Mississippi, Griffith's unit saw action at the battles of Iuka and Corinth. Afterward, the command transferred Griffith from one unit to another until he deserted in 1863 and made his way to Arkansas. At some point, he joined Cullen Baker's guerrillas, the same group that Bickerstaff joined almost two years later.[17]

According to various sources, Baker recruited Griffith, Bickerstaff, and other men like them for a pro-Confederate irregular force in Arkansas variously known as the "Frontier Rangers," "Independent Rangers," or "Southern Rangers," a group of deserters who became little more than thieves and murderers. They did oppose a group called the "Mountain Boomers," another irregular group of Union sympathizers.

As the war approached its end, Baker, Bickerstaff, Griffith and their men caught nine Unionists trying to leave the state and murdered them in the "Massacre of the Saline." The guerrillas next burned the homes of six Unionists and murdered six more men in Saline County. They robbed the homes before they torched them, loaded their booty onto wagons, and drove them toward Texas where the wagons and the goods disappeared into the northeastern part of the state.[18]

Baker, Bickerstaff, Griffith, and their band also preyed upon pro-Confederate families, doing anything they could to add to their collective wealth. Later, many former Rebels in Texas saw Bickerstaff, Griffith, and Baker as defenders of the Lost Cause who championed everything good about dear old Dixie, including slavery. Their actions in Arkansas contradicted that image because they attacked loyal Confederate families. They even levied tribute on Confederate sympathizers in Perry County, Arkansas, forcing them to pay protection money to remain secure in their lives and property. In time, Bickerstaff attracted a following independent of, but working closely with, Baker and Griffith, and their men.[19]

As the war reached its end, the renegades increased their activities to add to their wealth. They raided Federal scouting patrols and commissary trains and stormed into Louisiana to attack the Federal post at Natchitoches in addition to exacting their usual tribute from civilians. In the spring of 1865, Baker, Bickerstaff, Griffith, and their combined forces, again in southern Arkansas, massacred another group of pro-Union irregulars, some members of the aforementioned "Mountain Boomers." Some of the "Boomers" surrendered, at which time the "Frontier Rangers" disarmed and secured them. Baker, Bickerstaff, Griffith, and their men then butchered them and left their cadavers to rot. Afterward, the Baker-Bickerstaff-Griffith raids increased in frequency. According to hapless civilians, the marauders robbed, murdered, and committed other "dark crimes." The civilians were "terror-stricken." They appealed to the state for protection, but such appeals were in vain.[20]

Finally, the civilians in Southern Arkansas had enough of the Baker-Bickerstaff-Griffith atrocities and formed vigilante committees to target the desperadoes for destruction. Learning of these developments, the guerrillas staged one last giant raid. They murdered several men, burned various homes, and sent terrified women and children fleeing for their lives while trying to find temporary safety by hiding deep in the woods. All the while, the raiders continued collecting more booty, so much in fact that the treasures filled several wagons. Learning that elements of the vigilant committees and the Arkansas Militia were closing in, Baker, Bickerstaff, and Griffith pointed their horses and wagons toward the Texas line and scampered away.

Some sources claim that Ben Bickerstaff murdered two more black men because they blocked the way west to Titus County. The Arkansans pursued the renegades, who had to abandon much of their booty and scatter. Baker headed for the Sulphur River bottoms, his permanent haunt. While a few of his men stayed with Baker for a short time, Bickerstaff and his personal following rode on to Titus County.[21]

Of the troublesome trio, Griffith apparently had the hardest time. Separated from Baker and Bickerstaff, he escaped Arkansas by riding south into Louisiana where a Federal force captured him. Not knowing of his guerrilla background, Union commanders paroled him just as they did thousands of Southern soldiers at war's end. Before going home, Griffith had an altercation with a freedmen and murdered him. Then, he joined his family in Richmond, Arkansas, and quickly got into trouble again. In front of five witnesses, in broad daylight, he murdered the freedman William Cass, who also lived near Richmond. Cass was in the employ of Hardin R. Runnels, a former governor of Texas, who had championed secession in the Lone Star State.

Apparently, Runnels had become angry with Cass and paid Griffith to kill him. On the run from area lawmen after the killing, Griffith soon robbed three blacks of their weapons and assaulted another freedman, Samuel Willis. Thereafter, Ben Griffith was a wanted man and lived the rest of his life on the dodge. But he was a hard man to catch. He had no fixed home. Instead, he moved frequently and found river bottoms or thickets in which to hide. Even so, in the autumn of 1866, Griffith feared that the authorities in Arkansas were closing in, so he crossed into Texas and apparently first sought sanctuary with Cullen Baker. Griffith rode with Baker or Bickerstaff for the rest of his life.[22]

Bickerstaff's experience was different. When he returned home, he enjoyed a happy reunion with his parents, brother Black, and sister Amanda. Black had returned from the war unharmed and healthy although, like Ben, he had spent time as a prisoner-of-war. While talking with his family and with others in Titus County, most of whom were former Confederates, Ben Bickerstaff's ego led him to concoct a tale about his heroic deeds and about Federals who had persecuted him.

But even while enjoying the safety of home, among family and friends, he could not stay out of trouble. In the fall of 1865, he robbed and murdered a number of freedmen who lived in the Gray Rock vicinity. He did not need complex motives because, in his hatred, he refused to acknowledge the ex-slaves' freedom.[23]

Bickerstaff's actions were not unique in Northeast Texas. In March 1865, prior to the arrival of Union troops in Texas, the *Galveston Daily News* reported that the town of Clarksville in Red River County was "infested by roving bands of guerillas, who [were] plundering the country and people."[24]

These problems undoubtedly continued to exist because General Gordon Granger addressed them in his General Orders No. 3 and General Orders No. 4, issued on June 19, 1865. Granger had arrived earlier that day as commander of the first wave of Union troops to ensure that Texans abided by the Emancipation Proclamation and that Confederate forces in the state surrendered according to the terms that Lieutenant General Edmund Kirby Smith, commander of the Confederate Trans-Mississippi Department, had accepted on June 2.

In addition to proclaiming that Lincoln's Emancipation Proclamation would be enforced, Granger stated that "all lawless persons committing acts of violence, such as baditti, guerillas, jayhawkers, horse-thieves, & c., are hereby declared outlaws and enemies of the human race."[25]

Granger's orders had little impact in the Northeastern counties of Texas because increased criminal activities in Texas had become commonplace. Less than a month after the arrival of Granger's forces, the editor of the *Galveston Daily News* wrote that "every county exchange that comes to hand is teeming with accounts of robberies and murders, and lately wholesale arson has been added to the list."

The editor continued, "Men of all grades seem to have entered on the career of crime and doubtless find it profitable since they commit their deeds with impunity."[26] In this atmosphere of lawlessness, Bickerstaff found the life of crime too alluring to resist. He initiated his own criminal sprees that haunted the freedpeople and their white allies in the North Texas region for the next four years.

Bickerstaff recruited an ever-larger band of men, the total eventually amounting to thirty or forty gunmen, including Bill and D. Grissom; Elisha Guest; Charley, Ralph, and Horatio Weaver; Charley Farrow (or Farrar); and Lum Houston. Even the young John Wesley Hardin rode with Bickerstaff at times just as he rode with other Northeast Texas brigands. Like Hardin, all were young men who vowed to oppose the Reconstruction process and to continue fighting the Federals, native white Unionists, and freedpeople.

Guest was typical of such men. Only twenty-four years old in 1865, he stood six feet tall, sported steel blue eyes, had a fair complexion, and weighed approximately 170 pounds. Like other raiders, he committed sundry crimes, mostly plundering to enriching himself. Also like the others, he wrapped himself in the Confederate flag and claimed to represent the Lost Cause to gain supporters. For a time, local authorities--Confederates all--and ordinary citizens closed their eyes to the crimes of Guest, Bickerstaff, and their kind. Indeed, just before the war ended, Confederates placed men with unquestionable loyalty in all local and county offices in East-Northeast Texas.[27]

For example, Confederate Captain J. B. Anderson was installed as sheriff of Fannin County in January 1865. Anderson had served in James Bourland's Border Brigade, a unit that participated in the "Great Hangings" in Gainesville, Cooke County, in 1862, wherein Confederate authorities lynched more than forty accused Unionists who spoke out against conscription. After only a few months in office, Sheriff Anderson murdered several of his prisoners for the "crime" of Unionism or for desertion. The sheriff argued that he killed them only when they tried to escape. Conversely, Anderson failed to act when former Confederates committed heinous crimes.

One case in point involved Fannin County's Bob Lee, a former soldier who returned home, organized a guerrilla band, and began his own War of Reconstruction. He was so effective that people began to call him the "Man Eater." The moniker was apt, for shortly before his death in 1869, he bragged that he had killed forty men--white Unionists and freedmen--since

John Wesley Hardin frequently rode with Bickerstaff, Cullen Baker, and Bob Lee. He abandoned Northeast Texas and headed south only after the last of the guerrilla trio was killed. Courtesy of Bill O'Neal from his personal collection.

he had returned from the war.[28]

Lee was much like Bickerstaff, Baker, and Guest in that he became an efficient killer. Born in Arkansas in 1835, Bob Jehu Lee was the son of farmers Daniel and Polly Davis Lee. He was the oldest of three children born of their union. Shortly after Lee's birth, Daniel moved the family to Northeast Texas and established a new farm in Hunt County, where Bob and his siblings grew to maturity. As an adult, Lee established his own farm adjacent to his father's holdings.

In the census of 1860, he listed himself as a farmer, age twenty-five

Wildcat Thicket became the permanent headquarters of Bob Lee and his raiders. Whenever Bickerstaff and Cullen Baker were in Lee Country, they were safe at Lee's hideout. Courtesy of Carol C. Taylor

and the husband of Melinda, also twenty-five years old and a native of Arkansas. They had three children, the youngest being only one month old when the census taker recorded the information.[29] Bob Lee was not an imposing man. He stood five feet-eight inches and had dark hair and dark eyes. His complection was sallow, and he was clean shaven except for a thin moustache.[30]

When the war came, Bob and his brother William joined a unit that eventually became Company C, 9th Texas Cavalry, that saw its first action in 1862 at the Battle of Chustenahlah in Indian Territory. Next came the Battle of Pea Ridge, Arkansas. Since Ben Bickerstaff's company fought in the same battle, it is possible that they met either before or after the fight. Eventually transferred east of the Mississippi River, Lee's unit fought at various sites, including the Battle of Iuka and the disastrous battles of Franklin and Nashville where the Union destroyed General John Bell Hood's Army of Tennessee.

Sources paint a dark picture of Bob Lee's Civil War service. According to one contemporary account, Lee was guilty of war crimes. When Yankees fell into Lee's hands, he apparently robbed and killed them. He must have made profits, for he returned home with an abundance of gold coins, much more than he could have saved as a sergeant, his highest rank.[31]

Stationed in Memphis when the war's end was near, Lee deserted his unit and returned home. He embellished his war record, presenting himself as a "captain" and a war hero. In addition to his other war crimes, Lee kidnaped an underage black boy and enslaved him. He forced the lad to return to Texas with him and put him to work on his farm and that of his father. He refused to free the boy pursuant to General Granger's Galveston proclamation. The slave was still working for Bob Lee as late as July 1866.

The Lee family also contracted with some of the new freedmen to work their land. But after the blacks had harvested crops, the Lees refused to give the blacks their rightful shares of the bounty. Bob Lee then threatened the laborers with death unless they continued to work the land for the family's benefit.

Freedmen's Bureau Agent Hardin Hart, a noted Unionist and later a district judge, supervised the Freedmen Bureau's work in Hunt County. He learned of the Lee family's labor practices and of the young boy who had been enslaved. He led a detachment of the 26th Infantry to the Lee farms, intending to secure the release of all the blacks and to give the freedmen financial justice. Bob Lee refused to cooperate, grabbed his guns, and chose to fight. Outnumbered, he took flight to avoid arrest.

Forever after, he was a fugitive from justice, forced to live life on the run. Lee's biggest problem and one that eventually led to his death, was that he refused to acknowledge that slavery had ended. Like Bickerstaff, Baker, and their followers, he possessed a passionate, irrational hatred of blacks.[32]

The gunfight Lee had with Hart and the Federal troops was not the first occasion that he had captured great attention. In late 1865 Lee and some of his men were in a Bonham, Fannin County, drinking their day away. They became irate when they learned that a local Unionist had raised the United States flag from a downtown pole. They rushed out of the saloon

Bickerstaff's main headquarters was in this thicket in the White Oak Creek bottoms of Hopkins County. Courtesy of Carol C. Taylor

to avenge the insult. Bob Lee personally pulled the banner down and ripped it to shreds.

Even if lawmen had wanted to arrest Lee--which they did not--it would have been impossible because the Lee men on the scene outnumbered local law officers. In the following days, Lee and his band raided the countryside in Fannin County, killing or wounding several freedmen.[33]

Eventually, the forces of law and order determined that desperadoes like Bob Lee and Ben Bickerstaff threatened to destabilize the Northeast Texas region. As for Lee, he was forced into hiding at his "headquarters" in Wildcat Thicket near present-day Leonard in Southwest Fannin County from whence he emerged anytime he had informants tell him the movements of the authorities.[34]

Lee embellished his Confederate service record, he committed war crimes, and he definitely committed felonies soon after he returned home, but Lee was daring and charismatic. He had a lot of sand. Hailed as a leader who showed grit, determination, and courage, he quickly gathered a gang. Many young men gladly followed him to continue the fight to Yankees, beleaguered white Unionists, and the unfortunate and often defenseless freedpeople.[35]

Like Lee, Bickerstaff was forced to go into hiding. Ben and some of his men moved from Titus County into Hopkins County and established a camp in a thicket in the tangled bottoms of White Oak Creek, approximately four miles northwest of Sulphur Springs.[36]

But to elude arrest, he remained on the move, spending time in several of the area's thickets because they made good hiding places. All such places were similar, and all were contained in an approximate sixty-mile square of the Sulphur Forks watershed. The thickets represented Mother Nature gone wild. Each had a solid thick mass of trees, bushes, saplings, briar patches, thorn vines, brambles, and other plant growth. Such vegetation were almost impossible to penetrate and impossible even to see through.

The largest, Jernigan's Thicket, covered portions of Hopkins, Lamar, Fannin, and Hunt counties. Its length a little longer than its width, it was approximately ten-miles square. Visitors needed a large knife to cut through the tangled vegetation should they be foolish enough to enter it. It was named for Curtis Jernigan, whose family founded Commerce. In 1843

Jernigan shot and wounded a deer that scampered into the thicket and disappeared into the maze. Unwisely, Jernigan followed the deer, became lost, and wandered around in the mass for four days before he found a way out.[37]

Other area thickets included Wildcat, located northwest of Leonard; Black Jack Grove, near Cumby; Mustang Thicket, just south of Leonard; and Black Cat Thicket, northeast of Greenville. Also in the area were the Big Thicket and Choctaw Bottoms. Smaller masses were Tidwell Thicket, located north of Greenville; Hobbs Thicket, near Enloe; and Big Creek Thicket, north of Cooper. Alfred Howell testified about such places. He wandered around the perimeter of Black Cat Thicket in 1854. He later told his brother that if a person got lost in that mistake of Mother Nature, the person might never get out. He added that the maze was the home of wildcats, wolves, bears, and panthers. All of the masses--from the first mentioned to the last--were in the region where the gangs of Bob Lee, Ben Bickerstaff, and Elisha Guest roamed.[38]

Bickerstaff and his men likely murdered at least one resident of the Sulphur River bottoms. A Southern native, born in Limestone County in North Alabama, Matthew William Denning came to Texas with his family in 1857. A veteran of the Cherokee removals in the late 1830s, he chose to settle in the southwestern quadrant of Lamar County where he paid taxes until 1861 when he received a Red River Script Patent of 160 acres located two miles north of Pope's Bridge on White Oak Creek in Titus County, now Franklin County.

Denning chose the out-of-the-way place in the bottoms because he was a staunch Unionist and wanted pro-war Democrats to leave him alone. He refused to attend Confederate musters in either Lamar County or later, in Titus County. While he wanted isolation, he was brave enough to oppose the ex-Rebels after the war. Denning's Unionism brought him to Bickerstaff's attention. The renegade often hid in the bottoms not far from Denning's place. When Denning died in 1867 under suspicious circumstances, many people believed that it was likely that Bickerstaff had killed him.[39]

Many people also believed that Bickerstaff's brother Black had joined his band and could have participated in Denning's murder, but no hard evidence surfaced that actually tied him to his brother's wayward band.

Rather, Black built and ran a sawmill. Such work kept him busy. But, he apparently became a troublemaker. Some sources claim that Black often drank to excess every time he came to Mount Pleasant, Mount Vernon, or any other area town. He usually caused trouble with a black whip that he always bandied about. He seemed to enjoy picking fights and then whipping his opponent.

Black did not join his brother's band, but he was able to furnish all matter of intelligence to Ben Bickerstaff and his men and to provide them with safe harbor in his home. Even if Black did not join his brother, others did. Ben acquired a permanent following of guerrillas on whom he could always depend.[40] According to historian June Tuck, Ben Bickerstaff quickly established a reputation as a man who should not be provoked, for he would shoot and kill "at the least provocation."[41]

In the fall of 1865, Cullen Baker, now called the "Swamp Fox of the Sulphur," and his guerrillas rode into Titus County and joined Bickerstaff and his band of raiders. Baker's band included Matthew Kirby, Lee and Seth Rames, Jack English, George W. Barron, and others. It was only natural that Ben Griffith, Bob Lee, and their followers also rode with Bickerstaff and Baker on occasion. These men became a band of brothers in a loosely constructed army pledged to initiate what amounted to a Second Civil War in Northeast Texas.[42]

3 Initiating a Reign of Terror

While desperadoes such as Bickerstaff, Baker, and Lee continued their criminal careers, events taking place in Washington, D.C., and in Austin proved beneficial to the renegade bands in the northeast counties of Texas. As mentioned, President Abraham Lincoln had initiated the Reconstruction process in 1863 with his Emancipation Proclamation and his "Ten Percent Plan," which stated that a general amnesty would be granted to ex-Confederates who took an oath of allegiance to the United States; that high-ranking Confederate officials and military officers were temporarily barred from amnesty; and that once a tenth of the voters who had participated in the elections of 1860 had taken the oath within a particular state, the citizens of that state could create a new government and elect representatives to Congress.[1]

Radical Republicans criticized Lincoln's plan as being too lenient toward Rebels who had torn the Union asunder. They were also disappointed that Lincoln made no provision for the freedmen, beyond granting them their physical freedom. Many Radicals had been pre-war abolitionists guided by humanitarian motives. Many knew that only giving the former slaves their personal physical freedom of movement was not sufficient to prepare them for real freedom and citizenship.

Many Radicals wanted the federal government to take all steps necessary to protect the former bondsmen, but Lincoln believed that race relations were best left for the state governments to monitor. On April 14, 1865, an assassin's bullet took the life of the president, but the spirit of

Reconstruction to which he first gave voice continued to exist in the reconciliation efforts of his successor.[2]

Following the shock of Lincoln's death, Vice-President Andrew Johnson, a pre-war Democrat from Tennessee, became the country's new chief executive. In May 1865, he announced his plans for reconstructing the South. Because Congress was not in session when Johnson assumed the presidency, he initiated his own plan without congressional approval and therefore avoided an early confrontation with Radical Republicans who had opposed Lincoln's lenient process of restoring the Union.

Similar to Lincoln's "Ten Percent Plan," Johnson's program favored a speedy reunification of the Southern and Northern states. Aside from the abolition of slavery, Johnson's New South maintained many of the vestiges of the *antebellum* era. He appointed provisional governors in the former states of the Confederacy and instructed them to oversee the formation of state constitutional conventions and the creation of new state governments. Johnson made no provisions for protecting the civil rights of the freedpeople, preferring that white Southerners continued to dominate the affairs of their states.

Johnson issued an Amnesty Proclamation on May 29, 1865, which restored political rights to the majority of Dixie's whites, effectively ensuring their domination of the South's newly-formed governments because the white masses would vote for their "natural" leaders who had staunch Confederate credentials.[3]

President Johnson appointed Andrew Jackson Hamilton as Texas' provisional governor. Hamilton was acceptable to Radical Republicans in Washington, D.C., but his appointment proved controversial with many Texans, especially former Confederates and unrepentant secessionists. Though he became a noted Texas politician prior to the outbreak of the Civil War, Hamilton was a devoted Unionist. He refused to support the Confederacy. After serving a term in the United States House of Representatives (1859-1861), Hamilton won a seat in the Texas Senate in 1861 where he continued to espouse the Unionist cause. Plots against his life forced him to flee the state first to Mexico, then to various Northern states.[4]

Hamilton became something of a hero in the North and delivered rousing Unionist speeches in such cities as New York and Boston. He joined the Union Army in July 1862, taking the rank of brigadier of volunteers. The same year, he met President Lincoln, who appointed him military governor of Texas.

In 1863 Hamilton accompanied Federal forces that temporarily occupied Brownsville. When commanders recalled the units stationed there later that same year, Hamilton moved to New Orleans where he spent the rest of the war. Because of his service to the Union, many Texans considered him a traitor. Confederates, including those in Texas, apparently did not understand that they were the real traitors because they had tried to overthrow the United States Constitution by force.[5]

Hamilton arrived in Galveston on July 21, about a month after General Granger had secured the city. Although he had received little guidance from President Johnson, the provisional governor began formulating plans for reconstructing the state. His primary duty was to restore Texas to its proper place within the Union. Hamilton began at the local level. Within a month, he had restored civil government in eighty counties by appointing Unionists and a few Confederates to local offices even though violence committed by men such as Bickerstaff, Baker, and Lee was epidemic.

Next, Hamilton supervised the registering process for voters and the election of delegates to a state constitutional convention. Then, he monitored the convention to make sure that its members properly revised the state's governing document.

Crucial to these revisions was the ratification of the Thirteenth Amendment to the United States Constitution that abolished slavery; the acknowledgment that the act of secession was illegal and therefore null and void from its inception; and the recognition that the state's debts which had been incurred during the war were no longer valid. Once the convention completed its task, voters returned to the polls to approve the new governing document and to elect local and state officials. Providing President Johnson and Congress approved of the state's actions, Presidential Reconstruction would be complete in Texas, and it would once again become part of the Union.[6]

Hamilton cautiously moved forward with his plans. He feared that former Confederates and secessionists would seize control of the polls. Knowing that Radicals in Washington would block the state's readmission to the Union if the new civil government did not reflect a true spirit of reform, Hamilton delayed calling for the election of delegates for more than three months, hoping to appoint a strong contingent of loyal Union men to key political positions throughout the state, who would protect the polls from unrepentant Rebels such has Bickerstaff, Baker, and Lee. To do so, Hamilton depended on the Union League for support.[7]

Originally organized as a secret society in the North in 1863, the Union League's purpose was to bolster morale and give strong support to the policies of President Lincoln. Texans in exile in New Orleans formed a chapter of the Union League in 1865 and moved the organization to the Lone Star State when they returned in the summer of 1865. They worked with other pre-war loyalists to set up local league councils, the first founded in Galveston as the Loyal Union Association and headed by the Unionist Colbert Caldwell of Navasota.

The League expanded across Texas. Members vowed to continue their support for the Union and to oppose anyone who had voluntarily served or supported the Confederacy. The Union League became a powerful political force.[8]

In addition to his direct worries about politics and his strong support for the Union League, Governor Hamilton was more concerned about general lawlessness in Texas, especially in the Northeastern counties. He feared that violence would become a major barrier to his program of restoring the state to the Union.[9] His assessment was correct. The bands of brigands forming in Northeast Texas came to the attention of Brevet Major General George A. Custer. After suffering organizational problems and logistical setbacks, Custer's cavalry regiment left Alexandria, Louisiana, on August 8, 1865, crossed the Sabine River, and made its way toward Houston.

Before the regiment reached its destination, General Granger, whose headquarters remained in Galveston, ordered Custer's division to bypass Houston and march to the rural community of Hempstead, where the soldiers would find an abundance of grass and forage for their horses. Custer and his men remained there until the end of October before moving west to Austin.[10]

While stationed in Hempstead, Custer learned from scouting patrols that some of the former Confederates had formed bands in the Northeastern region of the state and were terrifying white Union men and freedpeople. (For more on Custer's views, see Appendix I). Custer's scouts reported on the activities of men such as Ben Bickerstaff, Cullen Montgomery Baker, Elisha Guest, and Bob Lee. The rogues had no fear of the Union military that was trying but failing to re-establish law and order.

Custer reported that the renegades attacked army patrols and commissary trains, while sheriffs and judges loyal to old Dixie protected the felons. Custer said that many people helped and protected the raiders because they always postured as defenders of the Lost Cause.[11]

In an open letter to President Johnson, Mrs. L. E. Potts's of Lamar County confirmed that Custer was correct in his assessment of Northeast Texas. A Unionist who went into exile during the war, she wrote: "In addressing you [Johnson] I do not address you as the Chief Magistrate only, but as the father of our beloved country, one to whom we look more or less for protection, but most especially the <u>poor negro</u>." Continuing, she said that "I wish my poor pen could tell you of their persecution here. They are just now just out of slavery only a few months, and their masters are so angry to have to lose them that they are trying to persecute them back into slavery."

She added that "it is not considered a crime to kill a negro. They are often run down by bloodhounds and shot because they do not do precisely as the white man says . . . there have never been any troops here and everything savors of rebellion."[12]

Potts said that "the Confederacy has destroyed and ruined mine and my children's property." She added that one reason that she had stayed in California during the war was the fear that her young thirteen-year-old son might be forced to fight and to die for the Confederacy (indeed, boys that young were killed during the war). "We left a large estate here which they confiscated and destroyed all that they could. The land is all that is left to us. They stripped it of all the timber and destroyed my houses."

But Potts did not beg for herself. She could live with the property losses. Rather, "for humanity's sake I implore you to send protection in some form to these suffering freedmen . . . I have stated only facts. The negroes need protection here. When they work they scarcely get any pay, and what are they to do." Potts closed her letter by asking President Johnson to send troops. (For more on Mrs. Potts and violence in Northeast Txas, see Appendix 2).[13]

Despite widespread violence in Texas, on November 15, 1865,

Governor Hamilton issued a proclamation that called on Texas voters to go to the polls on January 8, 1866, to elect a slate of delegates to a constitutional convention that would convene in Austin on February 7. Political strife engulfed the state as election day approached. In Ellis County, a candidate seeking election to the convention stated that "if he had the power he would have swept the last Northerner off the face of God's Earth."

After his comments, the crowd cheered so loud that the "glass fell out of the windows." In the same county, another prominent citizen stated that "if he now had the power he would sink the entire [national] Republican party forty thousand feet below the Mudsills of Hell."[14] Such political vitriol was common place in January 1866, and it carried over into the constitutional convention that met in February.

Delegates to the convention met between February 7 and April 2 and created a new system of government for the state. In the process, the delegates declared the Secession Ordinance null and void, repudiated the state debt, and recognized the end of slavery even though they refused to ratify the Thirteenth Amendment. In an effort to thwart Hamilton's plan to provide the freedpeople with limited rights, the delegates denied the freedmen the right to vote, to hold political office, to serve on juries, or to give legal testimony against whites in court. Before adjourning, the solons set June 25 as the date for the referendum on the newly-created state document and for election of new officials under its provisions.[15]

While Hamilton attempted to bring real political reform to the state, a new Federal agency tried to protect the freedmen in Texas. The Bureau of Refugees, Freedmen, and Abandoned Lands, more commonly known as the Freedmen's Bureau, arrived in Texas in September 1865. Created by Congress in March 1865, the Bureau's general function was to help Dixie's black community make the transition from slavery to freedom.

The Bureau's Commissioner was the one-armed General Oliver Otis Howard, who had great sympathy for the plight of the former slaves. Each Southern state had an assistant commissioner who in turn appointed sub-assistants to implement policies at the local level.

The sub-assistants were most important because they operated where people actually lived. The sub-agents handled local affairs day-by-day. They helped the new freedpeople establish schools. They used some Bureau funds to rent cabins or some other space for classrooms. They paid a partial stipend to teachers who volunteered to teach in the new schools. The agency had help from various Northern benevolent societies, the most active and important was the American Missionary Association that sent teachers, mostly young unmarried Northern women, to teach in the schools for blacks.[16]

Sub-agents helped freedpeople establish permanent meeting places for their religious congregations. Given a little Bureau money to buy materials, blacks built structures that could be used simultaneously for schools, churches, and civic meeting houses. Local agents had other responsibilities. As sharecropping became commonplace, they monitored labor contracts to ensure fairness to the white and black croppers.

Because many landowners tried to cheat the sharecroppers out of their share of the crops, usually a one-half share, agents had to settle disputes that arose over the bounty. Because local white judges and juries refused to provide freedpeople justice in court, local agents assumed jurisdiction, much like an appeals court, and ruled on the cases. Informally, local agents acted as marriage counselors. Some fined a spouse of either gender who committed adultery and forced wayward husbands to pay child support.[17]

Local agents had to work in a hostile white community with men such as Bickerstaff, Baker, and Lee who refused to give any rights to the former slaves. Most agents had no troop support except for a small personal guard, and some agents lacked even that. Some were retired officers of the Union Army. Others were still in the army serving on detached duty. Professional soldiers at least had the training and the will to deal with all manner of problems, including violence.

But, the Bureau was always undermanned. At the height of its expansion, only sixty-seven agents served in Texas, and all had more than one county to supervise. The Bureau was the first social agency in the nation, a grand experiment, but it was destined to a troubled life for lack of manpower and funds and was stymied by the hatred of a majority of Southern whites.[18]

Bureau agents had to deal with violent circumstances like those described in Mrs. Potts's correspondence to the president. For example, in Red River County, Elisha Guest, who often rode with both Bickerstaff and Baker, caused mayhem in Clarksville and its vicinity. He helped organize a local terrorist group that numbered approximately 100 men who had secret meetings in the bush near the Red River.

Just as Confederates had suppressed Unionists during the war, Guest's Klan group continued to do so during Reconstruction. A local Union man owned a gin on the outskirts of Clarksville. Terrorists led by Guest burned it, hoping to ruin the Unionist financially and drive him from the county.[19]

Although Unionists such as Mrs. Potts wanted to bring the Klansmen and desperadoes to justice, many former Rebels living in Northeast Texas were willing to help anyone who postured as a defender of old Dixie. Bernard Patterson, whose relationship with Bickerstaff had almost gotten him lynched during the war, and his family operated a farm in Lamar County. Bernard helped the Southern ruffians whenever they were near. His son, James Patterson, who became an attorney in Cooper, Texas, remembered that as a boy, he met and came to know such renegades as Bickerstaff, Guest, Bob Lee, and Simpson "Simp" Dixon, one of Lee's top lieutenants. They often stayed at the Patterson farm when they were in Lamar County.

The farm had a twenty-six-acre orchard, including three acres tangled by grape vines. The desperadoes always stayed in the orchard and hid deep among the vines. As a boy, one of James's chores was to take food and drink to the men whenever they were on the farm. An officer in the pre-secessionist club in Lamar County and a Civil War veteran, Patterson supported the desperadoes because, once again, they claimed to represent the Lost Cause, and all of them wanted to clean out the Yankees and native Unionists by any means.[20]

More than one Freedmen's Bureau agent stationed in Northeast Texas agreed that men such as Bickerstaff, Baker, and Lee represented continued Southern resistance and the refusal of the Rebels to accept the results of the late war. It was evident that Bickerstaff had become determined to resist Reconstruction. Known as a Southern firebrand, he shot first and asked questions later.

One Bureau agent created a list of the most notorious of the guerrilla leaders in Northeast Texas, and Bickerstaff's name was near the top. Other notable outlaws listed included not only Lee and Baker, but also Ben Griffin, Guest, John "Pomp" Duty, Simp Dixon, Dick Johnson, George "Indian Bill" English, Henry Farrar, and John Henderson. Another observer added "Wild Bill" Bateman, Wade Anderson, Phillip Simpson, and William "Bill" Taylor to the list.

Such men interfered with efforts to implement the Reconstruction process. They cared little for life, nothing for the law, and nothing for the stability of their regions. Death and destruction characterized their world. Among the general public, they became known as "nigger killers."[21]

As if to prove the forgoing true, in May of 1866 the twenty-five-year-old Guest killed a black man in Lamar County. Southern loyalists ran the county, so local authorities took no legal action; but, by October 1868, Unionists controlled the area, and a grand jury indicted Guest for murder. Because he was a fugitive, the authorities sent a description of Guest to various other counties, but no one could catch him.[22] Josiah Thompson, Bickerstaff's best friend, joined the ranks of the malefactors by murdering a Hopkins County freedman in 1866.[23]

The desperadoes of Northeast Texas kept abreast of politics, and they celebrated the outcome of the June 25 referendum on the new constitution and the election of James Webb Throckmorton as governor. The election meant that Hamilton's plan for reconstructing the state had, in essence, failed. Collin County's Throckmorton defeated Unionist Elisha Pease by a vote of 49,277 to 12,168, and Democrats took the legislature, results signaling that former Rebels now controlled the state.

The new governor was not a diehard ex-Confederate who refused to accept the outcome of the late war, but his conservative political views prevented him from becoming a supporter of the national Republican Party. Prior to the war, he had been a Unionist who allied himself with Governor Sam Houston. At the Secession Convention of 1861, Throckmorton became one of the immortal eight who voted against leaving the Union. Then, while waiting for the public referendum on the question, he returned home to campaign against deserting the Union. His zeal, coupled with that of Collin McKinney, won the day in Collin County when its people voted to support the national government.[24]

When statewide results demonstrated that a great majority of its voters had approved secession by a vote of 46,153 to 14,747, that fact gave Throckmorton pause. Following the firing on Fort Sumter in the Charleston, South Carolina, harbor, and Lincoln's call for 75,000 volunteers to crush the rebellion, Throckmorton became one of the first men in Collin County to join the Confederate Army.

Although he fought with distinction in several Civil War engagements, recurring health problems forced him to resign in 1863. He served in the Texas Senate in 1864 and apparently recovered from his health problems, for in December of 1864, he became a brigadier general of Texas's First Frontier District. The next year, Confederate General Edmund Kirby-Smith appointed Throckmorton Commissioner to the Indian Nations. As the president of the Texas constitutional convention of 1866, Throckmorton expressed his desire to restore Texas to the Union without giving freedmen full suffrage rights, thereby securing conservative Unionists and ex-Confederates support for his gubernatorial candidacy. With the overwhelming majority of the state's voters fitting into these two political factions, his victory in the race was predictable.[25]

The man Throckmorton defeated in the governor's race, Elisha M. Pease, was a veteran of the Texas Revolution and a pre-war governor, a Democrat who served two terms from 1853 to 1857. A Unionist with no interest in slavery, Pease allied himself with Sam Houston. In 1860 and 1861 he campaigned actively, hoping to convince the people that secession was folly and would damage Texas greatly. Just as a majority of voters rejected his pre-war Unionism, they rejected Pease again in 1866 by choosing Throckmorton.[26]

Once the state government was in place, the public waited to determine how a pro-Confederate, conservative legislature would deal with the new realities in Texas. Among the legislature's first actions was to create the Black Codes in 1866 that returned the new freedpeople to a status that greatly resembled slavery. Now codified, black Texans could not vote nor hold political office; could not serve on juries nor testify in cases involving whites; could not marry whites nor claim land under the Texas Homestead Law; and could not escape segregation on common carriers nor share in public school funds.

An apprenticeship law gave whites control of underage blacks either with parental consent or by the order of a county judge. Also heinous was the Contract Labor Code which forced blacks to sign twelve-month contracts for jobs lasting more than one month. The labor code gave employers certain judicial rights. They could fine workers who failed to perform their work; who damaged tools; who left without permission; and who were generally disobedient.[27]

Related was the Vagrancy Code. All local authorities could arrest idle blacks who had no apparent livelihood. Those who could not pay fines could be contracted out until they earned sufficient money to pay. The Convict-Lease Code entrapped blacks whom judges and juries sent to county jails or the state prison. Such unfortunates could be contracted out to private employers and forced to work for little but room and board.

The racial climate was such that renegades such as Bickerstaff and his men believed that they could continue to attack freedpeople and white Unionists so long as they continued to posture as Southern heroes who had been persecuted by Yankees and native Union men. At times they even claimed to be enforcing the state's Black Codes by keeping a close watch on the freedpeople.[28]

Bickerstaff and his men became members of what New York newspapers labeled "THE NEW REBELLION" along with other headlines that read "SULPHUR SPRINGS---ARMED DESPERADOES SCOURING EASTERN TEXAS---A REIGN OF TERROR." The story that followed was a report by Lieutenant Charles Vernou, who said that on August 30, 1866, Cullen Baker and a party numbering at least thirty men, including Bickerstaff, attacked him in the Bois D'Arc Creek bottoms in Lamar County. Vernou rode away, but the desperadoes chased him for several miles before he reached the farm that he had bought. He escaped his pursuers by riding into dense woods and hiding in a thicket. The attackers beat a black sharecropper in an attempt to force him to tell them where the Yankee lieutenant was hidden. They ordered all sharecroppers off Vernou's place after they had gathered their portion of the crops in the field but told the workers to leave Vernou's portion to rot. The raiders ordered the freedmen to return to their old masters and to serve them, else, they would all die. Vernou later said that the renegades visited Paris, the Lamar County Seat, as they pleased and that they intended to kill white Union men, Yankees--especially Freedmen's Bureau agents--and black leaders.[29]

For a time, Bickerstaff seemed to have pubic support, especially because he served the interests of the region's ex-slave holders and the Democratic Party. He found leaders of the various black communities and told them to announce the news that he would kill any freedmen not working or violating the Black Codes. Consequently, many whites continued to remain willing to harbor him, to supply him, and to act as his spies who told him when the authorities were near.[30]

An unidentified informant likely demonstrated sympathy by warning Bickerstaff in January 1866 that a Bureau agent was seeking him. Ben and some of his men rode southeast until they reached Panola County where they committed a robbery in February. Someone recognized Ben and gave the authorities that information. In March Panola County's grand jury indicted him for the crime, a fact that sent the renegades riding north until they reached Titus County.[31]

In October 1866, Judge Albert H. Latimer, a resident of Red River County since 1833, summarized some of the trouble that renegades were causing the black community: "Never in the days of slavery had there ever been know the wrong, the outrage[,] the oppression that now exists in all Northeastern counties of Texas towards the poor Negroes." Adding that blacks had "no rights whatever," he said that "instances of cruelty and violation of all law towards them . . . would make your heart bleed." The oppression was so harsh that Latimer's freed slaves "returned to [him] and besought [him] to return them to slavery so that they would have some protection."[32]

According to Latimer, the same conditions prevailed in Bowie, Fannin, Lamar, and all the surrounding counties. The lash, the judge said, was "now more cruelly administered than it ever was." Freedmen had produced and harvested "fine crops" on land rented from whites and for their efforts had been "deprived of everything upon some pretext--sought out by the landlord to engage in quarrels which would terminate in the most brutal punishment and dismissal without a dollar for the labor [or a share] of the crop."[33] Guerrillas such as Bickerstaff terrorized, robbed, and killed with impunity. No relief was in sight.

4 Living in Pandemonium Itself

While Bickerstaff continued his life of crime, his close associate Cullen Baker also helped destabilize Northeast Texas. Baker targeted William G. Kirkman, a new Freedmen's Bureau agent, for death. A military veteran, Kirkman had served his country well during the Civil War. Born in Jacksonville, Illinois, early in the 1840s, the mature Kirkman, six feet, two inches tall, volunteered to when the war came. He joined the 39th Illinois Infantry Regiment. A telegraph operator before the war, his superiors used him in that capacity until he was mustered out in January 1865.

After working as an operator in Chicago and Rockford, Illinois, he joined the Bureau. Kirkman's brother Joel, who worked at Bureau headquarters in Texas, talked William into making the move. The telegraph operator came to the Lone Star State in 1867 and took over Freedmen's Bureau Sub-District Fifty-Eight, with Boston in Bowie County as his headquarters from whence he served several counties.[1]

When Kirkman moved to Boston, located in the heart of Baker Country, he had only four men to assist him. Within three weeks he had his first encounter with Baker. Knowing that the desperado was a wanted felon, Kirkman led a detail consisting of Colonel DeWitt C. Brown and three cavalrymen into Cass County on July 24, 1867. The small Union force intended to arrest Baker, one of his lieutenants, L. R. Rollins, and any other renegades they discovered. The troopers searched the Sulphur River bottoms, but their efforts proved futile.[2]

Baker discovered their presence in the bottoms and began to track them, keeping a close watch on their every move. The hunters then became the hunted. After searching the area surrounding Baker's home and interviewing his neighbors, Kirkman decided that they were lying to cover Baker's trail. Yet, he could do nothing about it, so he and his men turned their horses and began the return trip to Boston. Soon after Kirkman's detail crossed the Sulphur River, Baker and several of his men ambushed them. The gun battle accomplished nothing.

Baker and his men withdrew after firing several volleys, after which Kirkman and his men resumed their ride back to Boston. The Bureau man was apparently unaware that Baker and several of his henchmen were still trailing close behind his detail.[3]

Reaching town the next day, Baker and some his men brazenly entered a store to purchase food and announced to several people that they had come to kill Kirkman. Alerted that Baker was in town, the Bureau agent and his men started toward the store. Before reaching it, Kirkman noticed

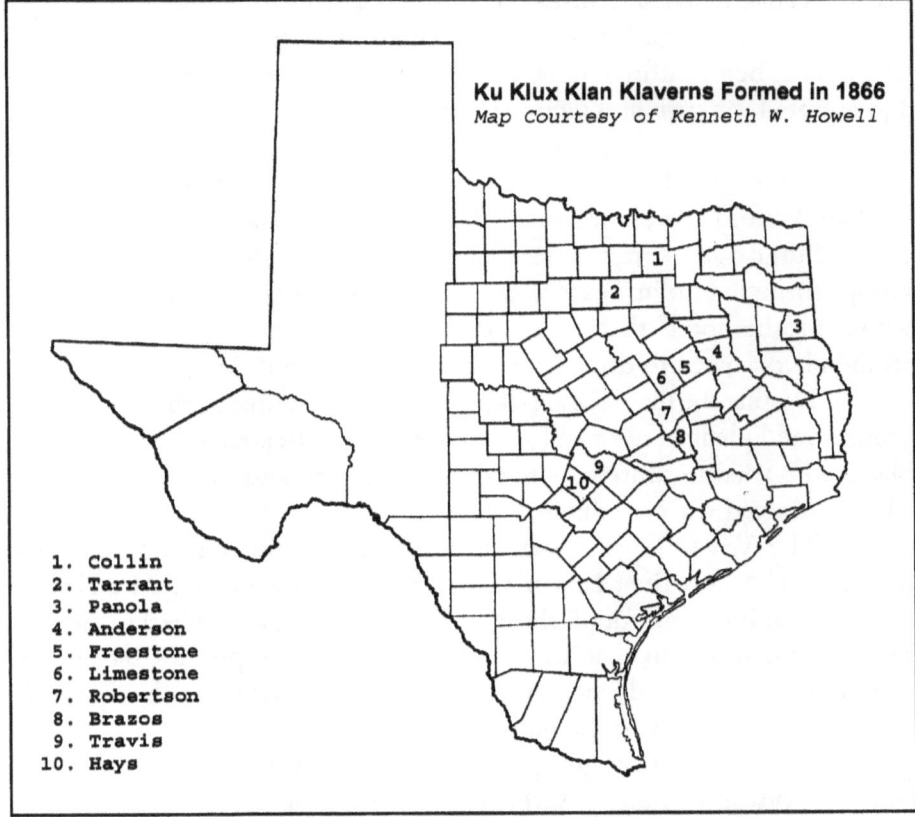

The map above indicates the number of terrorist Klan-like groups that existed in Texas by 1866. Courtesy of Kenneth Howell.

a gun projecting from a store window. The Yankees were able to take cover just as the town erupted with gunfire. When the smoke cleared, one of Kirkman's men, Albert E. Titus, lay dead in the street, and Baker had suffered a gunshot wound in the arm.[4]

Wounded and venerable to capture, Baker, along with his men, fled the scene. After they scattered, Baker sought safety and medical attention at the home of a sympathizer. Later that night, he slipped away from town. According to Kirkman, Baker was almost impossible to arrest because so many local people helped him. Baker also helped yeoman farmers and planters by running off sharecroppers after harvest so the owners could claim all the crops. According to Kirkman, landlords could hire Baker for "a few dollars" to kill any freedman in the region.[5]

As Baker recovered, Bickerstaff added to his stature in the judgement of many former Confederates. In mid-1867 he organized and became a co-leader of a Klan-like terrorist group in Titus County, a role that he shared with Elisha Guest. Various men in eastern Texas such as Ben Bickerstaff, Ben Griffin, Cullen Baker, and Bob Lee organized such groups and adopted the garb and tactics of terrorists.

Such organizations in Texas predated the rise of the historic Ku Klux Klan in Pulaski, Giles County, Tennessee; ex-Confederate General Nathan Bedford Forrest organized the latter group in late May or early June 1866. But, cavalry commander Colonel George Custer had noted violent groups springing up in Texas as early as the summer of 1865. He told of a white "brotherhood" that coalesced in Limestone and Freestone counties. Its members vowed to drive all blacks from their counties.

Despite the illogic of attacking their major source of cheap labor, the brotherhood pledged not to allow employment of freedpeople; to whip any blacks who tried to contract with white employers; and to whip any whites who contracted with freedmen.[6]

The *New Orleans Tribune* reported that in 1865 terrorists operated in Texas well before the Klans in Tennessee began organizing. The *Tribune* erred by calling the groups the Knights of the Golden Circle, the pre-secession organization that advocated creating an "empire for slavery" by conquering Central and South America in addition to the Carribean islands. The error related only to the name.

In Texas, terrorist groups formed in at least seventy-seven different counties, possibly more. According to historian Allen Trelease, Klan organizations, such as the one led by Bickerstaff, were most effective. They demoralized both the ex-slaves and white Unionists and contributed to the defeat of the Reconstruction process. The terrorists variously named themselves the Ku Klux Rangers, the Teutonic Brotherhood, the Knights of the White Camellia, the Pale Faces, the White Caps, the Red Hand, the Knights of the Rising Sun, and so forth.[7]

Regardless of the name under which they operated, the terrorist groups had two common purposes: first, to enforce strict white supremacy; and second, to cow native white Unionists along with the Yankees and reclaim the state for the Democrats. The terrorists spread chaos and death in their wake. Some sources credited Roger Q. Mills, once a Confederate colonel, as being the Klan leader who coordinated terrorist activity in Texas, but that view was likely overstatement. In fact, most groups operated at the county level and were autonomous.[8]

However, many such organizations cooperated with Klans in

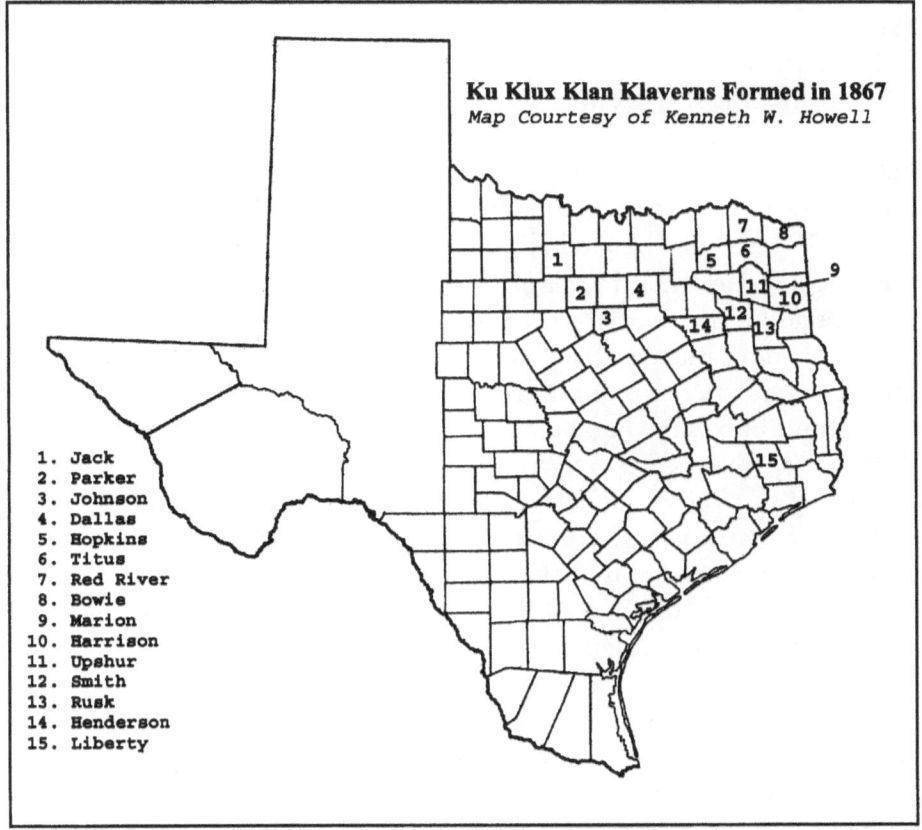

The map above indicates the number of terrorist Klan-like groups that existed in Texas by 1867. Courtesy of Kenneth Howell.

adjacent counties. By 1868, the majority of the counties in East-Northeast Texas had local Klan groups. Northeastern counties that had terrorist organizations included Hopkins, Lamar, Collin, Grayson, Red River, Fannin, Hunt, Bowie, Titus, Marion, Harrison, Upshur, Cass, Kaufman, Van Zandt, and Wood, as well as Ellis, Navarro, and Hill. According to one authority, the Klan only targeted blacks and the white Unionists who tried to protect them while leaving in peace the ex-Confederates and their sympathizers.[9]

Successful in Titus County, Bickerstaff also organized Hopkins County's Ku Klux Klan, known as the Ku Klux Rangers, and divided his time fulfilling his leadership roles in both counties. In the words of former slave Lee Pierce, Bickerstaff "was one of the main leaders of the [ex-Confederate] whites." After area blacks in Hopkins County organized an armed "militia" to protect themselves, Bickerstaff, Pierce said, led men who "killed several of the colored militia and wounded lots more" before the militia disbanded.

After the struggle with the militia, Bickerstaff knew it was time to run again. He rode south and entered Panola County as he had done once before. In mid-1867, a man named "Bickerstaff" reportedly committed a robbery in the county. The man was probably Ben Bickerstaff because authorities knew that he was in the area and already had been indicted there for an earlier felony. However, he returned to Northeast Texas once Panola's authorities started closing in on him.[10]

By now, Bickerstaff had successfully recruited and organized a small army, making it easier to intimidate (committing violence when necessary) freedpeople into following the will of the white community and remaining docile in sharecropping operations that amounted to a second slavery. According to one traditional source, the Bickerstaff- Guest-led terrorists rode area counties at night dressed in white with their faces hidden. Some adjusted their costumes to make them appear headless.

They rode up to the homes of African Americans, disarmed and robbed them, and threatened even worse treatment to any freedman who resisted. Bickerstaff, Guest, and their terrorist groups also operated in Cass County where Baker and his men probably joined them. One freedman recalled that a gang wearing white robes dragged him out of his home, hauled him into a nearby thicket, and ordered him to kneel for an execution-style murder.[11]

The victim, A. J. Hurdle of Daingerfield, in Cass County, decided not to participate in his own murder. He ran instead, managed to elude the provocateurs, and lived to tell the story some fifty years later. Under Bickerstaff and Guest, the terrorists developed more of a political function as Reconstruction proceeded. They warned freedmen to remain uninvolved with politics unless they joined the Democratic Party. They warned the freedmen to accept their status and whipped, shot, or hanged those who became active in the new Republican Party.[12]

Meanwhile, one of Bickerstaff's men came to the attention of the authorities repeatedly. Horatio Weaver had murdered immigrant Zara Sartin in Hopkins County on August 4, 1866. Local authorities, all former Rebels, refused to take action even though they knew that Weaver continued to visit his home in the county. Authorities also knew that Weaver spent much of his time with relatives who lived near Jefferson in Marion County, but, again, no lawman went after him.

Consequently, Sartin's wife, Amanda, wrote to Governor Throckmorton to ask him to intercede in the name of justice, something he did not do. She sent Throckmorton a description of Weaver, adding that he was a "sportsman fond of drink" and was "profane in common conversation."[13] Still, the renegade remained at large.

As Zora Sartin's death suggested, the War of Reconstruction continued. Captain Rand, still the Freedman's Bureau sub-agent in Marshall, had occasion to report on a trip from Tyler to Quitman to Sulphur Springs in April of 1867. He submitted a letter to superiors that was anything but positive. He held that the people were haughty and "still hold the party lines as strongly as during the war."[14]

Rand reported on crimes committed by Josiah Thompson, Bickerstaff's best friend and a member of Ben's guerrilla band. Authorities wanted Thompson because he had murdered a freedman. Rand next reported that Bickestaff's cohort Bob Lee and his men were busy in Grayson County, where they robbed and murdered a Unionist. Rand added that they "are a terror to all loyal people as they still claim to be fighting for the Confederacy." As well, the agent said that in Red River County--a primary haunt of Elisha Guest–unknown parties had murdered from twenty-five to fifty blacks.

Why Rand gave such a broad estimate is unknown. Local authorities believed that it was likely that Guest and his men were guilty parties in several of the killings. Rand added that civil law was a "farce" in Northeast Texas and that freedmen were cheated out of their wages and then were "mobbed" by whites if they complained.[15]

In large part because of Klan and desperado violence in the states of the old Confederacy and because Southern states had passed Black Codes that discriminated against the freedpeople, in May 1867, Congress seized control of the Reconstruction process. But, in Texas, even as the Federals were mobilizing, the Bickerstaff renegades staged a brilliant coup. In the summer of 1867, Ben Bickerstaff and his men, numbering at least twenty-five, captured a military commissary train near Sulphur Springs. The stores the train carried had come from Jefferson, site of a Federal garrison, destined for points west and southwest of Hopkins County. The fifteen-wagon, mule-drawn caravan contained arms, ammunition, food, clothing, and other essential supplies.

When the train was only a few miles from Bickerstaff's lair in the White Oak Creek bottoms, the guerrillas attacked, killing several troopers and wounding others before winning the day. Some of the teamsters were local men who worked the teams to earn a living for their families. The desperadoes spared their lives and set them free to walk back to safety. After the drivers had left, Bickerstaff's men unhitched the mules, claiming the animals as their own. They helped themselves to all the supplies that they could cart away. Then they drew the wagons together and torched them.[16]

While Bickerstaff captured the commissary train, one of his cohorts found trouble. Civil authorities in Lamar County found and arrested Elisha Guest, threw him in the Paris jail, and charged him with murder. By then, Guest had already killed a number of people. Earlier, he murdered a freedman in Lamar County, a crime for which he had not yet been indicted. In addition, he had been indicted for other crimes in Hopkins and Titus counties when he rode with Bickerstaff.

In May of 1867, Guest killed a white Unionist. That the victim was white, and from a county that had gone Unionist in 1861, was what motivated the local authorities to finally grab Guest. According to the report of Bureau Agent Albert H. Latimer, whose headquarters was in Clarksville in Red River County, Guest had murdered a number of freedmen in Lamar County and was "a perfect desperado and a terror to the black people in all this region of the country."[17]

Latimer, also responsible for Lamar County, asked his superiors for troops, for at least twenty men, some of whom he wanted to keep in Red River County. Others he wanted to station in Paris. Latimer said his entire Bureau Sub-District was out of control, a common observation of agents in Northeast Texas. He claimed that the Paris jail was worthless and falling apart. But he said the county sheriff was keeping a guard at the jail day and night to watch Guest. Despite the constant vigil of the sheriff and his men,

Guest escaped the dilapidated holding pen before he was brought to trial.[18]

Following Guest's escape, Colonel William H. Sinclair, the Freedmen's Bureau's Inspector, toured Northeast Texas. He commented on the chaotic conditions caused by renegades such as Bickerstaff and his raiders. White Unionists and the freedpeople, said Sinclair, were living in "Pandemonium itself," and conditions remained "deplorable." The inspector added that landlords refused to pay sharecroppers for their year's work and that blacks continued to toil in "servitude worse than slavery" because landowners no longer had a long-term ownership interest in what was now a free labor system.[19]

Gangs such as those run by Bickerstaff, Baker, and Lee (and Klan terrorist groups) beat, shot, and killed freedmen virtually every day. Sinclair reported that civil officers protected such murderers. White Unionists and blacks were helpless, he said. They watched known marauders, who had indictments against them "for the worst crimes," ride into and out of their towns. "Civil law is dead," exclaimed Sinclair.[20]

Sinclair took special interest in Guest, who was again riding with Bickerstaff and Bob Lee. Sinclair reported a horror perpetrated by Guest, who had now killed at least ten freedmen. The young hotspur got genteelly drunk and assaulted a pregnant freedwoman, whom he shot and wounded. While the woman was still alive, he "cut out her womb with its living contents" still inside, tore the fetus out, "and exhibited the fetus to others in his drunken glee."[21]

Despite such horrors, late in August 1867, law and order scored a victory. A party of soldiers arrested Baker in Honey Grove, a settlement located in Fannin County about fifteen miles east of Bonham. Although details are lacking, a problem developed because Baker decided not stay arrested. He managed an escape from jail, probably with the assistance of some local whites.[22]

Baker resumed his criminal activities, and on October 6, 1867, he and Bickerstaff raided another Union supply wagon coming out of Jefferson destined for Boston in Bowie County. Accompanying the two outlaw captains were L. R. Rollins, Jack Bell, Lee Rames, Guest, John Kelley, and possibly Ben Griffith, Matthew "Dummy" Kirby, and "Wild Bill" Longley. In the gunfight that occurred during the attack, the marauders killed two men and wounded another.

The renegades then made off with the loaded wagon and its team of mules, driving it to their hideout in the bottoms near the Sulphur Fork of the Red River. The place was in a swamp about twelve miles long and five miles wide. Baker had used it scores of times after he deserted during the war. He knew every inch of the place and believed that he and his men were safe there. Learning of the attack on the train on October 7, Boston's Bureau agent Kirkman and his personal guard went in pursuit of the villains, scouted the countryside, but returned to town once again empty handed.[23]

Meanwhile, the first sizable force of Federal troops arrived in the area after being delayed by an outbreak of Yellow Fever. Major Samuel Henry Starr, soon to be colonel, and two companies of the 6th Cavalry Regiment reached Mount Pleasant, the force aiming to quell the lawlessness in the area, with Bickerstaff, Baker, the Englishes, and Griffith becoming major targets. Before Kirkman went in pursuit of the raiders, he sent a message to Starr, gave it to a courier, and told him to get to Mount Pleasant as fast as possible. Starr took immediate action.

Because Kirkman was under a death threat from Baker, Starr detached six men and sent them to Boston to join the agent's four-man guard and to give Kirkman a better chance of both living and preforming his duty. Starr also ordered Lieutenant Moses Wiley to take four men, patrol the area around Boston, and arrest Baker if he could be found.[24]

At 3:00 a.m. on October 8, Wiley and his detachment left Mount Pleasant and rode toward Boston. All five men wore civilian clothes to give them a better chance of securing information than they would have had if they had worn their uniforms. Soon, Starr received word from an informant that Baker was in the vicinity with at least fifteen heavily armed men, a group too large for Wiley to challenge. During the afternoon of October 8, Starr ordered Lieutenant Jeremiah Wilcox and nine other soldiers to reinforce Wiley. Though neither Wiley nor Wilcox encountered Baker, they managed to capture John Kelley who was in the party that had attacked the supply wagon.[25]

After his successful raid, Baker distributed some of the stolen goods to his neighbors in Boston, Jefferson, and other towns. People in Jefferson were so impressed with Baker's generosity that they gave him a new shotgun and two new revolvers before calling him the "Robin Hood" of the Sulphur River. Learning of the townspeople's show of support and gathering additional intelligence about other civilians actively helping Baker and the other cutthroats, Starr questioned how he could bring law and order to Northeast Texas. He was further surprised to learn about the atrocities that white Texans were committing against the freedpeople.[26]

Even as Starr was getting his Texas education, military men in Northeast Texas continued their search for Baker and Bickerstaff. The outlaws knew how to fight and also when to run. For a few weeks Bickerstaff and his band were relatively inactive, hiding in Titus County. But in the latter part of 1867, they rode back into Hopkins County and set up their regular "headquarters" in the White Oak Creek and Sulphur River bottoms about four miles northwest of Sulphur Springs.

Much like men in Titus County, the majority in Hopkins County were Southerners who had voted overwhelmingly for secession (797 to 315) although the cotton culture and slavery were not as entrenched as in Titus County. Residents heartily supported the Confederacy by raising six companies for service in the Confederate Army in 1861.[27]

Thus, after the war, Bickerstaff could depend on the support of many locals because he continued to cast himself as a supporter of the Lost Cause who would take the battle to white Unionists and the freedpeople. Still, the gang moved frequently when necessary to escape the authorities. They spent time in Hopkins County's Black Jack Grove, now known as Cumby, and sometimes slipped into counties like Titus and Red River. They even ventured as far west as Grayson County and as far south as Van Zandt, Navarro, Ellis, and Hill counties. Everywhere the desperadoes went, they disrupted life by continuing to prey on the freedpeople, Federal soldiers, and anyone identified as a Unionist. By November, they were back in Titus County.[28]

Newly promoted Colonel Starr of the 6th Cavalry was still in command of the garrison at Mount Pleasant and still after Bickerstaff. He also served as the local agent of the Freedmen's Bureau. He was less effective than he might have been because his superiors had transferred many of his men to other posts. He had only thirty-five men, a number insufficient to corral Bickerstaff, who was then riding with rogues directed by Baker, Pomp Duty, Tom Emmett, and George English. Starr posted a public notice in the local newspaper, asking Titus County residents to form a posse or at least relay information about the desperadoes to him. No one came forward; even area Unionists remained silent out of fear. Again, for a time, the desperadoes had their way in Northeast Texas.[29]

Starr despaired. At one point in November 1867, he recommended to his superiors that all freedpeople be evacuated from Titus County to keep Klansmen and guerrillas under Bickerstaff from exterminating them. As if to prove that Starr was correct, in December of 1867, George English murdered two black men, including Gordon Riley on December 9.

According to witness U. J. Cason, a white man, the shooting occurred on his property, a farm located approximately a mile south of Snow

Hill. English apparently killed Riley because the man had a handgun; such a thing infuriated the murderer, who used a double-barreled shotgun to slay the man. Then English robbed the body of the revolver. Six whites witnessed the shooting, after which English said to them: "Gentlemen, I have killed me some meat down here[,] and I wish you all to understand that I did it." Next, he led a small group that murdered Jim Green on Christmas Day.[30]

In January 1868, Starr submitted another pessimistic report to his superiors, stating that the "disloyal element" expected that they could soon re-enslave the blacks. He added that he expected a rebellion in Northeast Texas at "no distant date." If one remembers the havoc caused by terrorist, Klan-like groups, and guerrilla gangs, one must conclude that Starr's prediction was a reasonable one, even though a full-scale rebellion did not occur. Rather, smaller groups of evil-doers continued their despicable ways.[31]

Although he was undermanned, Starr continued to patrol the area in hope of bringing the desperadoes to justice. After learning that the colonel was in the field, the raiders rode hard until they were back in Hopkins County to hide. They left when military authorities there took up their trail. They fled back to Titus County, Bickerstaff's old haunt, but they did not stay out of trouble there for long. Led by Bickerstaff and English, on February 22 four gang members visited freedman Ned Poindexter's home near Mount Pleasant. Wearing Klan disguises, they tied and blindfolded the man and his wife and robbed them of household goods, food, and clothing. Starr sent a squad to investigate, and the soldiers found and arrested one of the outlaws. But he escaped before they could get back to the garrison in Mount Pleasant. Once he received word of the escape, Starr sent a unit in pursuit, but the squad had no success.[32]

Conditions in Titus County did not improve in the months that followed. Now riding with Bickerstaff and Guest, George English continued to boast about killing blacks and Federal soldiers. In March, he allowed Sergeant Pearson, one of Starr's personal guard, to buy him a drink in a saloon in Mount Pleasant. Not recognizing the murderer, Pearson said that he had been sent to arrest English and asked if he knew the man. English said "yes indeed" before he drew his handgun and shot the sergeant in the head. When first hearing of Pearson's death, the wife of a local physician exclaimed: "I am glad of it, I wish every Yankee was killed."[33] A few days later, English also killed a freedman who lived near Gray Rock.[34]

African Americans continued to be favorite targets of the outlaw gangs. Starr exclaimed, "It is impossible to tell how many [blacks] have been killed within the last six weeks--No doubt a great number. The people dare no longer complain." He added that "a negro seen coming in the direction of Mount Pleasant runs great risk of his life. [The] outlaws have subdued the minds of the whole people, white and black. Terror reigns." Continuing Starr said that "a day probably does not pass without murder or robbery."

Concluding, he said that he had been advising "freedpeople and Union men to leave the country as fast as possible, but the colored people are too poor to act on my advice . . . The hatred of Yankees and freedmen is the creed of these people."[35]

With conditions deteriorating, the Union command inexplicably transferred Starr and his men in March 1868, a development that area Unionists believed would lead to disaster: To replace Starr and his men, a meager squad of fifteen infantrymen moved in under the direction of Lieutenant Adam G. Malloy. Such a development underlined the problems the Army had with its lack of manpower. Infantrymen proved no match for terrorists and renegades who were in their saddles atop good mounts. The killing continued.[36]

While George English was active in Titus County, Elisha Guest was contacted by his father who asked him to come home. Guest slipped away from Titus County and rode to his father's place in Red River County, about nine miles from Clarksville. Captain Charles Rand, still the Bureau man there, learned from an informant that Guest's father wanted his son to kill him (Rand). Since he had no troop support, the captain could only say that "I am on the lookout, will kill him if he don't me."[37]

Matters grew worse in Red River and Lamar counties in April. Bureau agent DeWitt Brown, now stationed in Paris, told superiors that the white people in Lamar County had organized yet another society "called the Ku Klux Klan," adding that area freedpeople had become so afraid of the terrorist groups and outlaw bands led by Bickerstaff, Guest, and Bob Lee that they had stopped complaining to the Bureau for fear they would be killed.

Brown added that "Rebels" intimidated white Unionists as well. Like most agents in Northeast Texas, he believed that the only thing that could bring peace to the region was for the military authorities to send more troops.[38]

5
Every Loyal Man in the State May Fall, May-July 1868

In the summer of 1868, Northeast Texas became the flash point in the War of Reconstruction. This came as no surprise to the people living in the region. During the two previous years, they had witnessed increasing conflict between the terrorists of the region and Federal authorities. In the fall of 1866, National Radical Republicans were successful in winning control of both houses in mid-term congressional elections.

The Radical's victory primarily came as a result of the unrepentant attitudes of white Southerners and their continue denial of full civil rights to freedmen. The Radicals set out to dismantle the failed Reconstruction policies of President Johnson and to implement a new process by which the former Confederate states could be readmitted into the Union.[1]

As a result, Congress passed the Reconstruction Acts, which called on each of the former Confederate states to register eligible voters, both black and white; to elect a convention to write a new state constitution; to establish state and local governments in compliance with the new state constitution; to ratify the Fourteenth Amendment; and to elect United States representatives and senators.

To ensure that the states fully complied with the measures of the Reconstruction Acts, Congress divided the Confederate states into five military districts and placed each district under the command of a major general who directed troops of occupation. Congress combined Texas and Louisiana into the Fifth Military District under the initial command of General Philip Sheridan.[2]

Sheridan took charge on March 19, 1867. From his office in New

Orleans, he issued an order stating that the current commanders in the states would retain their commands. For Texas, this meant that General Charles Griffin remained the head of the subdistrict of Texas. Griffin differed with the Throckmorton-led state government on policy. He was quick to inform the governor that his administration and the legislature, both filled with conservative Democrats and former Confederates, was a provisional government only.

As such, Sheridan and Griffin limited the authority of the civil government in the state by ordering that the governor could no longer appoint individuals to fill the vacancies in elective offices and that the state could not hold elections unless approved by military commanders. General Griffin also issued an order requiring all jurors to take the Test Oath of 1862, which stated they had never voluntarily supported the Confederacy, an order that made it impossible for the majority of white Texans to serve on juries.[3]

Governor Throckmorton attempted to obstruct military rule of Texas at every turn. His actions led General Sheridan to remove him from office in July 1867, replacing him with a moderate Republican and pre-war Governor Elisha M. Pease.[4] The military commander's action caused resentment. Conservative Democrats and former Confederates, many of whom were now barred from voting or holding office, plotted their return to power. One of their strategies consisted of turning a blind eye to the violence perpetrated against the freedpeople and their white allies.

Many prominent politicians even helped organize terrorist groups in their counties. Using the Klan and other terrorist organizations as a paramilitary arm of the Democratic Party, they hoped to regain control by intimidating voters who favored Radical Republicans policies and by keeping them away from the polls. Guerrilla groups in Northeast Texas fit well into the plans.

Early in 1868 Bickerstaff, John "Pomp" Duty, George English, and several other renegades caused one disturbance after another in Red River County. Of the wild bunch, Duty caused the most trouble because the county was his home. About thirty years old, he had dark hair, brown eyes, and stood about six feet tall. Even before the other desperadoes arrived, Duty often rode into Clarksville late at night and shot up the town.

A local Unionist said that Duty did it just for "fun." It was also rumored that he headed the county's Ku Klux Klan that did everything in its power to hurt the freedpeople. In February of 1868, the Klan attacked the teacher of a small black school in the county in broad daylight while school was in session. The raiders took the teacher outside and beat him in front of his class with clubs and large stones. According to one observer, Duty and Bob Rainey planned and directed the attack. Bickerstaff was with them and did his share of mayhem.[5]

After his foray into Red River County, Bickerstaff moved into Lamar County in May, riding with the desperadoes Cullen Baker, George English, Bob Lee, and Lee men Dick Johnson and Simp Dixon, along with several other guerrillas. They killed six or seven white Union men. A short time later, DeWitt Brown, still the Bureau's man in the county, learned that the renegade band had increased in number, with Bickerstaff and the others joined by "Indian" Bill English along with Dick Harper, Lee and Seth Rames, Elisha Guest, and Pomp Duty. Brown estimated that the guerrilla leaders had amassed more than 100 men.

Calling Bickerstaff and the others a "cabal of outlaws," Brown reported later that it was impossible to bring these men to justice because the malefactors had so much citizen support. They continued to ride unopposed into any town in the area without fear. Of course, likely fear of the terrorists silenced many whites who did not condone their criminal acts; that helped explain why the band was so free to do whatever the leaders wanted.[6]

In desperation Brown wrote to M. L. Armstrong, a Unionist who was elected to the state constitutional convention held in Austin. Brown bemoaned his fate. He revealed that Cullen Baker had vowed to kill him. The desperado had boasted that "Brown is my meat." The somewhat shaken Bureau agent informed Armstrong that the group of guerrillas had been openly camped in the bottoms of Bois D' Arc Creek. The agent speculated that the bandits hoped to lure him and his personal body guards to the area and ambush them. Brown knew that he did not have enough men to accomplish anything but his own death, so he remained at his headquarters, refusing to fight the outlaws on their terms.

Additionally, the agent reported that Guest and Bickerstaff had passed through Paris heading east. Brown predicted that Armstrong soon would hear of more violence and death in Red River and Titus counties. Already, they had done significant damage in Lamar, Red River, Hopkins, and surrounding counties.[7]

Although Brown had predicted that Bickerstaff would ride for Titus County, the renegade fooled him by traveling in the opposite direction.

With a group that included the Bowman brothers, G. G. and William, the Baptist preacher William Ellis, a man named Boardman, and other cohorts, Bickerstaff appeared in Navarro County early in June of 1868. His party robbed several freedmen of their weapons, clothes, blankets, utensils, food, and other valuables. They robbed one freedman in broad daylight on a public road near Corsicana.

Navarro County was not like Bickerstaff's typical haunts. Loyal citizens living in and near Corsicana worried that the outlaws might turn their attacks on the white Unionists in the county. They had heard of the atrocities committed against Unionists and freedpeople in the counties to the north and east of them. Fearing that their lives and property were in danger, some of the county's finest managed to accomplish what others had failed to do: They found and arrested the robbers.

It appeared that Bickerstaff and his men had finally met their match. But at camp in the late hours of the night, the renegades, who were not in chains, overpowered a sleepy guard, escaped, and hid in a countryside thicket.[8]

Despite their narrow escape, Bickerstaff and his men committed more robberies in Navarro County. Still in the company of Ellis and the Bowmans, between June 17 and June 23, Bickerstaff robbed six black families of all they had of value. The gang's activities were cut short when lawmen once again apprehended them and lodged them in the Corsicana jail. Despite their precarious position, Bickerstaff and his men benefitted from the blind justice administered throughout Texas by racist judicial officials. A justice of the peace let them go, saying that they only robbed "damned niggers."[9]

Before leaving Navarro County, the brigands attacked five more black families; stole four horses; shot two freedmen near Spring Hill; and committed other noted offenses. One victim was Henry Carruthers. The raiders went to his home on July 4 and tried to kill him, shooting at him three or four times. After Carruthers ran away, the guerrillas helped themselves to his household goods and his other supplies. They confiscated three horses and two saddles.

Another victim was Peter Bunton. They robbed him of everything that they could carry away. Military authorities also suspected them of the multiple rape of an underaged freedgirl. The military reported that civilian authorities in the county refused to form a posse and bring the renegades to justice, realizing now that Bickerstaff and his men only bedeviled the freedpeople.[10]

The Bureau agent who reported the atrocities of the Bickerstaff gang in Navarro County offered some profound thoughts to his superiors: "The condition of the freedmen of this place is worse than when they were slaves. In [the] time of slavery they had to bear only the abuse of their masters. Now, they bear the abuse of every drunken, worthless villain in the country . . . Riots and hangings are the order of the day."[11]

While the outlaw gangs terrorized loyal citizens and military men in the Northeast Texas region, events unfolded in Austin which further aligned conservative Democrats and former Rebels against the Radical Republicans' Reconstruction policies. Just two weeks after General Sheridan dismissed Governor Throckmorton from office, President Johnson replaced Sheridan with General Winfield Scott Hancock, a well-known Democrat who had doubts about the wisdom of the army's involvement with the politics of Reconstruction. Hancock issued General Order number 40 which forced military personnel who captured felons to turn over such men to civil authorities for trial.

The order hamstrung the military and led to more major crimes because oftentimes a civilian jury would vote "not guilty" if former Confederates were on trial. Hancock also took steps to restore civil authority in the Fifth Military District. He called for elections to be held between February 10 and February 14, 1868. The voters would decide if a state constitutional convention should be held and, if so, to elect delegates.[12]

Republicans did not constitute a majority of registered voters in the state. That fact was problematic for them. The Texas Constitution required the participation of the majority of registered voters to call a constitutional convention. Leading Texas Democrats came up with a plan to thwart the electoral process.

They called on Democrats eligible to vote to stay away from the polls in the hope that the state would not have the necessary majority of registered voters to legitimize a constitutional convention. Because of divisions in the state's Democratic Party, their plan failed. Enough Democratic voters went to the polls to validate the election results. The voting majority, slightly more than 51 percent of registered voters in the state, favored the convention by a count of 44,689 to 11,440.

The new black vote explained the lopsided victory, with African Americans voting 36,932 for the convention and only 818 balloting against. As well, 41,234 white registered voters failed to cast ballots, while 11,730 black registered did the same.[13]

Assembling on June 1, 1868, the convention included ninety delegates. Eighty were white and only ten were black, numbers indicating that white fears of "Negro domination" were groundless. The number of true carpetbaggers was also minimal. The majority were Southerners; yet, the new Republican Party dominated. The tiny Democratic delegation was hopelessly out numbered.

Their strategy was to remain united, hoping to become the swing vote if different Republican factions disagreed. Hamilton, former provisional governor of the state, led the largest Republican bloc whose moderate members supported Governor Elisha M. Pease. Hamilton's faction represented the Unionists of Northeast Texas, where majorities in a number of counties had voted against secession.[14]

Besides calling for the restoration of law and order, Hamilton's bloc favored agricultural and commercial interests and supported granting limited civil rights to black Texans. Heading another faction, James W. Flanagan advanced the issues of East Texas, the region favoring economic development; more railroad construction; and a possible division of Texas into smaller states. Flanagan's faction opposed granting blacks any rights. Unionist supporters from central and western counties comprised a third bloc. Led by Edmund J. Davis, James P. Newcomb, and Morgan C. Hamilton, their faction favored broad economic development and state division and also supported broad civil rights for freedpeople.[15]

George T. Ruby of the Freedmen's Bureau led the black delegation. The group favored broad civil rights for their community and lobbied for free public schools. Ruby (1841-1882) was a native of New York who became a journalist. After a tour of Haiti reporting for New England's *Pine and Palm*, he returned to the United States in 1864, moved to Louisiana, and became a teacher.

After a feral white mob beat and almost killed him in September 1866 for daring to open a common school for blacks, he fled Louisiana and took a job with the Freedmen's Bureau in Texas. Teaching in Galveston, Ruby also served as a correspondent for the *New Orleans Tribune*. Eventually, he became a traveling agent for the Bureau, going wherever he was needed.[16]

A natural politician, Ruby established local branches of the Union League wherever he went, that in addition to establishing local temperance societies. He joined the Republican Party and became a delegate to the

Texas Constitutional Convention of 1868-1869. After his service as a delegate, voters elected him to the state senate, where he represented the predominantly white Twelfth District. Although he was an active champion for the Texas black community, he did not seek re-election in 1873. In 1872, Congress passed the Amnesty Act, which restored voting privileges to many former Confederates who had been disenfranchised previously.

As a result, Democratic "Redeemers" captured both houses of the state legislature in 1873. Ruby realized that his chances for re-election were hopeless. However, while in office, he represented his constituents well. He was the type of black man that Bickerstaff, Baker, and Lee hated. He was not from the South; he was not a Democrat; and, while in office, he proved most capable, proving the fallibility of assumed "black inferiority."[17]

At the constitutional convention, the majority of delegates chose Davis as their president over Judge Colbert Caldwell of East Texas. Caldwell still played an important role; he headed the select committee that investigated rampant lawlessness in the state and compiled evidence against such outlaws as Bickerstaff, Bob Lee, and Cullen Baker.[18] (For Caldwell's report on violence, see Appendix 3). From Tennessee, Caldwell migrated to Arkansas, entered politics, and served a term as a state legislator before moving to Mansfield, Texas, in 1859.

In August 1865, Provisional Governor Hamilton appointed him judge of the Seventh Judicial District. In October of 1867, General Sheridan appointed him to the Texas Supreme Court. Over time, he became a stalwart moderate Republican who called on Federal authorities to destroy terrorists groups operating throughout the state.[19]

Many issues divided the convention, so much so that the tax money to support it ran out, that causing the delegates to adjourn until revenue from a special tax provided new funding. Reconvening early in December, the delegates went back to work but again adjourned after only partially finishing their task of writing a new constitution.

Exasperated military leaders gathered up what was finished, added clauses that made sense of the document, and sent it to the voters for their approval. That accomplished, Texans had a new constitution that created a free system of public schools, granted civil rights for the freedpeople, and centralized law enforcement. The latter reform eventually made it harder for terrorists like Bickerstaff, Baker, and Lee to operate.

But, until the measures could be fully implemented, the raiders continued to terrorize the loyal citizens living in Northeast Texas.[20]

While the convention delegates were in session, Bickerstaff and a few of his men returned to Hopkins County early in July and killed yet again. They murdered Charles Grimes, an elderly freedman, in a politically motivated incident. Grimes gave no direct provocation, but he was on the county's board of registrars, a position that the terrorists believed was above the status of a black man. In Hunt County, unknown parties attacked freedman Jim Brigham, who, like Grimes, was a member of his county's board of registrars. Unlike Grimes, Brigham survived.[21]

Bickerstaff next targeted the white Joe M. Easley because of his outspoken Unionist views. Late one afternoon in July, Bickerstaff and several of his men accosted Easley and several freedmen who worked for him as they were returning from the fields. Easley's farm was located about three miles from Sulphur Springs, and he was surprised that the wild bunch would operate in broad daylight so close to town. The freedmen scattered, while Easley sprinted to his horse, bounced atop it, and outran the raiders. After throwing the guerrillas off his trail, he returned home, forted up, and grabbed several loaded guns to defend himself and his wife. Still looking for Easley, the renegades returned to his place but decided that rushing the house was fool-hearted.[22]

They camped nearby and waited until morn. Apparently believing that he was safe, Easley appeared on his porch, went to his barn, and saddled a horse. He rode toward town where he had business. As he rode, Easley discovered that Bickerstaff and two of his men were following him. He left the road, reversed direction, and made it home before the villains could catch him. For five days and nights, Easley and his wife remained inside and vigilant. Bickerstaff and his men eventually abandoned their goal of killing Easley.[23]

Like DeWitt Brown before him, Easley also wrote to Republican politician M. L. Armstrong on July 17, explaining his travail. Easley told Armstrong that Bickerstaff was intellectually astute. The desperado continued to use statewide politics and the Lost Cause to his benefit throughout the rest of 1868. Casting his banditry as part of the ongoing struggle between the Federals and their allies and the pure former Confederate Democrats of Texas, he built a following and enlarged his gang while Democrats turned a blind eye to his antics because he was taking the fight to the "enemy."[24]

According to Easley, Bickerstaff and his band had returned to the

Sulphur Springs area only to escalate their race war against the freedpeople. They raided black homes, taking all weapons away from freedmen, leaving them defenseless, while warning them to practice deference in all matters relating to whites. The desperadoes drove some blacks from their homes because they were recalcitrant. The brigands killed or maimed freedpeople for no apparent reason other than the victims were black and supported the Republican Party.

The guerrillas were merciless toward their black victims, making no distinctions between men, women, or children. Easley added that the wounded could not receive medical care because physicians either sympathized with the murderers or were intimidated by them and refused to treat blacks. Easley asserted that many people who might have protested were afraid to send information by mail because the county's postmasters belonged to the Ku Klux Klan that Bickerstaff still directed.[25]

Bickerstaff and his band appeared to control Hopkins County. Upon learning that freedwoman Minerva James had complained to authorities about his atrocities, Ben targeted her. She claimed to know that Bickerstaff had killed Charlie Grimes because she had witnessed the slaying. She was the domestic servant of Herman Spencer, who had a farm about four miles from Sulphur Springs. Bickerstaff and four of his men found her at Spencer's place and took her away after threatening Spencer, telling him he would die if he interfered. The renegades stopped about a mile from the farm. They raped and otherwise tortured the woman before murdering her.

Shortly after killing Minerva James, the marauders burst into Buck Thomas's home and took a freedman who worked for him a short distance from the house and killed him, the specific cause of the slaying unknown. With Bickerstaff and his men close, a number of Hopkins County blacks simply disappeared, never to be seen again.[26]

Bickerstaff next targeted a white Unionist named Flowers because the man supported the Union League and opposed mob rule. Under the cover of darkness, the malefactors broke into Flowers's home and murdered him. The next day, as friends were taking his body to the local graveyard, the renegades rode up and fired into the crowd. They killed a man and a small boy and grievously wounded the boy's father, who received a ball in one of his lungs.

According to Joe Easley, no physician in Sulphur Springs would treat the wounded man because he was a Unionist, and the doctors in the area were all Democrats. Easley pointed out that the "Rebels" in Hopkins

County always "got up" some pretext for such violence, usually blaming the victims. "The would-be social class of rebels stand ever ready [to] fabricate falsehoods and [to] make excuses for all murders committed by their friends."[27]

Because the situation in Bickerstaff country was so desperate, Easley again wrote Hopkins County's M. L. Armstrong, who was then attending the state convention, and told him of the deadly doings of the renegades. Easley complained that military authorities had promised to send troops by July 1 to reimpose law and order and to protect the lives of area Unionists.

But, by July 17, the troops had not arrived. Easley said that he had tried to rally the Union men, but most were too afraid to confront the malefactors. Instead they hugged their farmhouses by day and slept hidden in the woods at night, believing their lives would be forfeit if discovered by Bickerstaff and his men. In disgust, Easley reported that he could raise only four men who had the courage to fight and that Bickerstaff had so large a force that he could easily overwhelm them.[28]

Easley said that he knew that Armstrong was "doing all [he could] in the convention to give protection; but if it comes at all (which I very much doubt) it will be too late for most of the prominent Republicans [of Hopkins County]. I know that I can't survive but a few days, unless there is a speedy change in our favor. They [Bickerstaff, his raiders, and the Klan] are recruiting daily. Every day makes them more bold and defiant. Every outrage they commit seems to increase their desire for something worse. I cannot leave my family to be murdered by them. I am bound to stay near them, so I can give them protection at night."[29]

On July 27, Easley wrote yet another letter to Armstrong. He reported that the guerrillas had dispatched three more men. Already, Bickerstaff and his men had murdered four men in the Starr family, with young Luke Starr being the last surviving male. Earlier, several of the Starrs had ridden with Bickerstaff and other renegades, but, for unknown reasons, Ben began to doubt their loyalty and started killing them, one by one. After Bickerstaff and his band besieged the Starr homestead, the son-in-law of Mrs. Starr, Everett Jackson, ventured outside to see what the desperadoes wanted. Bickerstaff shot him stone dead.

The killer then negotiated with the Mrs. Starr, who was one of three females in the house. He threatened to burn the place down with all inside unless they brought him all the weapons in the house, in which case Bickerstaff promised that Luke would not be assaulted.

Once Mrs. Starr delivered the weapons, several entered the house and made everyone come outside. Bickerstaff ordered Luke to sit on a nearby log. The women did the same, gathering around Luke, trying to shield the front of his body; whereupon, one of the renegades fired a double-barrel shotgun into Luke's back and, in Easley's words, "hurled him into eternity."[30]

The louts murdered the last of the Starr family's men. The third killing occurred near the forks of the Sulphur River where another freedman died. Easley closed his letter to Armstrong thus: "The wildest excitement prevails around the county. Union men are leaving. Eight families are leaving for the North today while a great many others are said to be making preparations to leave soon." After saying that he might soon be the only Union man in Hopkins County, Easley told Armstrong that "I shall stand at my post. I prefer death to submission. I know that Republican principles will prevail, though every loyal man in the state may fall, if not there is nothing left to live for."[31]

While engaged in his murderous campaign, Bickerstaff learned that another military commissary train was moving through Hopkins County. On July 15, Bickerstaff, Joseph Weaver, George Branch, and the Bowman brothers learned the route and overtook yet another train. After forcing the small squad of military escorts from the field, Bickerstaff and his men took control of the wagons.

Wagon master P. A. Tuck reported that he faced twenty men, each having a double-barrel shotgun and several handguns. Bickerstaff collected as many stores as he could into one wagon, burned another one, and headed to the safety of the bush. Tuck said that the robbers were most gracious. Not only did they leave him alive, but they also gave him a receipt for all the goods.[32]

Bickerstaff also gave the teamster a written message to take to Sulphur Springs. It may have been one of the longest sentences in the history of the English language:

> To the Commander of the Post of Sulphur Springs:
> The undersigned reached here yesterday evening and found five wagons loaded with military stores, and no one to receive them, and thinking the whole affair was humbug, I have thought it expedient and proper, a duty I owe my own reputation, and believing it a duty to an insulted and

oppressed people, I have by force of arms taken charge of the contents of said wagons, and will in time report to your headquarters.

Capt. B. F. Bickerstaff
Comd'g this Mil. Division

P.S. Should any soldiers be sent up this way, it is my intention to bushwhack and kill the last one of them.

B. F. B[33]

It is interesting that the Civil War sergeant, who was reduced in rank because of war crimes, now promoted himself to captain. About the teamsters: He left them standing in the road as he bid them adieu and hauled away the booty. Why the terrorists did not kill the teamsters remains a mystery. Nevertheless, Bickerstaff left no doubt in the minds of those living in the area that he controlled Sulphur Springs and Hopkins County. He was still fighting and winning the Second Civil War.[34]

As Bickerstaff and his men were tearing through Hopkins, his cohort Baker continued to terrorize loyal citizens in Lamar County. Still under a death threat, Bureau Agent DeWitt Brown reported that early in July, Baker, Guest, George English, "the Marshall boys," and other renegades remained encamped in a thicket along Bois D' Arc Creek. Brown feared that at least one of them was watching and that if he left town, the spy would relay the information to the others in the bush, and Brown would become a dead man.

Since he was alone and had no protection, the agent wanted headquarters to send him at least a dozen troopers. He referred to the recent "outrages" that Baker, Guest, and the others had committed in Red River County and in Fannin County, where they were joined by Bob Lee and his men. The agent added that an informant told him that Titus County was out of control because of Bickerstaff's actions.[35]

While Bickerstaff and Baker carried out their atrocities, Bob Lee was active in Hunt and Fannin counties. Lee and his men committed so much mayhem that the editor of the *McKinney Messenger* questioned, "How long will [Lee's] fiendish acts in Hunt and Fannin counties be permitted to go unnoticed, and the perpetrators be allowed to run at large [?]" The editor added, "Law and order must prevail in Texas or we are a ruined people."[36]

During the month of July, the various outlaw gangs raided Red River, Upshur, and Titus counties. On several occasions the terrorist groups donned disguises and helped planters and yeoman farmers run off sharecroppers so that the landlords could claim all the crops.

The activities were such that a Bureau agent stationed in Marshall, a military stronghold in Harrison County, reported that lawlessness in the region was on the increase. The agent advised superiors that troops were needed, especially in Red River, Titus, and Upshur counties. He added that the desperadoes had murdered several blacks in the area, commenting that "these men kill [N]egros for the pure love of killing."[37]

After attacking the supply train near Sulphur Springs, Bickerstaff and some of his men joined Baker, "Indian Bill" English, and their gang members in Red River County. They were with Ben Griffith just before he met with his well justified demise. On July 20, 1868, Griffith rode into Clarksville about sunset, armed with three sixguns and a double-barrel shotgun which he held cocked across his saddle.

Several men welcomed him to town, and he became quite talkative. He said that Baker, Bickerstaff, Guest, English, and about twenty-five other men were assembled in the bush near town. Others probably riding with the outlaw party were Pomp Duty and John Henderson, who had earlier tried to murder Captain Charles Rand, the Bureau agent who manned his post in Clarksville.[38]

Griffith reported his latest doings, proudly saying that he and the other assassins had been "below" (probably referring to Titus or Hopkins or both); had murdered three Yankees and four freedmen; and had looted a commissary train before burning it. He spoke of the next action planned. The group intended to move west and attack another train destined for the forts on the West Texas Indian frontier. Griffith dismounted, cocked shotgun in hand, and went in the saloon to have his canteen filled with whiskey.

After coming out and jumping back atop his horse, he told his audience that he would be on the Boston Road should anyone want to come after him. He shouted "Look out niggers!" as he rode away. Rebel yells and the laughter from the white crowd filled the air.[39]

Just outside town, Griffith stopped to torment a teenaged black male, Charles Dyer, who was making his way along the road. A bystander ran to tell Bureau Agent Rand who had earlier been assaulted and severely beaten by local white malefactors. Rand, the county sheriff, and two other men formed a posse--no one else in town volunteered--and went after Griffith. One posse member fell behind because his mule refused to run, but the three other men rode on. The threesome found Griffith's just out of town, still berating young Dyer.

The renegade had drawn his sixgun and was threatening to kill the lad, but seeing the posse, he spurred his horse for a getaway. He hoped to reach the safety of the nearby terrorist camp in the bush.[40]

Griffith did not get there. Shots from the posse knocked him off his galloping horse. He fell to the ground dead. A runner reached Bickerstaff and the others and told them the news, after which they disappeared rather than deal with spunky lawmen and a Bureau man who did not back down. But just before the bothersome band left the area, they sent a messenger to tell Rand that he would soon die.

After noting that threat, Rand had Griffith's body buried in the Clarksville Cemetery, and he paid for it with funds the dead man had in his pockets. Rand sent the rest of Griffith's personal possessions and his horse to headquarters.[41] As a postscript to Griffith's death, *Flakes Galveston Bulletin* added, "there are those who will canonize Ben Griffith because he was killed by a U.S. officer."[42]

When Rand reported the details of Griffith's death to superiors, he mentioned the death threat before asserting that Clarksville was "divided in sentiment, [and] I don't know who my friends are. I do not want to retreat, but to stay here alone with not a soldier within 60 miles[,] and every second man a sympathizer with the desperadoes, is to say the least unpleasant."[43] (For Rand's report, see Appendix 4).

Griffith's death caused a firestorm around Clarksville. Baker, Bickerstaff, and other guerrillas believed that a majority of people in Red River County would celebrate Rand's demise. As the guerrillas plotted their next move, rumors circulated through the streets of Clarksville. One of the most disturbing to reach Rand was that Griffith's relatives in Arkansas wanted to avenge his death and were on their way to Clarksville to find his killer. This rumor later proved to be true and might explain why Bickerstaff and Baker did not immediately storm the town--they were simply waiting for reinforcements.[44]

With the outlaws virtually at his door, Rand took evasive action. He avoided his office and forted up in the county courthouse and worked from there. He did his office work and ate his meals with a cocked handgun resting within easy reach on his table while always sitting with his back against a wall to forestall any attack from behind.

At night he moved around inside the courthouse, hiding in

different places to sleep, never staying in the same place twice, while "young rowdies" led by Bickerstaff, Baker, and the others, virtually "treed" Clarksville. They shot up the place while drunkenly cheering for Jefferson Davis and President Andrew Johnson, the pre-war Democrat from Tennessee who was struggling to defeat Congressional Reconstruction. The renegades loudly cursed Rand and dared him to come into the open. For ten days, he toughed it out, awaiting the arrival of a squad of soldiers that he had requested from his superiors.[45]

Rand's luck changed for the better on August 1 when a squad of troops from Marshall, disguised as civilians, arrived and met him in the courthouse. That night, the squad, with Rand in tow, slipped out of town and rode for twenty-eight hurried miles to put distance between them and possible confrontation. When they finally camped, the men alternated watch duty through the night to protect against a surprise attack.[46]

Soon, they reached the safety of Marshall, a town well garrisoned and relatively secure. Captain Rand later learned that fifteen gunmen from Arkansas (probably some of Griffith's relatives and friends) arrived in Clarksville the day after he and his rescuers left. Reinforced, Bickerstaff and Baker might have caused an armageddon by attacking Rand and the other Federals.[47] Once in Marshall, the agent took time to recuperate, saying that "I am wore from exhaustion and constant anxiety day and night."[48]

After the incident in Clarksville, Bickerstaff and about fifteen of his guerrillas moved into Van Zandt County to begin a carnival of robbery and terror, as always targeting the same groups--white Unionists and the freedpeople. Bickerstaff and his men set up camp at Jordan Saline, using the site as a temporary military headquarters. The outlaws started making their ususal rounds, robbing the homes of the area's blacks. At one point, they came heavily armed into Canton. This surprised some townsmen because Canton was a Unionist stronghold where most people would not support violent men such as Bickerstaff.[49]

The band hoped to change that. They assaulted Unionist W. R. Moore because they learned that he had spoken out against them. They hoped that the Moore incident would intimidate the town's other Unionists. They left Moore for dead, but he defied the medical "odds" by remaining alive although his injuries troubled him for the rest of his life. After partially recovering, Moore continued to speak out about the lawlessness in the Northeast Texas region.

Although the desperadoes left Canton and returned to Jordan

Saline, they were most unhappy that the place was a Unionist stronghold. Bickerstaff sent the town's leaders a message. He threatened to burn down the entire village if Unionists interfered with his rapacious plundering.[50]

While Bickerstaff and his men raped Van Zandt County, Baker returned to Paris to rid Lamar County of its Bureau man. Learning of their approach, DeWitt Brown took refuge in his office and waited for military assistance. The guerrillas reached Paris before Brown's reinforcements arrived. Literally minutes before the terrorists reached his office's front door, the agent was able to slip out a back exit, mount his waiting horse, and make his escape through the woods.

Baker proclaimed to the people of Paris that he intended to shoot the agent "into mincemeat" once he found him. Further, the marauder announced that he had appointed himself as the new Bureau man in town, and he warned local blacks that they must abandon the Republicans or suffer the consequences.[51]

Brown took refuge on a farm that he had purchased when first arriving in the area. Informed of his movement, Baker and his men laid in wait for Brown at Rocky Ford on Bois D'Arc Creek. As Brown forded the creek, the outlaws ambushed him, shooting his horse out from under him. Amazingly, the wounded steed scrambled to its feet. Brown jumped back aboard and was able to escape. When he arrived at his farm, he discovered that Baker had arrived there ahead of him and had forced the freedpeople who were working for him to retreat to the woods. Only one freedman remained behind.

The terrorists had beaten him severely, and he was unable to escape with the others. After almost being killed, Brown continued as the Bureau agent until early November, but he found it impossible to carry out his duties because local terrorists continued to threaten his life.[52]

Shortly after the incident at Brown's farm, Baker left Lamar County to reunite with Bickerstaff, Lee, and others in Hopkins County to help continue what some journalists still called the "New Rebellion."

6 The New Rebellion, August 1868

Following the events of July 1868, the entire nation began to hear of the bloodbath in Northeast Texas. The Northern press began following what reporters called the "Texas troubles."[1] Local Republican newspaper editors took the military to task for not doing enough to control the state's lawlessness. Even some former Confederates complained that matters were entirely out-of-hand. The Democrat and Confederate veteran Charles DeMorse, editor of the *Clarksville Standard*, exclaimed: "How long the Government of the United States or its military representatives in Texas, will bear this sort of levying of tribute, we are somewhat curious to see."[2]

The editor of the *Marshall Texas Republican* wondered how long the Federal troops would allow men such as Bickerstaff, Baker, and Lee to dominate Northeast Texas and continue "levying tribute" from the military and civilians.[3] The editor of the *Paris Vindicator* believed that conditions in Northeast Texas were so bad that he suggested "buying off Lee, Bickerstaff & Co., by paying them a liberal subsidy."[4] In September, *Flake's Galveston Bulletin* reported that in Hopkins County "there are [white] Union men who have not dared to sleep for an hour for months."[5] Despite the *Bulletin*'s hyperbole, the general meaning was clear: Unionists were losing the Second Civil War in Northeast Texas.

Although he was late to act, General J. J. Reynolds, now commanding Texas, responded to the rise in violence by ordering Lieutenant Charles A. Vernou, then working in the adjutant general's office, to take command of a squad and tour Northeastern Texas to investigate the disturbances made by Bickerstaff, Lee, Baker, and all their cohorts. After a three-day ride to the vicinity of Sulphur Springs to begin his investigation, Vernou was welcomed to the area by Bickerstaff and a party of his men that included Branch and the two Bowmans. They ambushed and murdered two of Vernou's troopers.

Enraged by the incident, Reynolds took immediate action. He placed a $1,000 reward each on the heads of the unholy trinity: Bickerstaff, Baker, and Lee. Reynolds announced that bounty hunters only had to deliver one or all of the troublesome trio dead or alive to the post commander at either Austin or Marshall. The general later expanded the reward to include most of the trinity's top lieutenants.[6]

After killing the two troopers, Bickerstaff and some of his men immediately fled the area only to pop up in Jefferson on August 17. According to the judge of Marion County, Bickerstaff entered the store of a "Col. Taylor" in mid-afternoon on August 18 and asked to speak with him privately. When the two thought they were alone, Bickerstaff asked Taylor if he belonged to the Democratic Party. After Taylor said "Yes," the renegade told him to tell all his Democratic friends to stay off the town streets on that night and the next.[7]

Bickerstaff told Taylor not to ask for an explanation except that people would be safer at home than on the streets. The judge later received a written note, probably sent by Bickerstaff, telling him not to go home that night and that all would be explained later. The note was signed "a friend." Other Democrats, including the local mayor, visited with Taylor and the judge and urged them to take the advice. Taylor went to the home of a Democratic ally and stayed with him for several nights. The judge also managed to hide.[8]

Bickerstaff informed the public that he had 150 men encamped nearby and that he was prepared to kill all Bluecoats and native Republicans in Marion County or to drive them out of the area. The Unionists' response was, for once, swift. A loyal Republican sent a rider to the garrison of Federal soldiers in Marshall to ask for help.

Meanwhile, Republicans in Jefferson assembled a "police force" of about fifty armed men who showed the public that they intended to quell any disturbance that the Bickerstaff guerrillas initiated. When he learned about those fifty policemen armed to the teeth and ready, Bickerstaff called off his planned attack. He and his men soon left the area and returned to Hopkins County, hoping to find better opportunities for mayhem.[9]

Criticized for failure to take action sooner, General Reynolds began formulating a plan to bring peace to Northeast Texas by initiating a military crackdown to break up the gangs of Bickerstaff, Lee, and Baker, and other desperadoes such as Pomp Duty, Elisha Guest, and the English brothers. Early in August while still formulating his overall strategy, the general ordered the commander at Fort Richardson on the West Texas Indian frontier to detach a squad and send it to Hopkins County. The duty fell to Lieutenant Thomas M. Tolman, soon promoted to captain, to lead thirty-seven cavalrymen to Sulphur Springs, where they were to establish a garrison.

The Hopkins County area was an obvious target for Reynolds because of the Bickerstaff gang's antics and also because of the multi-county Klan activities led by both Bickerstaff and Guest. Moreover, Lee and English and their bands, along with Baker and some of his men, had all been sighted in Hopkins County recently. They were there to add more firepower for Bickerstaff's campaign of destruction.[10]

The Federals reached Sulphur Springs on August 10. The first order of business was to build a stout garrison. Luckily--given the local war that would soon develop--it proved to be a good one. Surrounded by a wooden stockade ten-feet high with open ports to fire through, the camp enclosed an entire city block bounded by South Davis and Magnolia Streets east and west and Main and Conally Streets north and south. The stockade had elevated, interior ramparts so sentries along the wall could see any trouble coming their way. Inside were the headquarters, the barracks, and a small jail.[11]

When members of Bickerstaff's gang (those who remained behind while he was in Jefferson) realized what was happening, trouble immediately followed because the military had greatly underestimated the extent of opposition in Hopkins County. Learning that Federal troops had arrived in the area, Bickerstaff's men held a meeting in Old Tarrant, the county seat before Tolman moved the county government to Sulphur Springs.

In Bickerstaff's absence, one of his lieutenants, Henry Farrar, led the meeting. All in attendance agreed to fight the Bluecoats and, if possible, kill them all. They also established a policy of "with us or against us" and applied it to county residents. Civilians were either to join them or be treated the way the guerrillas intended to treat the Union invaders and their supporters.[12]

As soon as Tolman rented land in town and his men began

constructing the garrison, a major incident occurred. A number of the younger men in Bickerstaff's band, led by Henry Farrar and Jack Grissom, tried to carry out their pledge to kill the soldiers. They taunted the troopers, even as the Yankees worked to finish constructing their fort. The young hotspurs loudly asserted that they would never submit to Northern rule and denounced the United States government, using pejoratives as they did so. Some older townsmen joined the scene, coming heavily armed as they did so. A powder keg was about to explode, but Grissom made a mistake that took his life and caused the civilians to retreat.[13]

Grissom came out of the pack, approached a corporal, and began to harangue him. The corporal, probably a raw recruit sent to Texas to prove his mettle, quarreled with the desperado. As their argument became heated, Grissom produced a pistol in one hand and a small derringer in the other. One of the corporal's cohorts saw Grissom pull his weapons, and in a flash he aimed his own carbine at the renegade and fired. The trooper's bullet killed Grissom and put a fitting end to the argument. All the soldiers in the small squad heard the gunfire, mustered, and confronted the mob. The citizens chose to retreat rather than fight the troopers, some whom were battle-hardened veterans of the late Civil War.[14]

Despite Grissom's death, Bickerstaff's men continued to gather in the area around Sulphur Springs and committed atrocities, perhaps hoping to draw some of the soldiers away from their garrison where they would become easier targets. Farrar and others went to the "Mount of Rocks" just east of Rock Creek and built a strong fortified headquarters from which they made daily raids. They bushwhacked troopers who were couriers and stole army supplies. John Vaden was now Bickerstaff's second-in-command. One of many rabble rousers who had been too young to serve in the late war, Vaden was but a teenager who intended to make a name for himself as a desperado whom the Yankees could not stop.[15]

Vaden taunted the Federals by using clever ruses, usually by taking advantage of area blacks. On August 14, just four days after Tolman and his troopers reached Sulphur Springs, the outlaws whipped a freedwoman and let her go. After the woman reported the assault, Tolman sent a seven-man patrol under Sergeant Edward Grey, a twenty-nine-year-old native of Tyrone County, Ireland, to investigate. Grey took along a freedmen who knew the area. They found and arrested the man who had beaten the woman.

Unable to find any other raiders, the patrol started their return to headquarters with their prisoner, not knowing that the terrorists had arranged an ambush. Young Vaden had an estimated twenty to thirty men who simply overwhelmed the small squad. The renegades struck within about a mile of town. Delivering a hail of bullets, the guerrillas murdered Grey, two other troopers, and the freedman who was acting as the guide. The killers then liberated the prisoner. The death of Private John Miller, a twenty-six-year-old native of Londonderry, Ireland, was particularly brutal. A brigand shot the young man off his horse and then approached him on foot. The boy begged for a drink of water, and the renegade said that, indeed, he could have some water. Just after that statement, the murderer shot the young trooper point-blank in the head. The last thing the boy saw was a sixgun pointed at his forehead.[16]

After hearing of the attack from a courier, Tolman led a relief squad that reached the scene of the ambush not more than twenty minutes after the murders, but all the killers had vanished. In his report, the Captain Tolman explained his plight. He said that he had only twenty-four men left, a few of them too sick for duty, adding, "I am unable to do anything at all. The town is surrounded by bush whackers and murderers and they threaten to drive the troops away, outrages are committed every day."[17]

Tolman asked his superiors for reinforcements. He wanted no less than 200 men (two full companies). He had talked with Bickerstaff under a flag of truce, Tolman said, and the raider had claimed that he could raise from 250 to 350 men to wipe out the Federals. Bickerstaff even threatened to bring in artillery after learning that Cullen Baker had come into the possession of two cannons.

That the desperado had manpower was not in doubt. On August 1, before the Yankees had arrived, Bickerstaff (passing through before continuing to Van Zandt County) had come into town with from 140 to 150 men, riding in two by two, that fact suggesting that Ben had intelligence about the troopers' movements, the fact also suggesting that Bickerstaff controlled the town. But Tolman finished his report optimistically. If he had enough men, he said, he could corral the entire gang organization in Northeast Texas, including the outlaw chiefs: Bickerstaff, Lee, the Englishes, and Baker.[18]

In mid-August, Vaden, who like Bickerstaff was from Titus County, committed more mayhem. Riding his race horse, a sorrel mare, he staged a one-man raid on Sulphur Springs. Using the main street, he spirited his mount through town. As he passed within forty feet of the military stockade, he fired a couple of wild shots to announce his presence. He rode past the Cotton Hotel (one source says El Rancho Hotel) and spied Tolman and his wife sitting out on the hotel gallery (Several of the married men whose wives accompanied them had rented rooms in the hotel). The hotspur fired a round that missed Tolman's head by inches. As he continued his ride, he saw a freedman known only as "Old Grimes," a leader of the local black community. Vaden gunned Grimes down while continuing his dash out of town. By the time the Federals put together a patrol to pursue, Vaden had vanished into the countryside.[19]

Reacting to Vaden's one-man raid, Tolman tried to disarm the town. He ordered a patrol to scout the entire vicinity and to confiscate the arms of any men wearing them, but the "gun order" was ineffective. Too many men had guns at home. Next, some of the Bickerstaff men, possibly led by Vaden, stole into town late at night. They got to the back of the local hotel without being seen. They set the hotel on fire, hoping to kill the Federals and their wives or drive them into the open so they could be shot. A hotel employee noticed smoke and gathered enough men to put out the blaze before it could spread and cause major damage.[20]

The Bluecoats could not take effective action to stop such outrages because their reinforcements had not arrived. The inaction was noted by the bandits who became more audacious. Bickerstaff rejoined his men late in August and learned of the actions that had taken place in his absence. He began to plot new attacks on the loyal citizens of the county and their Federal guardians. Bickerstaff and his men--their number including Vaden, Bill and D. Grissom, Charley and Rash Weaver, Charley Farrow, and Lum Houston, all young hotspurs--still operating in and around Hopkins County, corralled a freedman and assaulted him before allowing him to escape near the small garrison at Sulphur Springs.[21]

The former slave ran to town and complained to Tolman who probably realized that the guerrillas had set up another trap, but he hoped that some show of force might be beneficial. Out went another small squad of cavalry, guided by the freedman, who rode into another ambush wherein the guerrillas murdered three of the squad and wounded several others. Bickerstaff and his men suffered no casualties because they were well concealed in a thicket guarded by a copse of black jack trees. A runner reported to Tolman even as the battle raged. The commander sent another squad, but the killers had fled by the time the rescuers arrived.[22]

Leading the raiders, Bickerstaff struck Sulphur Springs itself. The guerrilla leader had been much impressed with Vaden's account of his dash through town, so Bickerstaff decided to repeat his young hotspur's bold attack on a grander scale. Bickerstaff picked about twenty of his men who had the fastest horses and led them on a lighting raid. Riding rapidly through town at night, they shot at several Yankees who were near the local hotel and another group who were near the general store. They fired at all freedman in sight before disappearing into the darkness before the Federals could react. As the raid and subsequent events proved, Bickerstaff's guerrillas controlled the area, and many whites in Hopkins County belonged to the Klan, which meant that the renegades had a large support network.[23]

Bickerstaff's raiders were not always successful in eluding the authorities. Soon after their raid on Sulphur Springs, a patrol captured John Nelson and John Dickson and put them in the guardhouse. Both also rode with Elisha Guest whose headquarters remained in Lamar County. The three had murdered an old freedman who lived near Caney Creek in the Pennell hamlet in Hopkins County. Although Guest escaped and apparently left for Mexico, Nelson and Dickson stood trial for the murder and, in a travesty of justice, a pro-Democratic jury acquitted them.[24]

Bickerstaff assembled even more ruffians who surrounded Sulphur Springs, some of whom went into town and laid siege to the garrison that protected Tolman and his small command. Bickerstaff audaciously sent a message to Tolman, saying that he could assemble 350 men to drive the Union men out. The outlaw told Tolman the truth. Within a short time, the scourge gathered even more than he had predicted. Approximately 500 men, including some of Bob Lee's raiders, consolidated behind Bickerstaff. Believing that he was in total control, Bickerstaff warned Tolman that if the troops did not leave, he would exterminate them, that he would kill them all.

Tolman reported via a courier to his superiors that with only the small force under his command he could do nothing, especially because the Rebels continued to receive the help of local civilians who provisioned them and warned them of any approaching authorities. The outlaws did not fight military-style, Tolman added. Instead, he said that "the desperadoes . . . greatly outnumber us and fight from the bush."[25]

Tolman turned even more of his attention to Bickerstaff and his raiders. After gaining some information about affairs in Northeast Texas, Tolman wrote the adjutant general's office with an overall strategy for dealing with the region's lawlessness by putting cavalry in the field. Tolman told his commanders that he desperately needed reinforcements, at least 200 more cavalrymen, and all the supplies they would need for a military campaign against the terrorists.[26]

Tolman wanted some of the men and some of the supplies to concentrate at Pilot Grove because the village was in Bob Lee's territory. The captain feared that Lee would use the problems in Hopkins County to open a violent campaign in Grayson, Hunt, Fannin, and Collin counties, the area that Lee regarded as his own. Tolman wanted the rest of the reinforcements to join him in Sulphur Springs. He told his superiors that Northeast Texas needed even more troops to "put down the desperate gangs of Bickerstaff, English, Baker, and Lee, all of which are connected together."

Tolman advocated a virtual war of attrition: "The best method to get rid of them would be to send a large force to move from Pilot Grove, near where Lee operates down through this part of the country, and to keep the force in the country till the desperadoes and outlaws are [killed or] driven out."[27]

Tolman wanted a force large enough to hound the outlaws; to chase them all over Northeast Texas; and to pick them off one by one if necessary. He intended to use any means necessary to bring an end to the Texas War of Reconstruction. The war had become personal, especially since the guerrillas had killed several of his men and had attempted to kill the officers' wives by burning down the hotel where they stayed. He was more than ready to give the desperadoes an appropriate send-off while putting them straight on the road to hell.[28]

Struggling to form his own effective strategy for subduing the miscreants of Northeast Texas, General Reynolds wisely decided to follow Tolman's advice. He called for an increase in troops in the region, using Sulphur Springs as the major pivot from which all action would swing. The general announced that Captain Adna Chaffee would lead the military effort, with Tolman as second in command. A native of Ohio, Chaffee had fought in the Civil War as a member of the Union's 6th Cavalry. He saw heated action during the Peninsular campaign and fought in the battles of Antietam, Fredericksburg, and Gettysburg, where he was wounded.

After recovering, he served under General Philip Sheridan for the duration of the war; by the end of the conflict he had risen to the rank of first lieutenant. Promoted to captain, Chaffee was stationed at Fort Griffin in January 1868. He saw action against the Quahadi Comanches, after which his superiors promoted him to brevet major. Over time, he had become a no-nonsense, brave officer who could handle the campaign against Northeast Texas' guerrilla bands and terrorist groups.[29]

Late in August, Chaffee left the Indian frontier and led two cavalry companies to Sulphur Springs. The general had heard from Tolman and from Vernou. Reynolds now understood the gravity of the problems such men as Bickerstaff, Baker, and Lee caused; and he was ready to launch a major assault on the criminal elements in Northeast Texas. The general intended to keep at least 100 cavalrymen in the field at all times to pursue; to hound; to arrest; to kill lawbreakers like Bickerstaff, Lee, and Baker; or to drive them from the region. His instructions to Chaffee were clear: "You will proceed to Sulphur Springs, Texas, and from that point as a rendezvous you will take the field and continuing generally in it until the bands of desperadoes commanded by Bickerstaff, Lee, English, Baker, or their confederates are broken up or driven from the country."[30] (For more on Chaffee's orders, see Appendix 5).

By September 1868, Reynolds had developed a more detailed plan, one that involved even more soldiers, to bring order and security to Northeast Texas. He ordered an additional regiment of infantry to reinforce the small garrison at Marshall and to wait there for further instruction. Cavalry would have been preferable, for the gangs of Bickerstaff, Baker, and Lee "were all well mounted and organized."[31]

Men afoot could not hope to cope with mounted, heavily armed men such as Bickerstaff and his fellows in crime. But, General U. S. Grant, commander of all the United States Armies, had ordered a reduction in cavalry regiments, part of a post-war demobilization effort, one that complicated matters in Northeast Texas. Even so, Reynolds was ready to use what troops he had. In a general order, Reynolds renewed the rewards for all the major guerrillas in the area.[32]

Next Reynolds ordered Lieutenant Colonel Samuel H. Starr, commander at Fort Richardson, to detach sixty or seventy more cavalrymen to lead a wagon train to reinforce Chaffee and Tolman, while also bringing needed supplies for their men. Reynolds ordered Captain (soon to be Colonel) Walter B. Pease of Company D, 17th U. S. Infantry, to reinforce the troops at Sulphur Springs, to take command, and to send a squad of men to Pilot Grove, the hamlet in Grayson County in the heart of Bob Lee Country.[33]

Once he arrived in Sulphur Springs, Pease reported that he was stationed in an area that was the most lawless in Texas. He wrote to his superiors, telling them that the Federals would need at least six months to clean out the region. Anticipating action soon, Reynolds ordered the Sulphur Springs contingent *not* to target non-violent supporters of the renegades and *not* to destroy private property of civilians. Then, by name, the general listed the quarry of Chaffee and Tolman: Bickerstaff, Lee, the English brothers, Pomp Duty, Guest, Baker, and their men.[34]

By the fall of 1868, statistics confirmed Captain Pease's views about widespread violence and major turmoil in Northeast Texas and most of the rest of the state. State grand juries had issued 5,000 indictments for murder since the end of the war, but authorities had carried out only one legal execution in the state, the condemned being a freedman in Houston. Loyal citizens in almost all of the Northeastern counties reported that active Klan-like terrorist groups continued to operate inside their respective borders.[35]

Concurrently, the Northeast Texas renegades continued their destruction. In addition to frequently riding with Baker and Lee, Bickerstaff maintained his association with other Northeast Texas desperadoes who often rode with his brigands.

The list of names of the outlaw leaders now included George and "Indian Bill" English; James Lockhart; Tom Emmitt; Abb Stephens; William Weston; Seth and Lee Rames; Charles Favirs; Josiah Thompson (Ben's best friend); Charley and Rash Weaver; Charley Farrow; Lum Houston; James and D. Grissom; Joe Winters; Thomas Wilkinson; Henry Traylor; "Wild Bill" Longley, once the latter had moved into Northeast Texas; and others. Their mayhem forced Federal authorities to station more men in garrisons at Clarksville, Sulphur Springs, and Mt. Pleasant.[36]

All the desperadoes were "products" of the Civil War and refused to let it end. Accustomed to violence and willing to fight, all had committed crimes and were on the run from Federal, state, and county authorities. But in their view, they were members of the "New Rebellion" that many Northern newspapers mentioned. According to one editor, they were "rough and ruthless."[37]

There is a little evidence that "rough and ruthless" Bickerstaff had a lighter side. William B. "Billie" Wortham, who lived in Austin in the 1920s, related a tale about the desperado. Wortham grew up near Sulphur Springs in the 1850s and 1860s. When he was but a boy, he had a pony that mysteriously disappeared. Suspecting that Bickerstaff or one of his men had stolen his mount, the boy bravely ventured into the guerrilla's camp in the bottoms of White Oak Creek. Boldly confronting Bickerstaff, Wortham stated his mission. Impressed with the boy's sand, Bickerstaff asked him if he were the son of "Colonel Wortham," late of the Confederate Army. Billie replied that he was. Bickerstaff smiled and told him to inspect the grounds to see if his horse was there. When the boy found his pony, the outlaw gave it back to him and sent him on his way.[38] That episode must have drawn chuckles from Bickerstaff's men because they knew him as a hardened killer who rarely had compassion for anyone.

Bickerstaff's opposition to Reconstruction reform, including the expansion of rights to the freedpeople, led him to propose a "military alliance" with Baker and Lee. The three would unite their gangs and continue the resistance, with Baker taking overall command as "captain" of the combined bands, and with Bickerstaff and Lee serving as "first lieutenants." Such a formal consolidation never took place, but the unholy trinity continued to ride together and to sometimes pool their men.[39]

Democratic leaders continued to support much of the regional violence whenever it flared anew. Many continued to sanction the outrageous actions of outlaws and Klansmen, seeing them as undermining the Republicans and the Reconstruction process. Looking forward to the former Confederate take over of the state, there were many "KKK Clubs." Leaders prepared barbecues for Democrats, encouraging them to vote the "right way." There also was intimidation of white Unionists and blacks. The county judge of Hopkins County forever complained about Bickerstaff in this regard, holding him responsible for most of the county's problems.[40]

Such was the nature of the Texas interior in August 1868: Many Democrats allowed the violence because it suited their goals, while Republicans and General Reynolds were now determined to make a direct assault on lawlessness. But, before any military effort could be mounted, there was the matter of Tolman, still stuck in the Sulphur Springs garrison with approximately thirty men, all trying to survive Bickerstaff's siege. Tolman was a hardened fighter. He was essential for Reynolds's "crackdown" to succeed. He had to be saved.

7

The Devil Be Damned, September 1868

Once other military men understood Tolman's dangerous situation, they moved to save his command. They intended to break the siege of Sulphur Springs. The renegades, helped by Klansmen, had stopped all couriers and supply wagons from reaching the garrison. They had cut off all the captain's communications. Tolman's command became isolated and needed outside help. The troops were running out of food, wood, and, more important, water. Despite the siege, a lone courier slipped through Bickerstaff's lines. He carried a message to Lieutenant J. H. Sands, the commanding officer of a small squad at Pilot Grove, to inform him of the developments in Sulphur Springs and of the woeful condition of the troops trapped inside the garrison.[1]

To relieve the beleaguered Tolman and his men, Sands seized the initiative. On September 3, 1868, he ordered his thirty-five-man contingent to march to Sulphur Springs. In his later report, Sands estimated that the number of Bickerstaff's force at 500 men strong. Though the lieutenant's estimate may have been exaggerated, likely Bickerstaff's ranks had increased because many of the otherwise sober citizens of Hopkins County had gleefully joined the siege. They bawled about burning out the Federals and killing them. As luck would have it, Sands--in addition to his small contingent--had at his disposal Lieutenant Vernou's small detachment from the Fourth Cavalry and a Lieutenant Larenburg's force from the Seventh Infantry, both units stationed near Pilot Grove.[2]

With Vernou in overall command, Sands ordered a detail in Sherman to take up the march and to join his contingent along the trail.

Sand's men covered twenty-three miles on the first day even though the march took the Bluecoats though dense thickets that were in the heart of Bob Lee Country. Sands took precautions. He was a professional no-nonsense officer, like Tolman. He shifted to a war footing. He sent out skirmishers to prevent a surprise ambush. He placed guards around Vernou's supply wagons. That night Sands set out pickets. He was ready to fight a pitched battle if necessary. In the second day's march, Sands's relief column covered fifty-six miles, a logistical feat that was hard on both men and animals, especially in the summer heat of Northeast Texas.[3]

Sands marched into town to relieve Tolman and found the command "under arms and ready to give us a volley." Bickerstaff and his men scattered just as Sands's forces reached the outskirts of town. The retreat suggests that they might not have known how many soldiers were approaching, or perhaps they simply wanted to avoid a fight with professional soldiers who had lately won the Civil War. Vernou commented that "Capt. Tolman and his command [were] in a desperate position," having been surrounded for a week by "at least two hundred men who have made all manner of threats if he did not submit to their terms. They . . . stopped his wood teams, and . . . tried every manner to cut him off."[4]

Vernou told his superiors that "I cannot give you any idea of the state of affairs in this [place]. The whole population of this county with few exceptions are in arms against the Government, and it will take not only a large force, but the most decided measures to put it in any sort of shape."[5] Like Vernou, Sands was pessimistic, saying that "the people all through the country we marched, evince the same spirit of lawlessness and resistance to civil law and only await a leading spirit to become as rebellious as those about Sulphur Springs. More troops are badly needed in this country and at this post [Sulphur Springs] which I should not be surprised at any moment to have attacked."[6]

Tolman had acted bravely, holding his post against vastly superior forces. But, he was a disciplined military officer up against a civilian mob of riff-raff who hesitated to engage in stand-up battles, preferring to do their fighting from ambushes when they had stealth coupled with superior numbers.

Later, an informant told the Federals that a farmer who lived about three miles from town was one of the leaders of the desperadoes, the messenger adding that some of the guerrillas were congregating on his farm. The "farmer" turned out to be Henry Farrar, one of Bickerstaff's trusted lieutenants. Tolman dispatched Sands and approximately fifty men to go to the place to investigate. The lieutenant and his men surprised about 150 raiders who were gathered there. A fight ensued wherein several horses were the only fatalities before the outlaw band, their superior numbers notwithstanding, fled.[7]

A few days later, Tolman received a "tip" on the whereabouts of Bickerstaff and his raiders. The informant claimed that they were hiding in a thicket about two miles from Sulphur Springs. Tolman sent Lieutenant Gustavus Schreyer out with all his squad, while Sand accompanied him and brought twenty-five of his own men, with Vernou accompanying the whole command. When Schreyer reached the thicket, he ordered a "charge" right into the heart of it. The detail wounded two of Bickerstaff's men before the terrorists escaped. Schreyer captured several horses and approximately twenty small arms. The detachment suffered only one man wounded and two dead horses. Heartened by Schreyer's "the devil be damned" aggressive action, Vernou told superiors that "Capt. Tolman will now be able to act on the offensive."[8]

The Yankees were successful in breaking the siege of Sulphur Springs; in subduing and scattering the enemy; and in sending them scampering for the thick bush near the farm. They chased the fleeing raiders, killing two and capturing a few more. That night Sands set out pickets to prevent a surprise attack. With no effect, Rebels fired on the pickets about midnight, but the guards returned fire and quiet returned. The next day, a guerrilla force led by Bickerstaff attacked a commissary train led by a Lieutenant Robinson near Sulphur Springs. When Sands learned of the incident, he led a twenty-five man relief column to save Robinson and his men. Sands's force surprised some of Bickerstaff's men and chased them into nearby woods. Later praised by his superiors, Sands managed to win his battle. Bickerstaff broke off the engagement and fled rather than confront the savvy officer and his column. The men saved the train and proved that they could be successful against the riff-raff opposing them if they had sufficient manpower and logistical support.[9]

The following day, Sands rode out of Sulphur Springs with a detachment of about fifty men, intending to return to Pilot Grove. About ten miles out of town, his skirmishers ran into another surprise attack led by Bickerstaff but managed to drive their enemies into a dense thicket. Sands tried to pursue them but found it impossible because of the thick bush. Back in Pilot Grove, Sands wrote his superiors, saying that "more troops are needed in this country."¹⁰

New developments proved Sands correct. Even before Sands delivered his report, blacks found a note nailed to a tree near a freedman's village in Lamar County, along Sanders's Creek:

> Notice is hereby given to all it may concern that Biggerstaff [*sic*] & Co. And Bob Lee & Co. Will visit this neighborhood on the 12th inst., and will continue from day to day until the Radical Party is exterminated or shows a perfect willingness to support the Democratic Party for any and every office whatever, this notice is principally intended for Charles Lee, and the other colored gentry living between the Red River and Sanders' Creek. All that cannot comply with this order had better hunt holes in the earth at once. We hope that all those who belong to the Conservative Party will sustain us.
> Yours, Friends to the Constitution and enemies to Congress.¹¹

The warning demonstrated that Bickerstaff, Lee, and others of their kind understood the political situation in Texas. They believed that they had good chances of survival if they continued to give lip service to the Lost Cause. As long as their violence helped the cause of the Democratic Party, it appeared that they could continue their criminal actions unchecked.

DeWitt Brown, still serving as the Bureau agent in Lamar County while awaiting a replacement, acknowledged that Bickerstaff, Bob Lee, and other robbers controlled the county and that it was impossible to enforce the law. The renegades were particularly hard on freedmen. According to Brown, "the freedpeople of this county have been generally robbed of their horses, clothing, arms, money, and other articles of that nature. They have been denied the legitimate fruits of their labor. They have been run off from their crops. Many have already left the county." Brown disgustedly reported that bands of up to sixty men "stomp through the country stealing all that is valuable (Brown's underlining) belonging to freedmen and Union men. Some freedmen have been murdered in cold blood and many have been whipped."¹²

Brown added that there was an agreement between local Democrats and the robbers to control the freedmen politically. If a black in Lamar County agreed to vote Democratic, he would be given "a Certificate of

Protection." Freedmen refusing to accept "protection" faced "immediate death." Continuing, Brown informed superiors that the Bureau "is extremely unpopular here" and that the local civilian government was as well because the public knew that local officials were cooperating with the Bureau. He concluded that "nothing short of martial law will do this country any good."[13]

Later, Brown learned that Baker was back in Lamar County, trying to recruit men, especially Klansmen, to lead another attempt to clean out the Union troops stationed in Sulphur Springs and the surrounding areas. In frustration, the agent wrote headquarters that "this is to certify that the Bureau of Refugees, Freedmen, and Abandoned Land in this Sub-District is powerless [and is] in the hands of its enemies. A corrupt public, aided by the Ku Klux Klan, has defied both the Bureau and the civil authorities. Troops are the <u>only means</u> (Brown's underlining) of restoring authority and of protecting this Sub-Assistant Com. From assassination!"[14]

Writing to General Reynolds, Paris civic leader M. L. Armstrong claimed that Brown's words reflected reality in Lamar County, adding that "bad men commit offenses" in the county "and take refuge in the Choctaw Nation."[15] A short time later, Brown told headquarters that his life was in "great danger." He pleaded that "unless I get help soon," the "desperadoes will kill me."[16]

Meanwhile, Bickerstaff, Vaden, and other gang members continued to persecute blacks and white Union men. One of the targets was Elijah "Lige" Reynolds, who was raised on a farm about five miles west of Sulphur Springs. He faced a tremendous decision when Texas seceded in 1861. A Unionist, he refused to commit treason by joining men who wanted to violently overthrow the United States Constitution. Although he had to leave his wife and two children behind, Reynolds fled to Mexico. From the Mexican coast he sailed to New Orleans where he met General Edmund J. Davis, a future governor of Texas. Reynolds volunteered for service in the 1st Texas Cavalry (Union), commanded by Davis.[17]

Reynolds remained with Davis for the rest of the war. When the regiment sailed from New Orleans and returned to northern Mexico, he participated in raids across the Rio Grande. He was among the first Union troops to occupy Texas and mustered out in 1866 while he was stationed in San Antonio. He returned to his Hopkins County farm near Sulphur Springs and tried to resume civilian life. But Reynolds's war record and continuing support for the Union were well known. One day he rode to town to pick up a few supplies. After loading the goods in his saddle bags, he began his return trip home. Although Lige Reynolds could not sense danger, a Bickerstaff man saw him ride into town and quickly rode out to tell Ben.[18]

Lige never reached home. Bickerstaff, Vaden, and several others caught him on the road and took him into a thicket where Vaden shot him off his horse. That round was lethal. The guerrillas dragged the corpse further into the thicket before leaving. Search parties found Lige's body four days later. Besides the victim, the search party also found the corpse of Reynolds's favorite dog. During the attack, the canine had tried to defend his master.

When Vaden dismounted to steal Reynolds's packages and rob his pockets, the dog attacked and bit the young hotspur on the calf of one leg, the bite leaving a permanent scar. Enraged, Vaden murdered the animal on the spot and draped its dead body across Reynolds's chest. Later asked by friends why he killed Reynolds, Vaden gave a short inaccurate reply: "He was an infernal Yankee."[19] Actually, Lige was but a loyal Texan who refused to support Dixie's suicidal war to save human slavery.

Even as Vaden was murdering Lige Reynolds, Chaffee and Tolman took to the field to implement General Reynolds's plan to kill the renegades or to chase them all over eastern Texas if necessary. Helped by only a handful of civilian Unionists led by Lewis Peacock whose farm was located near Pilot Grove, Chaffee and Tolman employed harsh tactics to get results. Locals soon began to refer to the two officers and their men as "Chaffee's Guerrillas."

Many civilians who had helped Bickerstaff, Baker, and Lee found themselves treated brutally. The punishment for some included being strung up by their thumbs, a tactic used by Bickerstaff during his days as a forage sergeant during the Civil War. Many Unionist observers noted, however, that the bloody business of finding Rebel murderers forced harsh measures to bring the law breakers and their accomplices to justice.[20]

Although Tolman later faced a military tribunal that reprimanded him for the brutal discipline that he imposed on his own men and that he meted out to civilians, the tactics brought some success. Chaffee and Tolman chased outlaws such as Bickerstaff, Lee, Baker, and other raiders across all of East-Northeast Texas. In a three-month campaign, the Federals traveled more than 1,000 miles.

Troopers caught and killed several of Bickerstaff's gang brave enough to come into the Pilot Grove saloon. They were looking for Bob Lee or some of his men. They might have been hoping to put themselves under Lee's protection so that they could enter his hidden headquarters in Wildcat Thicket. Though they did not find those whom they sought, the guerrillas decided to spend the day in the local grocery (saloon) and drink their life away, while generally raising hell with other men there. They made a terrible mistake, for the noted Unionist Peacock was in town; learned of the trouble in the saloon; alerted the Federal squad; and then helped them dispatch the drunken desperadoes.[21]

Despite the Federal crackdown, in September 1868, Bickerstaff and some of his men returned to Red River County and recruited local Klansmen for a new campaign to spread terror and violence. Eight disguised men raided the home of a freedman during broad daylight. Later, forty men surrounded another black man's home at night. Several burst into the place and rousted the family, who had to watch as everything they had of value was carted away. After going back to Hopkins County, Bickerstaff and his men were joined by Henry Farrar and his wing of the gang. Jointly, the renegades raided the homes of several more blacks.[22]

According to J. H. Fowler, interest in the coming elections ran high, and such men as Bickerstaff and Farrar did work that benefitted former Confederates who controlled the Democratic Party. The failure of the national Republicans to convict President Andrew Johnson of impeachment and remove him from office emboldened the Texas Democrats, who correctly believed that they would soon be returned to power. As Fowler put it, there was a "close alliance" among outlaw gangs, Klan terrorists, and the old secessionists. Fowler added that blacks in Red River County who agreed to support the Democratic Party received "protection" from the raiders, just as freedmen did in Lamar County.[23]

By mid-September 1868, the troubles caused by terrorist groups in Northeast Texas once again made an impact in Washington, D.C. Reports coming to the secretary of war painted a bleak picture of affairs in Northeast Texas. Mentioning Bickerstaff, Baker, Lee, and Jack English by name, one report referred to an attack by Bickerstaff and thirty of his men that had resulted in the murders of a sergeant, another enlisted man, and a civilian guide, the writer adding that Bickerstaff could raise up to 250 men when necessary. Such information illustrated the range, power, and danger of Bickerstaff and others of his ilk. That information also provided the necessary documentation to justify the ongoing military crackdown in Northeast Texas.[24]

In late September, Chaffee led another patrol through Northeastern Texas, gathering intelligence on the location of various outlaw bands in the region. Some of the information that he gathered was false. One informant told Chaffee that Bickerstaff had gone to Heelstring in Ellis County, which was not true. However, the major received some credible intelligence. He learned that many of the renegades, including Bickerstaff, had moved their families out of the region. Bickerstaff's wife moved to Hill County to a farm that her husband acquired earlier.[25]

Chaffee apprehended some of Bickerstaff's gang members while patrolling the region around Sulphur Springs. One of Chaffee's officers, Lieutenant Schreyer, recognized James W. Stringfellow as a guerrilla leader who was living at Tarrant in Hopkins County but who was wanted in Kansas for belonging to the renegade band that burned Topeka. Stringfellow had been making incendiary speeches, urging the citizens of Hopkins County to support Bickerstaff and to join the war on the Federal troops in the region. Chaffee arrested Stringfellow, took him to Sulphur Springs, and tossed him into a lock-up.

Of the renegades remaining in the area, Henry Farrar had become Bickerstaff's deputy and continued to lead them. Local military patrols eventually forced Farrar and the others to leave the vicinity, too. Farrar headed southeast hoping to make contact with his leader.[26]

Late in September, Colonel W. B. Pease arrived in Sulphur Springs to assume command of the post. He told superiors that as he was riding into the area, he found the town relatively quiet. He reported that the build up of troops at the post was responsible. Chaffee's entire command was there, as were Vernou's men, Sands's column, and a company from the 15th Infantry Regiment.

Pease's first action after taking command was to send Schyreyer and seventeen men to meet a commissary train coming from Waco, destined for various posts in Northeast Texas. The train only had a small guard and was coming through the area where Lee and Bickerstaff's men lurked. The Army did not want another supply train to be stolen.[27]

While troops in Sulphur Springs tried to bring justice to Northeast Texas, Bickerstaff returned to Titus County. He now traveled with George English, the felon who settled in the county after coming to Texas from Louisiana late in the 1850s. Shortly after their return, the two desperadoes caused major incidents not far from Gray Rock. Both men got drunk and began tormenting freedman Lum Kinchin, who was brave enough to argue with them. English shot Kinchin dead.

Next, they stopped at a small house in the countryside. As they dismounted, Bickerstaff saw a young black teenager, known simply as Flock. The renegade ordered Flock to come get his horse. When the youngster walked up to the outlaw, Bickerstaff drew his gun, intending to kill him. The head of a white family who lived in a house nearby intervened; he talked Bickerstaff into letting the boy live.

Curiously, Bickerstaff then told a whopper. He said that a Yankee had killed his father during the war and that, for revenge, he was going to kill all the freedmen who crossed his path. Perhaps the outlaw mistakenly believed that his father had been killed during the more recent struggle between the regional terrorists and Federal troops because Union soldier had visited Seaborne Bickerstaff's farm on more than one occasions looking

Ripley Creek ran through the Bickerstaff homeplace. Along the creek, Ben and his brother James honed their skills as marksmen while hunting small game for the family table. Courtesy of Carol C. Taylor.

for his renegade son. Regardless, Ben let the youth live; next, in his drunken state, he laid down on the porch of the house and passed out next to English who was already asleep. The next day, the two desperadoes had vanished.[28]

While Bickerstaff plagued Titus County and the surrounding areas, other terrorists were causing havoc in Hunt County. Early in September, area guerrillas found the nephew of District Judge Hardin Hart--a noted Unionist who complained frequently to authorities about the lawlessness in the Northeastern part of the state--in Hunt County without protection. They murdered him. Authorities believed that Bob Lee and his raiders were the killers. The murdered man's mother and widow witnessed the killing and signed a joint affidavit implicating Lee in the murder plot, but the Hunt County Sheriff failed to take action, probably because of collusion with the murderers or, perhaps, because of fear.[29]

Colonel Pease, the former Freedman's Bureau agent, still commanding the post at Sulphur Springs, went to Greenville and ordered the sheriff to go after two of the alleged killers, one named Wings and the other named B. Harris, both of whom belonged to the Lee gang, both sometimes riding with Bickerstaff.

An informant, the young seventeen-year-old Unionist Finley Graham, the son of the noted Unionist Robert B. Graham of Hunt County, who earlier had joined the raiders intending to expose them, told Pease that he had witnessed the murder of Hart. Graham said that he would testify in court in return for immunity, a favor easily granted, for the colonel was working with his father and had cooperated with the scheme to infiltrate the gang.[30]

Finley Graham had an interesting past. Like the rest of his family, he was a committed Unionist who opposed secession, but during the Civil War he served as a member of the "Greenville Guards." During Reconstruction, he became a Hunt County voter registrar, holding that post from 1867 to 1868 before he moved to Grayson County. How such a Unionist gained the confidence of former Confederates is a mystery.

After Graham delivered his information, Pease ordered the sheriff to summon ten mounted men. Because he did not trust civilian authorities, Pease ordered Lieutenant William Van Horne and a six-man squad of troopers to accompany the posse. A problem developed when civilians summoned by the sheriff refused service either out of fear or in a show of support for the villains who had killed young Hart.[31]

Learning that civilians were not cooperating, Pease explained to the populace that they must cooperate with civilian authorities and enforce their own laws or that the military would be forced to take charge and that he would station troops among them. Ten volunteers step forward.

At 4:00 p.m., the military-civilian posse then rode for the farms of the murderers. The sheriff sent three back to town because they had purposefully "forgotten" to take their weapons. Concurrently, the disgusted Van Horne set out pickets on the roads leading to the suspects' homes to stop any spies who might try to warn the murderers. Close to nightfall, just as the posse was reaching the house of one of the raiders, Van Horne, a former Bureau agent, saw two parties of six to eight men riding toward the house from opposite directions. When the strangers saw the soldiers, both parties took to the woods for cover.[32]

On reaching the house, the posse noted that the place was forted-up, ready for battle. It was a dog trot log cabin with chinks between some logs removed to make holes from which to fire rifles, shotguns, and handguns. Within the house, a speaker tauted the posse: "Come on damn you, we are

Thicket near the homes of Wings and Harris who escaped into it to foil the authorities. Courtesy of Carol C. Taylor.

ready for you."³³ Although gunplay remained a possibility, the sheriff convinced Wings and Harris to surrender peacefully after Lieutenant Van Horne promised that they would remain in the hands of civilian authorities rather than be tried by a military commission.

The lieutenant's men then searched the place. Inside the house, besides Wings and Harris, were five heavily armed men, some women, and several fretful children. They were left in peace. After being arrested, Wings bragged to Van Horne that if the posse had arrived a few minutes later, their friends would have arrived, and a "fierce resistance" would have been offered.³⁴

Although it was twilight, after Wings and Harris agreed not to try to escape, the sheriff foolishly allowed them to ride their own horses to Greenville, nine or ten miles away. The twin terrors did not keep their pledges. When the riders reached a strip of woods near a ravine, Wings and Harris let out yells; spurred their mounts; raced them toward the woods; and disappeared into the darkness. Their cries were a signal because unseen parties in the woods answered with their own yells. Graham was still riding with the gang to gain more information. He later told Van Horne that about fifty men, twenty-five or so on either side of the road, had been riding parallel to the posse's route. The guerrillas were prepared to attack if necessary to liberate their cohorts. Although Van Horne did not know how numerous the enemy was at the time, he wisely decided not to pursue with his small squad, especially not through a thick forest in the dead of night. On behalf of Wings and Harris, the ruffians soon threatened to kill young Hart's mother and widow because the two women had identified Hart's killers.³⁵

Before Pease left Greenville, a leading Rebel told him that the renegades had learned that Graham was an informer, that the young man would be dead within one hour after the Federals left town. The colonel did the logical thing: He took Graham with him along with Judge Hart's young crippled son who had been in the posse to arrest his cousin's killers. After Pease and his men returned to Sulphur Springs, several men implicated in Hart's murder surrendered to civil officials, but Wings was not among them. At least fourteen heavily armed renegades accompanied those who surrendered, a sign that new trouble was afoot.³⁶

Once in town, several raiders fired pistol rounds into Judge Hart's tavern where the younger Hart's mother and widow were hiding. One renegade shouted that the two women "should leave the county, that they [the gang] would not allow them to live in it." About forty raiders picketed all the roads leading to Greenville. Some members of the bad bunch openly proclaimed that there would be a trial and that their friends would be declared innocent because there would be no eye witnesses. The guerrillas warned that no one who testified against the murderers would leave the town's public square alive. Local authorities had no choice but to postpone their investigation and their prosecution of the crime.[37]

Straightaway, approximately 150 men attended a meeting in the rural neighborhood where Wings and Harris lived. They unanimously voted to fight to stop the conviction of their friends. Some said that they could raise another 125 allies and would have ample fire power to drive the soldiers out of Hopkins and Hunt counties. Colonel Pease later claimed that many of the men belonged to the Hunt County Ku Klux Klan. An informant said that many of the men had come from far and wide in groups. One contemporary source reported that Bickerstaff and Guest were present, as were many others from throughout Northeast Texas. They introduced themselves as "Bob Lee men"; "Bickerstaff men"; "Henry Farrar men"; "Marshal men"; "Pomp Duty men"; and so on. Mentioned earlier, some men had learned the identity of Pease's informant Finley Graham. B. Harris, his son Thomas, James Babb, and Thomas Coker vowed to kill the young brave heart. Because of the threat, Graham went into hiding for a time and temporarily escaped from the Second Civil War ongoing in Northeast Texas.[38]

8

In A State Worse Than Open War, October-December, 1868

In October, Bickerstaff rode into Marion County with Cullen Baker and a few other heavily armed men. They set up a camp in the bush but slipped into Jefferson at night to prowl around the town. They made contact with the area Klan group, the Knights of the Rising Sun and joined them to rid the county of a troublesome Union man. On October 4, they and others murdered Unionist George W. Smith, a storekeeper in Jefferson. Though he was white, he had become a major leader of area freedmen, trying to protect them from fraud and from being cheated out of their crop shares. A Civil War veteran, Smith had fought for the Union during the conflict, serving in a New York brigade. Attracted by cheap land that had deflated in value, he moved to Texas after the war and bought a farm.[1]

Settling in Jefferson and opening a general store, he joined the local Union League (also known as the Loyal League) and worked closely with the local Freedmen's Bureau agent. He became a delegate of the constitutional convention of 1868-1869, representing the interests of both blacks and whites living in his area. Smith joined the Republican Party, and his colleagues placed him on the party's executive committee.

According to many who knew him, he was a good man with few vices. He was "gentle" in his habits and "never visited brothels." He never drank alcohol and was careful with his language. He had good manners and reasonable habits. Even so, most of Marion County's former Confederates detested him, pejoratively labeling him a Yankee carpetbagger. Opposing him was the powerful organization, Knights of the Rising Sun. The number of its members may have topped 100.[2]

Earlier, in May, unknown parties attempted to assassinate Smith and failed, but they caught a freedman who was with him and cut the black man's throat from ear-to-ear. They also took Smith's suitcase and shredded it and its contents, including his convention documents, but Smith escaped. One observer believed that Jefferson would soon be on the "verge of eruption." In August, a band of the Knights tried to make that prediction come true. They waylaid Smith in a nighttime ambush, with several men firing at him in unison.

The Yankee and another friend, freedman Anderson Wright, shot back, wounding two of their attackers. Afterward, several of the Knights brought charges of assault with intent to kill. Pro-Confederate civil authorities aligned with the Democratic Party arrested Smith and Wright and tossed them into an insecure jail. Federal troops who had just arrived to establish a garrison tried to protect the prisoners. Major James Curtis led the fifteen-man squad, members of the 15th United States Infantry Regiment. Once again came the absurdity of a squad of infantry afoot having to cope with raiders who had good mounts. After an examination of affairs in the area, Curtis noted that whites committed "unblushing fraud and outrage" upon the freedmen and that little notice was paid whenever blacks were murdered.[3]

Curtis ordered several of his men to take their shotguns and follow him while he "scoured the country" for desperadoes. When he learned that Smith and Wright were in jail, he sent the rest of his men to protect them while he led the other squad on their patrol. Before Curtis returned with the balance of his force, at least forty disguised Knights, possibly more (one source says 120), approached the jail, and easily disarmed the Federals there. Then, through an open, barred window, they shot Smith repeatedly just as Curtis was arriving at the scene.[4]

The disguised Knights, with Baker and Bickerstaff accompanying them, were so numerous that they easily overpowered Curtis and his men. While some of the terrorists kept guns trained on the soldiers, several of the Knights went into the jail, got into Smith's cell, and, again, shot their victim repeatedly. The crazed terrorists did not stop shooting until they had emptied their guns. General Reynolds was so stunned by the murders in Jefferson that he issued General Order No. 15, on October 12, 1868, the order forbidding anyone to wear a mask. According to the order, military officers would arrest all violators.[5]

Bickerstaff was still in Marion County when a number of freedmen organized a militia to protect themselves against the Knights of the Rising Sun, the leaders of which constantly threatened area blacks with extinction and often assaulted various of their number. The Knights willingly helped landlords who had sharecroppers on their land. The terrorists--in numbers meant to be threatening and overwhelming--drove both white and black croppers from the land just after harvest, thereby allowing the owners to claim all the crops. According to one freedman, Dick Walker led the black men who met regularly at the African Methodist Church in Jefferson. They exchanged news, plotted strategy, and drilled in military fashion.[6]

The possibility of armed blacks fighting back alarmed many whites. Led by Bickerstaff and Henry Fowler, an area farmer, about thirty heavily armed whites marched to the church, and, with little thought at all, started shooting through the windows when the leaders of the militia were meeting. They killed several blacks and wounded a number of others. Bickerstaff and his men crushed the militia movement, leaving the freedpeople to live in terror while the Knights or other white terrorists roamed freely in the county. Blacks in the countryside often slept hidden in wooded areas at night out of fear that the renegades would raid their homes with murder on their minds.[7]

After the raiders attacked the black militia group, Bickerstaff and his men left the Jefferson area and rode back to Hopkins County. But, the military presence in there, coupled with the $1,000 reward on his head, made the place too dangerous for Bickerstaff. He knew how to fight and kill, but he also knew when it was time to run. For a time, he vanished.[8]

While Bickerstaff made his way out of Hopkins County, Cullen Baker rode back to Boston, Bowie County, and began plotting his revenge on the Bureau agent stationed there, William T. Kirkman. Baker apparently never forgave Kirkman, nor DeWitt Brown, for wounding him during their shootout in Boston in July 1867. Having rid the region of Charles Rand and believing that he had also run off DeWitt Brown, now it was time to deal with Kirkman.

At approximately 2:00 a.m. on October 7, 1868, Baker, Elisha Guest, and several other renegades assassinated Kirkman. The agent had established a record of fair dealings with the area's black community. Local Unionists praised him while those loyal to the Lost Cause condemned him. The Freedmen's Bureau was being phased out, and agents such as Kirkman had to make plans for the next stages of their lives. On the night of October 6, Kirkman worked late into the evening trying to finish his paperwork and get his files in order.⁹

Still working in his office, he heard noises outside at about 2:00 a.m. He then made a terrible mistake. Alone, he went to the office door, opened it, and stepped out to see what the ruckus was about. He was dead before he hit the ground. Baker, Guest, and two other men had been making the noises, and the agent did exactly what they expected him to do. From the shadows, the felons fired sixteen rounds at Kirkman, while he fired only once. Shotgun blasts penetrated his breast, side, and shoulder. But the fatal shot came from a revolver bullet that went into his brain from the right side of his head.¹⁰

Although the shooting could be heard for blocks around, only a lone black man was brave enough to approach the corpse. Other people were terrified that the killers might set upon them. They stayed in their homes, cowering. Their fears may have saved them because the murderers did not leave town. After waiting almost an hour, Baker, Guest, and the other men approached the body to confirm that Kirkman was dead. Each was heavily armed, all four having a double-barreled shotgun and several revolvers. The assassins robbed the corpse of a revolver and took Kirkman's horse.¹¹ Affairs once again in Northeast Texas appeared to be deteriorating even as Chaffee's Guerrillas remained in the field.

Reporting to superiors early in October, Colonel Pease drew a darker picture of the Northeast Texas region than ever before. Referring to events that occurred in Hopkins County during the previous month, he told his superiors that small parties of Bickerstaff and Farrar's gang had been "prowling about" in the vicinity of Sulphur Springs, hiding in the bush, looking for any military weakness that would allow them to attack. With Farrar in command while Bickerstaff was away, on the night of October 3 some of the renegades fired on a patrol whose men returned fire with no damage done to either party. Much worse, Pease said, the Bickerstaff forces tried again to set fire to Sulphur Springs on several occasions.¹²

In the most recent failed attempt, the raiders stole into the kitchen of the local hotel, diagonally across the narrow street from the garrison, about 10:00 p.m., where Pease continued to share a room with his wife. The arsonists were discovered and ran away before they could start a blaze. Also there were the post surgeon and several officers in the cavalry and their wives. Clearly, the guerrillas were trying to murder such men because their leadership was vital to the post. As well, Pease feared conditions would worsen as the election season wore on. About the arson: The colonel convinced civilians in town to organize a fire patrol to save their property because it was probable that the marauders would try to torch the entire place, just as they had tried in the past. A blazing fire might spread and engulf the whole downtown area.[13]

Pease feared that more trouble would soon develop. The people of East Texas, he said, were organizing more Ku Klux Clubs, "fully officered" and "thoroughly armed." The guerrillas became bolder as their numbers increased. Lee and Bickerstaff were involved, and young Graham was still under a death threat. Pease believed that the only way to restore order was to have Chaffee and Tolman continue their campaign against lawlessness. The colonel's report left no doubt that the Second Civil War was still ongoing.

Pease was even more distressed by the end of October. He told his superiors that he had not been able to devote time to uplifting the freedpeople. All he could do was to try protect them with the troops under his command. He suggested to his superiors that they should hire spies to gather information on the divisive elements in the population.[14]

Pease said that he could only control Sulphur Springs, not the countryside. "Numerous [racial] outrages are reported . . . in this and surrounding counties--whipping, robbing, etc., but they come to me in the shape of rumors and I have not the data to make a specific report."[15] Some observers wondered how Pease used his troops. He had one company of infantry, good for the town, and one company of cavalry, good for the countryside.

Some people wondered why Pease could not do something to bring the Bickerstaff rabble to justice. In fairness to the colonel, however, his men had an entire sub-district of several counties to patrol. One company of cavalry, about 100 men, could not patrol the entire district while coping with the constant chaos caused by Bickerstaff and other renegades.[16]

As if replying to his critics, Pease elaborated on his view of the situation:

> There is no use denying the fact, that this region is in a state worse than open war: The great majority of the people are openly inimical to the Government, and the troops are . . . objects of special hatred . . . and it is boasted that in a certain event the soldiers will be driven from the county by force. I consider it imperative that the troops at the various posts be

... placed in a position to defend themselves against any force before the results of the November election are known. The whole people of the region are (with a few exceptions) organized into Ku Klux Clubs ... divided into companies, fully officered and thoroughly armed.[17]

Despite his negative assessment, Pease had some good luck. After terrorists had threatened his life, the Unionist Edward Musgrove, called a "citizen refugee," sought and received asylum in the local garrison. In return for Pease's protection, Musgrove became a scout and guide for the colonel's patrols.[18]

Still trying to gain control of Hopkins County and its environs,

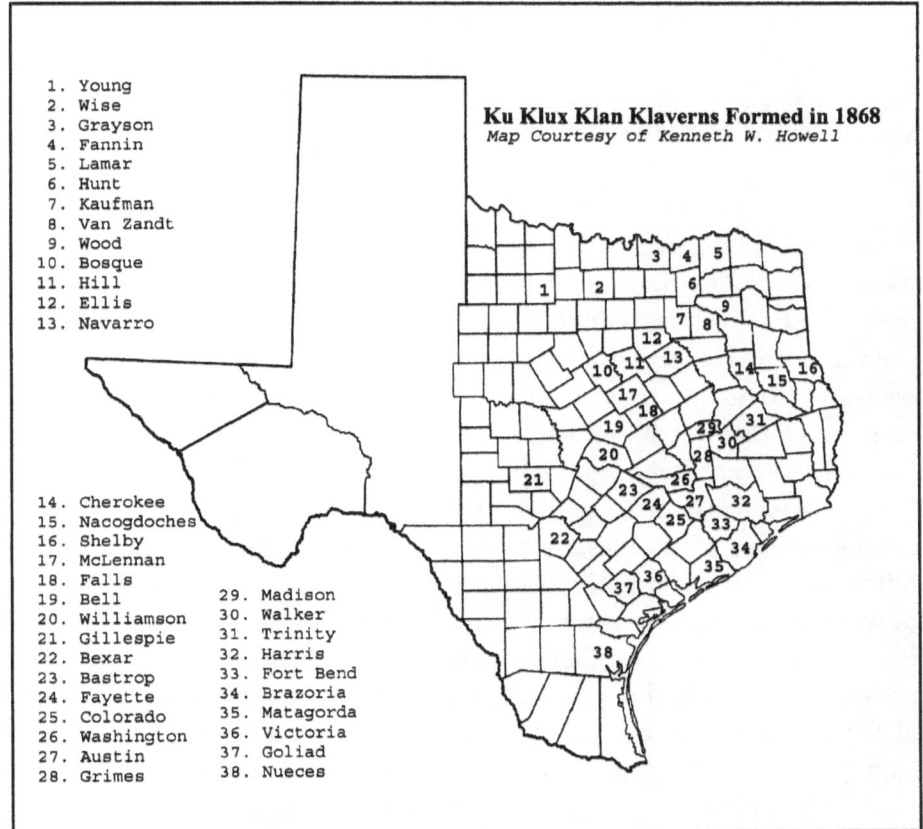

Map indicates the number of terrorist Klan-like groups that existed in Texas by 1868. Courtesy of Kenneth Howell

Pease empowered the citizens' fire patrol to arrest anyone carrying weapons other than soldiers or other employees of government. He established an 8:00 p.m. curfew for Sulphur Springs, again giving the fire patrol the authority to arrest any "suspicious parties" lurking around town after curfew. Pease told the citizen's patrol to use lethal firepower if necessary to control malefactors.[19] Clearly, the colonel was a no-nonsense officer, much like Chaffee and Tolman.

The critical situation in Northeast Texas caused by Bickerstaff and the other guerrillas prompted General Reynolds to send a discouraging report to the Army's adjutant general. The Texas commander said that "armed organizations, generally known as Ku Klux Klans exist, independently or in concert with other armed bands" in many parts of Texas, "but are most numerous, bold and aggressive east of the Trinity River." Reynolds reported that the purposes of these violent organizations appeared to be "to disarm, rob, and in many cases murder union men and negroes, and as occasions may offer to murder U.S. Officers and soldiers; also to intimidate everyone who knows anything of the organization, but who will not join it."[20]

The general noted that "civil law east of the Trinity is almost a dead letter. In some counties the civil officers, are all, or a portion of them, members of the Klan, or some other armed band. In other counties where the civil officer will not join the Klan, or some other armed band, they have been compelled to leave their counties." Reynolds averred that "the murder of negroes is so common as to render it impossible to keep an accurate account of them." He said that "perpetrators of such crime have not heretofore, except in very rare instances, been punished in this state at all."[21]

Reynolds referred to the murder of George W. Smith in Jefferson, adding that he had to pull some troops from the frontier and order them to Jefferson to deal with the Klan-led terror there. Reynolds in effect said that he was in a "no-win" situation. Weakening frontier defense emboldened the Plains Indians to continue their resistance, but the general said that he could not allow anarchy in the settled portion of Texas. He concluded: "In view of the present conditions of this state, and the revolutionary attitude of a large portion of the population, I . . . request that another Regiment of Infantry be ordered to this state, to rendevous at Marshall and Jefferson."[22]

In reality, to handle the troubles in East-Northeast Texas, Reynold needed more than just one more regiment of 1,000 men: Most likely, he needed a full corps, but such would never be forthcoming, given demobilization and the lack of Northern will.

In October 1868, even as the woebegone Reynolds pled for more men, Major Chaffee led a patrol to capture Bickerstaff. Chaffee left Sulphur Springs on October 16 and took his detail to the Sabine River bottoms where Ben Bickerstaff and his men had been terrifying black families. About twenty miles out of Sulphur Springs, an informant told Chaffee that he had seen Bickerstaff riding with a man named Porter and Taylor Bowman, when they were crossing the Sabine on Dement's Bridge. The major estimated that his quarry was about three days ahead of him. Chaffee and his men rode hard to gain time. They first went to the "Brook place," formerly Bickerstaff's home. The guerrillas had stopped there temporarily but had left still well ahead of the Bluecoats.[23]

Once the detail reached the Brook farm, Chaffee learned that

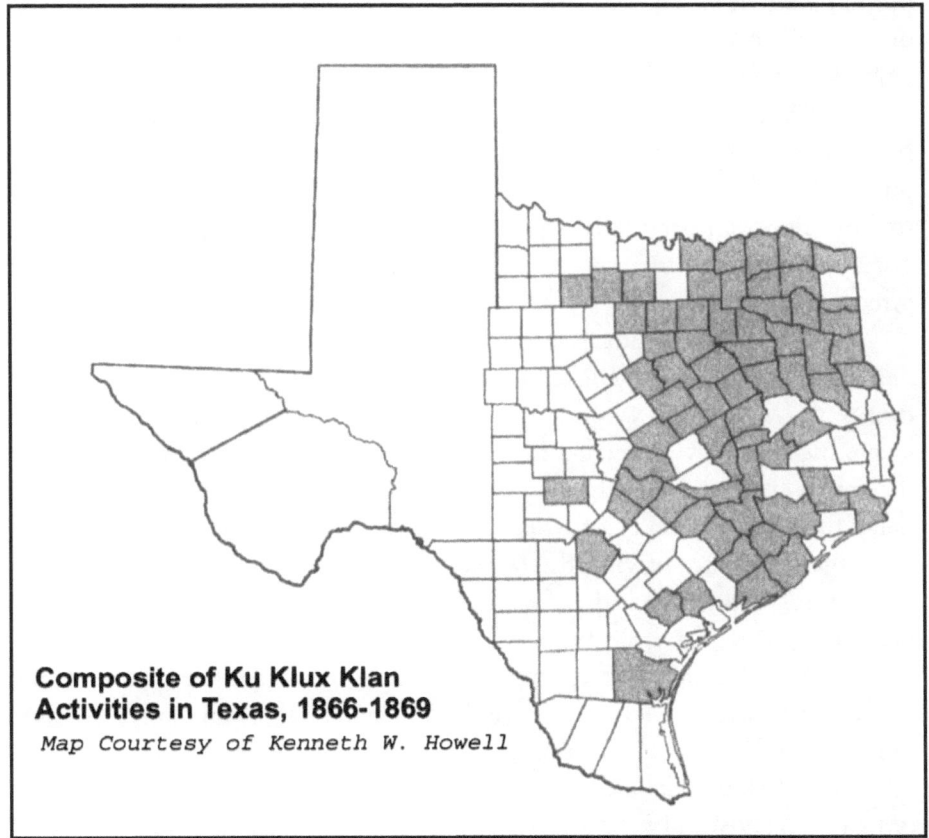

Map indicates the number of terrorist Klan-like groups that existed in Texas from 1865 to 1868. Courtesy of Kenneth Howell

Bickerstaff and his men had taken the road to Gray Rock where Ben's parents lived. The Yankees stayed on the trail of the raiders. When Chaffee believed that he was closing the gap, he sent a courier back to Sulphur Springs with a request that Colonel Pease send an officer and another detail of men to Gray Rock as fast as possible. Pease sent Lieutenant Schreyer and several men. Once Schreyer's detail arrived, the lieutenant surrounded the house of Bickerstaff's parents at 4:00 a.m. on October 18.

Although Bickerstaff and Porter slipped away, Schreyer arrested Seaborne Bickerstaff, Taylor and G. G. Bowman, and three other men. The lieutenant impounded five horses and three mules, all stolen, and took them back to Sulphur Springs. Before reaching the post, Schreyer arrested several more of Bickerstaff's men: A. G. Vandiver, George Branch, William Bowman, and the good Reverend William Ellis. All the men had actively participated in many of Bickerstaff's robberies and murders. Schreyer dumped his captives in the post guardhouse, where they joined three more of Bickerstaff's band: J. M. Frame, C. W. Stokes, and Cornelius Jones.[24]

Pease praised Scyreyer and his men for demonstrating "energy, promptness, and fearlessness." Continuing, Pease said that the men left the post on October 17, with less than an hour's notice, rode through a dark and stormy night, and made thirty miles before sunup. They captured their quarry, rode back, and reported their successful mission to Pease at 2:00 p.m.[25]

While Lieutenant Schreyer tasted success, Chaffee remained in the field. He picked up Bickerstaff's trail from Springfield to Quitman thence to Winnsboro where Chaffee lost Bickerstaff's tracks.[26] Failing to locate his quarry, Chaffee led his men to Hillsboro in Hill County, where the raider had established a new place about six miles east of town. The detail found the place, but Bickerstaff was nowhere in sight; he had escaped once again. Before leaving the farm, the major impounded several horses and mules. Other stock there consisted of cows and calves; Chaffee asked the county sheriff to hold them subject to orders from headquarters.

After talking to several people in the area, the Yankee leader learned that no one west of the Trinity River knew Bickerstaff's real name. He used the aliases of "Wilson" or "Jones," depending on where he was. Chaffee could not pick up Bickerstaff's trail at the farm and had little choice but to return to the post. This time Ben was riding east to get away from Chaffee.[27]

Bickerstaff did not stop until he reached Marion County. He began new operations there, a place where he had earlier had so much success in robbing and killing freedmen. Cullen Baker and his men gleefully joined Bickerstaff's renegades there. Using the alias of "Franks," Ben was with Baker when the latter launched his last campaign of terror. On October 24 between 2:00 and 4:00 a.m., Bickerstaff and Baker, accompanied by a gang member, rode to James Salmon's place about five or six miles from Atlanta in Caldwell County. The journey was prompted by revenge. Baker believed that Salmon had become an informer for the authorities and had helped the military track him nearly a year before. He also believed that Salmon had taken part in the gunplay that ended the life of his friend Seth Rames, a marauder who rode with Baker or ocassionally with Bickerstaff.[28]

Once the disguised killers, each dressed as Union soldiers, reached the porch of the home, they claimed to be Federals and asked Salmon, whom they had rousted out of bed, to come out. When Salmon opened the door, the villains rushed in and overpowered him. Next, according to Thomas Orr, who would soon kill Baker, the guerrillas "instituted a general carnival of plunder and robbery." They sacked the place. They opened trunks and closets, taking anything of value, including cash, coins, arms, and ammunition. They slit and searched bedding, looking for more loot.

When they left, they took a saddle, a bridle, saddlebags, and a mule. They also took Salmon with them, leaving his wife on the porch begging for mercy as they rode away. Although the killers told her that they would not harm her husband, some distance from the house, they murdered the man. His wife heard the shots and well knew what that meant. Without her husband, she slowly wasted away.[29]

After killing Salmon, the renegades remained in the Jefferson area, terrorizing other peaceful folks. They murdered three more freedmen in two separate attacks. But Bickerstaff and Baker's plundering in Marion County was about to end. Military men coming out of the post at Jefferson, took up their trail. Lieutenant A. G. Malloy and Captain James Brown managed to arrest one of the raiders, Joseph Weaver, who had been with Bickerstaff the previous summer when the guerrillas robbed the military train in Hopkins County. Authorities also suspected him of several murders. The Federals held Weaver in the guardhouse in Jefferson until they returned him to Sulphur Springs to stand trial.[30]

To escape a dragnet, Baker and his men rode north while the Bickerstaff men slipped away to the southwest and disappeared into Navarro County again. Soon, two men, one fitting the description of

Bickerstaff, began harassing several black sharecroppers. Soon, Ben ran again, this time to Wood County.[31]

Concurrently, Captain Tolman continued to take the fight to the enemy. He went after Wings, one of the killers of young Hart, who was rumored to be hiding in Wood County near his farm. Arriving at the place, the captain found only Wings's wife. Tolman believed that Wings was hiding in a nearby thicket and that his wife was taking him food and water, but Tolman could not find him. The captain learned from an informant that Bickerstaff had been seen in the county, along with his constant companions, one Porter and one of the Bowman brothers, who had escaped from jail. Tolman picked up their trail but lost it when they crossed the Sabine River. Like Chaffee, he decided to go to Bickerstaff's place in Hill County. Tolman reached and searched the place, but Bickerstaff was nowhere to be seen.[32]

The captain did find a large cache of stolen property, including government commissary stores and a wagon that belonged to a freedman in Jefferson. Tolman followed Bickerstaff's trail until he reached Ellis County, where he found and arrested Porter and the Bowman brother, but Bickerstaff was not with them. He had managed to slip away once again. Tolman and his squad then took their prisoners to Sulphur Springs. The captain and his scouts had covered a circuit of about three hundred miles.[33]

That Tolman found a wagon from Jefferson indicated that Bickerstaff's range was greater than some of the other guerrilla leaders. He stuck as far south as Navarro County, also raiding into Wood, Van Zandt, and Hunt counties, Hunt being Bob Lee Country. Whenever Lee learned that Bickerstaff was near, he and some of his band always found the bushwacker, cooperated in his schemes, and accompanied him back to Hopkins County when the death-dealing was done. On at least one occasion, Bickerstaff, Lee, and some of their men held a meeting, wherein they renewed their earlier threats to kill all freedmen caught between the Red River and Sanders Creek. Bickerstaff again negotiated with Lee and Baker about a formal alliance, but one never materialized.

Still, the renegades remained in contact and continued to work together closely to defeat the Reconstruction process while simultaneously enriching themselves with booty, the latter being their main goal. Bickerstaff, Baker, Lee, Guest, English, and other outlaws—the whole sorry lot remained active and violent as did the region's Klans.[34]

Bickerstaff and other desperadoes created such a desperate situation that the entire nation heard more about the "Texas Troubles" than ever before. To counter this bad publicity, H. C. Mack, in his *Texas: Information for Emigrants*, minimized the number of guerrilla raiders and the inordinate amount of violence in the state. He believed that reports of violence greatly reduced the emigration the state needed for further economic expansion. Mack argued that the Northern press exaggerated the problems of Texas. He admitted that the state had a "few famous characters" and mentioned Bickerstaff, Baker, and Lee by name, but he defended them by blaming Reconstruction policies, occupying forces, native white Unionists, and the freedpeople for causing all the bloodshed.[35]

While Mack was lying, on November 2, Colonel Pease took a squad of eighteen men to the Hopkins County farm of one Withers, rumored to be hiding gang members on his land. A search turned up nothing. Bickerstaff and his men still had a knack for vanishing when the authorities came too close.[36]

With lawmen and federal troopers close on their trail, Bickerstaff, his associate Matt Kirby, and a few other men slipped away from Hopkins County only to pop up later in Johnson County. Before leaving the area,

Captain Tolman lost Wings' trail after the guerrilla crossed the Sabine Ricer Courtesy of Bill O'Neal

however, Bickerstaff visited his parents who still lived on their farm near Gray Rock in Titus County. An Army informant saw him and alerted military authorities. A squad of troopers rode to Seaborne Bickerstaff's place and surrounded it before sunup on a cold winter day. Not knowing that Ben had already left, they hailed the house at sunrise, asking for surrender. Both of Bickerstaff's parents came out of their home and indeed surrendered, but the leader of the squad did not believe them when they reported that their son had fled. The troopers fired repeatedly into the house until they thought that anyone inside must be dead. A search proved that Ben's parents had told the truth.[37]

The squad arrested Bickerstaff's parents, charging them with harboring a felon. Although the military commander at Mount Pleasant allowed Mrs. Bickerstaff to go home, a squad took Seaborne to the Jefferson garrison and tossed him into a cell, officers later moving him to Sulphur Springs. The commander there hoped that having Bickerstaff's father in custody would lure the gunman into the open. However, like most desperadoes, Ben put his own safety first. He did not try to assist his father. He fled instead.[38]

Seaborne Bickerstaff remained in custody until mid-December. Still commanding the Sulphur Springs garrison, Colonel Pease finally released him on $3,000 bond. The officer cited Seaborne's age and his health problems (a pulmonary disorder) as the reasons for releasing the old man. While Seaborne caused no problems in the future, Pease cited the same reasons for releasing John Marshall, Sr., a member of Bob Lee's gang who sometimes rode with Bickerstaff. Marshall returned home, reestablished his ties with Lee, and helped the Lee and Bickerstaff raiders commit more devilry.[39]

To add to that devilry, Cullen Baker--called by one newspaper editor "Bickerstaff's lieutenant"--issued a manifesto in the fall of 1868, one that claimed allegiance to the Lost Cause. Hoping to curry favor with former Confederates, Baker wrote:

> Bowie County, Texas
> November 14, 1868
> Editors of the *Jefferson Times*:
>   Permit me to publish a statement in your paper in order to place myself right before the Government and the people of the country. Various rumors have circulation

through the country in regard to my course of conduct . . . I deem it necessary to declare my sentiments and intentions for the future . . . I am strictly in favor of the enforcement of the civil laws of the country by the legitimate authorities; and I now declare that it is my purpose to protect the quiet citizens . . . either white or black in pursuit of their avocations. This is my native country, and my interests are identical with those other citizens of the country; and I hope to remain in the counties of Davis, Bowie, and Marion, and the adjoining counties of Eastern Texas . . . The white man and the black man will be perfectly safe in my hands so long as he leaves me alone.[40]

Baker denied that he had committed any crimes. His statement was a master stroke in shifting blame from himself to his "enemies," those enemies including Union soldiers and members of the Republican Party.[41]

Meanwhile, Colonel Pease had military business that involved Bickerstaff's marauders. Pease had a quartermaster's check of $4,000, but to cash it, he had to send a courier to Shreveport, Louisiana, to find a bank that could handle that amount of money. He knew that the route included passing from Sulphur Springs through Marshall before reaching the bank, and he realized that the courier would have to ride through areas controlled by Bickerstaff and Baker. Robbery and murder were in the offing.[42]

Some of Bickerstaff's men learned of the $4,000 check and where it was going. Tom Emmett and a man named Carpenter, both Bickerstaff men, tried to raise a small force that could take the money when the courier made his return trip. Pease decided that his courier needed an escort for protection and that perhaps the escort could turn the trip into a scouting patrol that might capture some of the terrorists. Pease organized another dragnet, hoping the raiders' lust for the $4,000 would lead them to make mistakes that would result in their capture or their deaths. On November 17, he detached Lieutenants Schreyer and H. Horton and nine enlisted men to guard the courier.[43]

After Schreyer's squad left, Pease ordered Lieutenant James Burns and six enlisted men, dressed in civilian clothes, to follow Schreyer as far as Gray Rock. Burns was to seek any source of information about the location of the desperadoes. After scouting Gray Rock, the lieutenant and his men, as per Pease's orders, went to the home of Bickerstaff's parents and looked about for signs of the gang. It was a job that Schreyer could not do, for he had earlier arrested both of Bickerstaff's parents; but they had never seen Burns. Once Burns and his men arrived there, the lieutenant discovered that their quarry was not there, but Ben's mother Francis was.[44]

Burns told Mrs. Bickerstaff a woebegone tale about his contingent being escaped prisoners who were still fighting for the Confederacy. All they wanted to do was to live long enough to kill as many Bluebellies as they could. Bickerstaff's mother fell for the ruse and told the "escaped prisoners" the route to travel through the area to escape detection. She told Burns that her son had not been in the area since Lieutenant Schreyer had captured and arrested her and Bickerstaff's father Seaborne. She claimed that when she last saw her son, he told her that he was going to ride for Mexico. That may have been a purposeful prevarication, for no other sources suggested as much.[45]

After Burns left the Bickerstaff farm, Burns and his men rode southwardly toward Gilmer. During the trip, Burns told the people whom he encountered the "escaped prisoners" tale, saying that he and his men only wanted to join the Bickerstaff guerrillas who were causing so much pain to the military. All along the road, civilians hearing Burns's tale promised to do all that they could to help him. They gave the "escapees" provisions and provided fodder for their horses. Some gave the equivalent of military advice, such as not to travel on the main road and to scatter if seen.[46]

Burns and his men reached the outskirts of Gilmer at 9:00 a.m. on November 19 and hid in nearby woods after an informant told Burns that Van Horne and fifteen men, including a civilian guide, had arrived at sunup. Pease had ordered Van Horne into the field and had sent him to Gilmer by a different route, hoping that one column or the other would encounter the renegades. Both Van Horne and Burns learned that Schreyer and his men had reached the area earlier and had ridden on toward Shreveport. Burns and Van Horne rendezvoused, but neither man had accurate information about the location of the guerrillas.[47]

After the troopers found that the renegades were not in Gilmer, they went to the Wiles Plantation after learning from an informant that Bickerstaff and eight of his men had been there the week before, had whipped a number of freedmen, and might still be at the plantation or nearby. En route, Burns met Tolman and his squad of seventeen men who had been through Mount Pleasant before turning for Gilmer, staying west and south of Burns. Earlier, along the road to town, the captain's squad met a farmer who told them that Bickerstaff had been using the road but was ahead of them by about three weeks, adding that the Bickerstaff party had stolen three horses from another area farmer.[48]

Meanwhile, with the dawn, Burns directed his men to the Wiles plantation, rumored to be a place where the renegades often hid. Burns arrived at the plantation on November 20 at 8:00 a.m. and learned that disguised "Ku Kluxers" had whipped two black men and shot at another who ran away. As well, the "Kluxers" had murdered one freedman about two weeks before. After finding nothing of interest after a search of the area, Burns and his command rode toward Daingerfield. Like Tolman, Burns learned that one of Bickerstaff's men, Tom Emmett, was hiding on the farm of a Mr. Heffner, located between Daingerfield in Paschal County and Cheatams Ferry on Big Cypress. Once near the ferry, Burns and his men stopped for a meal at a Mr. McCains's place. McCains believed Burns's story about being escapees from a Yankee stockade. The man became a fount of knowledge about the doings of the desperadoes.[49]

McCains told the lieutenant that "Col. Baker" was raising a force and planning to attack the garrison in Sulphur Springs to "clean out" the "Damned Yankees," and to free all the men in the guardhouse. Baker claimed to have artillery and said that he intended to blow the fort "to hell" if necessary. He threatened to hang all the Bluecoats at the destroyed site if any survived the bombardment. Burns asked McCains that if Baker and Bickerstaff were such bad men, did they not need to be arrested? McCains answered, "No, they should not" because all they were after were the "damned Yankees and niggers." Like other military men, Burns noted that the majority of the white people protected the renegades as long as the citizens did not have to endanger themselves.[50]

After determining that Tom Emmitt was not in the area, Burns and his men rode on to Coffeeville in Upshur County where the lieutenant once more learned that men such as Bickerstaff and Baker stood in high esteem with the locals. After learning nothing more in Coffeeville, Burns's command rode toward Gilmer but within minutes met Tolman and his men on the Gilmer Road. Burns suggested that Tolman "arrest" him and his men, all in civilian clothes, and return to Coffeeville with the "prisoners."[51]

Burns hoped that the locals would trust him more if they understood that the Yankees were after them. Tolman led the "prisoners" back, and talked with townsmen, asking them if they knew the "escapees."

To a man, the locals told the captain that Burns and his friends were "all right." One man whispered to Burns, telling him that the townsfolk were willing to do anything they could to get them released, saying that after Burns mentioned that at least two of his companions had committed crimes and if tried in court, they would go to the penitentiary for life.

Still, the whites supported Burns but told him nothing of Bickerstaff or Baker. With his "prisoners" in tow, Tolman led his men back to Cheatam's Ferry and sent Burns and fifteen men to Parson Heffner's house. Burns and his squad surrounded the place before hailing the house and asking for Bickerstaff and Tom Emmitt. Heffner allowed a search, but Burns found nothing although one person mentioned that Emmitt had met Bickerstaff there earlier but that neither had been back after they joined forces. With Burns, Tolman, Van Horne, and other field commanders finding nothing, they became discouraged and returned to Sulphur Springs where they learned that Colonel Pease had other problems.[52]

An informant had told Pease that Henry Farrar, the Bickerstaff lieutenant who was usually on the run, was back on his family's farm which was only approximately three miles from Sulphur Springs. Freedmen working for Pease were cutting timber for the post quartermaster near there. Farrar and others attacked the men and chased them back to the garrison. On November 21, Pease ordered Lieutenant C. G. Gordon to take ten men, ride to Farrar's place, and investigate the episode.

At the site of the timber operation, Gordon arrested a young man named Jones and questioned him. Jones told the lieutenant that Charles Farrar, Henry's brother, and some other renegades had been there the day and night before and had chased away the freedmen, after which they rode to hide in a thicket in the White Oak Creek bottoms.[53]

Gordon reported what he knew to Pease, who ordered Lieutenant D. Chance to take twelve men to reinforce Gordon and to scour the woods for Farrar's hiding place. The search was unsuccessful, and the squad returned to their garrison. In their absence, Pease had arrested one Sewell, Henry Farrar's father-in-law. Calling Henry Farrar "one of the leading spirits" of the Bickerstaff guerrillas, Pease told superiors that he jailed Sewell for fear that he would alert Bickerstaff of the military's actions. Next, Pease sent Gordon and a squad to search several houses in and around Sulphur Springs where Charles Farrar might be hiding. It became another fool's errand. Gordon's search turned up nothing.[54]

Pease soon received intelligence that Will Withers and several more

Bickerstaff men had come back into Hopkins County and were trying to round up more men to make an assault on the garrison. They intended to drive the Federals out and free all prisoners that Pease had incarcerated. Pease decided not to await an attack. On the evening of November 26, he organized forty men into four detachments of ten each of mounted infantry. Tolman, Van Horne, Burns, and Gordon commanded the four detachments. Each had a guide and had a different part of Hopkins County to search.

In addition, Lieutenant Chance had ten infantrymen, afoot, who searched Sulphur Springs and its immediate vicinity. Although the searches turned up nothing, the five field commanders heard much talk from county residents and learned that members of the gang were nearby, but the officers concluded that the desperadoes were too afraid to remain in their homes. They hid in the bush in locations hard to find. Once again, the military men had failed to apprehend the outlaw leaders. Also important, Pease reported to superiors that "nefarious parties" still committed "outrages" against freedpeople in the area, but he said that many blacks were now afraid to complain, especially since so many of Bickerstaff's men were in the area.[55]

More action came soon. Pease learned that a group of four men had murdered freedwoman Julia Porter, who lived about eight miles northwest of Sulphur Springs, on Sunday evening, November 28. The murder seemed senseless because the woman was, according to the colonel, an "inoffensive creature" who was "almost imbecile." Pease knew that the killers belonged to Bickerstaff's raiders. The colonel theorized that she must have witnessed the four men committing a crime and they dispatched her so that her silence would be permanent. The inquest confirmed the woman's identity and gave the cause of death: a shot to the left breast, the ball burying itself eight inches into Porter's body.

The fact that Bickerstaff and his men had killed a woman was not unique in Texas. Freedmen's Bureau agents partially documented more than 2,200 violent incidents that occurred in Texas between 1865 and 1868. Of the number, 1,698 involved white attacks on blacks resulting in injury or death. Of that 1,698, whites assaulted 281 black women whom they beat, whipped, raped, shot, or set on fire. Whites killed at least two score of those women.[56]

Even as Porter was being killed in Hopkins County, more trouble erupted in Lamar. Two men had committed sundry crimes, including murder. Most likely they were Bickerstaff followers or, perhaps,

Bob Lee's men. In either case, Pease wanted them corralled. On December 20, He ordered Lieutenant H. E. Scott to take twenty men, sweep Lamar County, and arrest the renegades. Scott performed well. He found and arrested Daniel Franklin after discovering him in Jackson Hendricks's home, located about twelve miles south of Paris. The squad took Franklin to Paris where Scott took over the local jail, put irons on his prisoner, and tossed him into a cell.

On December 22, a freedman learned that Scott was now after another scourge, Ben Cummins, a murderer who had lately killed a freedwoman. The freedman turned informer and told Scott that he could find Cummins hiding on a farm about five miles from town. Scott sent a detachment after the killer. The squad searched thoroughly but could not find Cummins. Scott heard a rumor that Cummins had quit Texas and was riding for Missouri.[57]

By the end of the year, several marauders, most of them Bickerstaff men, were on ice in the Sulphur Springs guardhouse, all charged with bushwhacking. Those captured included Brunch, A. G. Vandiver, John Marshall, Sr., Reverend William Ellis, Cornelius Jones, C. W. Stokes, Hardegree, France, Franklin, and Hicks. Many others had already been processed and were serving time elsewhere.[58] The three primary outlaw leaders--Bickerstaff, Baker, and Lee--still remained at large, but their reign of terror would come to an end in the early months of 1869.

9

Send All of Them to Hell, January-February, 1869

After raising hell in Hopkins County, Bickerstaff and some of his men slipped back into Navarro County in the Cross Timbers of North Texas. Instead of finding large areas of thickets or brushy conditions surrounded by rolling prairies, they found rolling prairies surrounded by thickets. The land was much drier than the northeastern area of Texas, and Black Jack and Post Oak trees abounded in thickets of briars and poison ivy. Going by the name of "Thomas" and probably allying himself with the family of John Wesley Hardin, Bickerstaff established a base near Corsicana from whence he began terrorizing the county's black community and white Unionists. Usually in the company of several of his men, he went heavily armed. According to one area newspaper, "thefts were committed, plantations were visited in the absence of their owners, [N]egroes were assaulted . . . and robbed."[1]

Before authorities could move against them, Bickerstaff and his men slipped into Hill County to a spot between Oquilla Creek and the Brazos River about five miles northwest of Peoria. They set up a camp near the farm that Ben had recently acquired there.[2] He had a happy reunion with his wife, but, as usual, he could not stay out of trouble.

While Bickerstaff and his men plotted their next wave of crimes, the forces of law and order had a major victory. On January 6, 1869, a party led by Thomas Orr killed Cullen Baker and one of his men, Matthew "Dummy" Kirby. Military authorities still directed by Chaffee and Tolman had put so much pressure on Baker that he and his band had to stay on the move almost constantly.

The pressure was such that Cullen scattered his men in December of

1868, with different men heading to all points of the compass. With Kirby, Baker went back to Cass County, a place where he was usually safe.³ Though he continued to evade Federal and civilian lawmen in his old haunt, Baker ironically became the victim of local people who had previously aided him. One of those people was Thomas Orr.

Orr was born in Henry County, Georgia, in 1844. As a youngster, he helped his father William develop a profitable farm, while studying the land surveyor trade. Later, he sensed opportunity in Arkansas and migrated there. He soon found work. He became the surveyor of Lafayette and Miller counties and established the town site of Texarkana. As settlers moved in, Orr became the town's first mayor. He established a street railway, a first in the area. He promoted civic and cultural life. Indeed, he brought the first opera house to Texarkana. He led a normal life even though he suffered from a physical disability. He had rheumatism that had attacked his right hand and made it almost useless.⁴

By January 1866, Orr had grown tired of the surveyor trade. He took a teaching position in Bloomberg, Arkansas, just half a mile east of the Texas-Arkansas line. Orr's new job put him in Cullen Baker territory, for the villain roamed freely on both sides of the Texas-Arkansas border. The men developed deep hatred for one another because of their shared affections for the same woman. Baker's first wife, Martha Foster Baker, died on March 1, 1866.

Spending little time mourning, within two months, Cullen had taken up with Martha's sister, Belle, and asked for her hand. She rejected him, instead marrying Orr. Forever after, Cullen hated the crippled man. Not understanding the depth of Baker's animosity, on June 2, 1866, Orr approached Line Ferry which would get him across the Sulphur River. Cullen had established that ferry and was present when Orr arrived. Baker attacked the one-handed Orr and gave him a horrible beating.⁵

Why Cullen did not kill the crippled man is unknown. Perhaps he had real feelings about Belle and realized that he would lose her forever if he killed her husband. Or it may have been because Orr was a local man, and Baker usually left the local white people alone while bawling that he was fighting for the Lost Cause and the soul of old Dixie. Exceptions were white Unionists and the freedpeople. At times, his supporters helped him hide from authorities and provided him with food and his other needs.

In letting Orr live, it is also probable that Baker maintain a loosely interpreted sense of honor when it came to killing family members. While the codes of Southern honor might allow an individual to beat and harass a family member, Southern people considered it unacceptable to kill them. Whether Baker liked it or not, Orr was his brother-in-law. It is reasonable to assume that was the only reason that Baker did not kill him.

After he recovered from his beating, Orr learned everything he could about Baker. Orr was horrified by what he discovered. He soon understood that Cullen was a murderer and that he committed outrageous attacks even on women and children. Orr feared for his life because he had become "an enemy to a person who was but little better than the great arch-demon of the infernal regions."[6]

Orr was probably right, for Baker continued to harass him. He and

Civil War deserter and outlaw Cullen Baker was killed in 1869 by a group led by his brother-in-law, Thomas Orr. His grave rests in Oakwood Cemetery at Jefferson. Photo by Bob Bowman

a cohort, Lee Barnes, rode to Orr's schoolhouse shortly after the beating and harangued him in front of his class. Baker demanded money because Orr had not paid for using the ferry on June 2, the day he assaulted Orr. Although Orr paid him, he and Barnes continued disparaging him for some time before they left.[7]

The incident prompted Orr to talk to others. He learned that most people feared Cullen and wanted to stay away from him. Orr, however, found a few men who wanted Baker brought to justice. They formed a committee and rode to Line Ferry to talk with the arch-fiend. Because they were armed and too numerous to fight, Baker agreed to change his behavior, generally, and to leave Orr alone, specifically. Baker had no intention of keeping his word. Moreover, Baker had always drank to excess, especially after his wife died, and now he was drunk most of his waking hours. When Baker was drunk, he usually spun completely out-of-control. Despite his pledge to leave Orr alone, Orr took precautions. He carried a shotgun and a sixgun everywhere he went.[8]

Baker's slide into a type of drunken insanity continued until he began tormenting and killing other local whites in the county. If the South's code of honor ever influenced Baker that was now in the past--vengeance and blood ruled the day. Late at night on December 7, 1868, he and his men raided the home of William Foster where Orr and Belle Foster Orr were living. They captured Orr, who did not fight because he was concerned about the safety of his in-laws and his wife. Orr was not the only prisoner Baker had collected. There were three others who, according to Baker, must die. When they reached a suitable spot, Cullen left the road and went into the woods far enough to find a suitable tree. There, he and his men lynched Orr and two other prisoners. The fourth was temporarily spared because the villains only had three ropes.

Believing that Orr was dead, Cullen ordered his body cut down so the rope could be used to hang the last victim. Unknown to Baker, Orr's neck had not been broken; that Orr had not lost consciousness; and that Orr well understood his plight. Once cut down and the rope removed, he could still breathe. He feigned death until the desperadoes left.[9]

After he returned to the Foster's home, Orr plotted a counterattack. He believed that he must kill Cullen to survive. Once the renegade learned that Orr still lived, the desperado's rage and fury were endless. He vowed to find the crippled man and kill him on the spot. By now, many of Baker's closest cohorts had slipped away after judging him to be unstable. Dummy

Kirby, however, stayed with him. As his life drew to a close, Baker continued to look for Orr who went into hiding.

The desperado also continued to bedevil the Foster family. But on the day of his death, he made a terrible mistake. While on the Foster's property, he demanded whiskey for himself and Kirby. Both became genteelly drunk and passed out in the yard. So it was that on January 6, 1869, at about 11:00 a.m., Orr and a few other men emerged from hiding and shot the two guerrillas dead. Baker never woke up, but Kirby raised his head once before dying.[10] Orr and his men did a great service for the people of Northeast Texas. The area now had two less brigands, Baker probably being the worst of the whole bunch because he was so lethal.

While Baker was meeting the devil, January 1869 found Bickerstaff in the company of his good friend Josiah Thompson, a saddle-maker and resident of the Johnson County town of Alvarado. Thompson roamed both Johnson and Ellis counties in company with several other raiders. Among other crimes, Thompson was wanted for murdering a Hopkins County freedman in 1866. The motley crew were in Hill County when they learned that Johnson County Sheriff E. M. Heath, who also functioned as deputy tax assessor/collector, planned to take a large amount of tax money to Austin. Heath left Alvarado on January 20, 1869, supposedly not knowing that the renegades were setting a trap for him.[11]

The former Confederate Major William H. Cathey, a despicable Bickerstaff man who hailed from Comanche Peak in Johnson County, intercepted Heath on the public road near Hillsboro. Cathey's purpose was to distract the sheriff. Heath later said that he saw four mounted men ahead of him, but because cattle were near, he assumed that they were drovers. The sheriff said that he lost sight of them as they disappeared around a bend of the road ahead which was flanked by a thick forest.

Cathey delayed the sheriff long enough for Bickerstaff and several of his men to rush to the scene with guns in hand to take control. They wore black masks, but there was no doubt who the men were. One fired a warning shot at Heath to get his attention. The highwaymen disarmed and blindfolded both Heath and Cathey before taking them into a thicket about 400 yards away.[12]

The guerrillas escaped with $2,800 of Johnson County tax money, a small fortune, in addition to taking Heath's pistols (two Derringers) and his watch. They also took $1,000 from Cathey after which they took Heath back to the road and sent him on his way. Released later, Cathey returned to Hillsboro to inform authorities that he had been robbed. Heath and Cathey thus survived but returned to Alvarado empty-handed and embarrassed. Several local leaders, including District Judge Anthony B. Norton, believed that Heath, Cathey, and their assailants were part of a swindle, that Heath had cooperated with the supposed robbers.[13]

The redoubtable Republican Anthony Banning Norton was born in Mount Vernon, Ohio. He graduated from Kenyon College in Gambier, Ohio, and was admitted to the bar later that year. Norton helped lead the Ohio Whig Party before migrating to Kaufman County in Northeast Texas in 1855. In Texas he affiliated with the Know-Nothing Party. He served as state representative from Kaufman and Henderson counties from 1857 to 1861. He became a close ally of Sam Houston and wanted to save the Union. In 1860 he urged the nomination of General Houston for president of the United States.[14]

While he did not run for president, Houston did capture the Texas governor's chair in 1859 and repaid Norton for his support by appointing him adjutant general of the Lone Star State in 1860. Concurrently, Norton accepted the editorship of the *Austin Southern Intelligencer*, a powerful Unionist newspaper. After Texas seceded from the Union, Norton remained in the state until forced to flee in the fall of 1861 due to the hatred that secessionists had for him. He went to his old home in Mount Vernon, Ohio, but returned to Texas when the war ended in 1865.

In 1866 voters elected him to the constitutional convention as the representative for Kaufman, Henderson and Van Zandt counties. The delegates appointed him chairman of the Committee on the Conditions of the State. By 1868 he had joined the Republican Party, and Edmond J. Davis appointed him judge of the Fifth Judicial District of Texas, a district that included Dallas, Johnson, and other counties.[15]

Early in April 1868, Judge Norton reported that "assassination, murder, robbery and larceny are heard on all sides," and four months later asked for a military escort in order to hold court in Ellis County.[16] Norton believed that Cathey's complaint about losing $1,000 of his own money was a cover to make him appear to be victim and thereby to clear himself of any blame for robbing Sheriff Heath.

Norton's belief about a swindle was reinforced when Heath later did nothing to corral the Bickerstaff gang. He refused to go after them even when he had warrants. Nevertheless, the Texas Legislature later released Heath from any obligation and ordered the state comptroller to credit

Johnson County for the amount of money stolen.[17]

Judge Norton also suspected Cathey and Heath because the two had known each other for an extended period of time. Both were former Rebels who had raised companies for service in the Confederate Army in the early years of the Civil War. Both had served with distinction in the Trans-Mississippi theatre during the conflict. Cathey, who reached the rank of major, became a prisoner-of-war following the Confederate surrender at Arkansas Post. The Federal command sent Cathey and many of the men in his unit to Camp Chase, where they endured many of the hardship associated with Civil War POW camps.[18]

After being exchanged, Cathey served with Hood's Texas Brigade until it was destroyed at the battles of Franklin and Nashville in 1864. At the end of the war, Cathey was with General Joseph Johnson's command when it surrendered at Durham Station, North Carolina, on April 26, 1865.[19]

As for Sheriff Heath, he had lived in the county since its formation in the mid-1850s. Citizens elected him as one of the commissioners who helped to organize the new county. He later became the first justice of the peace in Johnson County and served as tax collector in 1859.[20] In holding such offices before the war, he was required to swear an oath of allegiance to the United States Constitution, a pledge that caused him problems during the Reconstruction era.

In 1862, to avoid the Confederate Conscription Act, Heath organized a company of Johnson County men who joined the 20th Texas Cavalry that was mustered in neighboring Hill County. Part of Cooper and then Gano's Brigade in the Trans-Mississippi Army, Heath was taken prisoner in July 1863. After his release in February 1865, he served with General Stand Watie in Indian Territory until the end of the war, surrendering with his command at Doaksville, Indian Territory, on June 23, 1865.

After the war, Johnson County voters elected Heath sheriff. Simultaneously, he served as deputy tax assessor-collector. After having sworn to uphold the United States Constitution, then taken part in the Civil War, Heath was unable to register to vote until Congress removed the disability.[21]

Suspicious of both Heath and Cathey, Norton wrote to Governor Elisha Pease about his doubts. He told Pease that Cathey had recently given Bickerstaff one of the best horses in the state and that Cathey frequently quartered the guerrilla and some of his men at his farmstead. According to Norton, Heath pretended to fear Bickerstaff and was absent from the court for most of its last two terms. The judge could get little done without his sheriff. Norton's grand jury had indicted Bickerstaff and his close friend Thompson, but there was no one to serve the papers or to make arrests. The judge asked the governor to send dependable lawmen or troops. If that were done, Norton promised "to capture the whole layout."[22]

Judge Norton was a valuable source of knowledge for Governor Pease. He reported that violent incidents had reoccurred countless times in Van Zandt County. Consequently, Pease finally convinced the army to send in Captain Samuel Steelhammar, who established his headquarters in Canton. He cleaned up Van Zandt County by arresting a number of Bickerstaff's men, but Steelhammar was cautious, especially after one of his officers was ambushed on a county road. On January 4, 1869, Steelhammar ordered Lieutenant John Little to take a squad of six men to Jordan Saline, about fifteen miles from Canton, to investigate a case of fraud wherein a landlord had allegedly cheated a black cropper out of his portion of the harvest in the previous summer and fall.[23]

Little and his men began their return trip about 3:00 p.m. When the men reached Aston's Furnace, a superior number of heavily armed men, some belonging to the Bickerstaff gang, attacked the soldiers. About 150 yards from the troopers, five renegades emerged from the woods and started shooting at the squad, its members returning fire. The feisty lieutenant believed that he and his men could handle the affray until he realized that the desperadoes had laid a trap. A second group, hidden in a thicket by the road, opened fire on the troopers, catching them in a crossfire.

Thinking fast, Little ordered his men to dismount and charge into the thicket to eliminate the shooters there. When the troopers aggressively attacked, the men in the bush scattered in many different directions. Possessing nerves of steel, the lieutenant then ordered a direct assault on the men on the road, but they rode away before the cavalrymen could get close enough to engage them. Wisely, Little chose not to pursue, for he knew that he might lead his men into another trap; yet, he knew that to attack and to fight was the only way to eliminate such lawless men.[24]

With brave men such as Lieutenant Little taking the field aggressively, Steelhammar brought law and order to Van Zandt County until headquarters transferred him and his contingent so they could passify another troubled area. According to Judge Norton, the malefactors, some belonging to the old Bickerstaff gang, others riding with different bands, reappeared as soon as the troopers left. The desperadoes renewed their reign of terror. That forced military commanders to act again, this time sending Captain C. S. Nelson to Canton.[25]

As long as troops remained posted in the county, peace prevailed. But, as always, when the place seemed pacified, the command transferred Nelson and his men, dispatching them to another trouble-spot that was out-of-control; then, Van Zandt's troubles flared anew. There seemed to be no end to the misery that dangerous desperadoes could deal out. To make a bad situation worse, a local justice of the peace allowed a number of Ben Bickerstaff's men to make bail, and once free, they resumed their normal practices of murder and mayhem. Once again, Van Zandt County descended into chaos.[26]

Meanwhile, Bickerstaff's friend in crime, Elisha Guest, came to the attention of authorities again in February 1869 when he murdered one of his own, a man appropriately named "Smith." Guest still had a price on his head, and the man succumbed to temptation. "Smith" rode to Paris and gave the local lawmen information about Guest's location. Smith then left Paris, crossed into Red River County, and went to Guest's camp near Jonesboro. An informant must have told the desperado about Smith's treachery.

When Smith arrived in camp, he dismounted, approached Guest, and put out his hand for a handshake. In close quarters, Guest whipped out a sixgun and shot the man in the head. Afterward, Guest and a few of his men stayed in the Jonesboro area for a time and committed their usual crimes of robberies and assaults.[27]

Shortly, Bickerstaff again became a headliner for the *New York Times* because the newspaper continued to track the "New Rebellion" in Texas. A correspondent, who had not heard of Baker's death, identified Baker as dominating extreme Northeast Texas; English and Bickerstaff as controlling Titus and Hopkins counties; and Guest as terrorizing Lamar and Red River counties, a grand jury in the latter county having lately indicted him for murder; and the cutthroat Bob Lee as the power in Grayson, Fannin, Hunt, and Collin counties.

According to the newspaper, the marauders had multiple motives, one of which was pseudo-political. They were determined to intimidate military men, native white Unionists, the freedmen, and anyone else whose opinions differed from their own. They continued to give lip service to the

Lost Cause and claimed to be Confederate to the core, but, according to the *New York Times* editor, that stance was a ruse to justify their crimes. The editor's Texas correspondent confirmed that the killers had many supporters, and other people were either apathetic or afraid to oppose the lawless bands who were fighting the second part of the Civil War.[28]

On February 20, 1869, Bickerstaff and a cohort, riding fine bay horses, invaded Smith County again. They confronted a family of freedpeople, who--like a number of black families--lived near the forks of Richland and Post Oak creeks about three miles from Springhill, in a recently settled enclave then known as the "Freedmen's Colony."[29]

Finding the husband gone, they ordered the wife to provide corn for their horses and supper for themselves. She complied. After determining that she had no money, they went to the cabin of another black family. They forced the husband to allow a search of his dwelling. Again finding nothing of value, they approached yet another nearby cabin, the home of freedman Ben King and his family. Finding him gone, they barged into the cabin and demanded that King's sister give them all of their valuables. There were none, except an old Enfield rifle that the robbers seized. King rode up just as Bickerstaff and his cohort were leaving. They demanded his weapon and his money.

After harsh words--King was not willing to stand passive while being robbed--one of the desperadoes shot him in the shoulder, the ball going to "his vital parts." King had not drawn a gun and did not do so after being shot. Instead, he ran away but only covered about twenty yards before he fell dead. Afterwards, Bickerstaff and his man mounted up and rode away.[30]

Bickerstaff and his men faded away and next appeared in Ellis County. Sheriff Peter Williams learned that "a band of outlaws [is] congregating in this [county]. . . I believe them to be . . . the Bickerstaff clan and also believe that their intention is to organize for action this Spring."[31]

Members of the gang stopped frequently at the homes of freedpeople and "forced them to furnish them with food and their horses with fodder and, without paying, are off again." The sheriff said that there were many strangers whom observers saw stopping and congregating in Brockvile (today's Bristol), about eighteen miles northeast of Waxahachie. Brockville was then unofficially known as Heelstring where dancing was a popular pastime. The place drew the likes of Bickerstaff and other lawless characters.[32]

Williams added that some people were helping the villains,

voluntarily feeding them and alerting them of the movements of the authorities. The sheriff talked about Stephen Merideth who had joined Bickerstaff. Merideth had earlier murdered Ellis Countian Charles Stricken in 1866. Later, he murdered a freedman in Sulphur Springs. But in Ellis County, he had so many friends who protected him that it was impossible to arrest him.[33]

Bickerstaff used the alias of "Bryan" and tried to remain quiet for a time. But his men could not stay out of trouble. Gang members Merideth and William Gillian assaulted Sheriff Williams in Waxahachie in broad daylight, the event leading to Merideth's disappearance and Gillian's arrest. Released on bond, Gillian returned to Hopkins County and killed another freedman; whereupon, he back-tracked and rejoined Bickerstaff in Ellis County only to be arrested again and put on trial. Staying at the local hotel, still using the alias Bryan, Bickerstaff intervened to save his man.[34]

In court, gang members Norman Dustman and a man named Pateet gave spurious testimony, trying to clear Gillian. That proved unnecessary. Gillian escaped during the trial. Because of murder threats, the woebegone Sheriff Williams stopped traveling around the county alone. He became most ineffective. Worried beyond belief, he wrote to Governor Pease, asking that a "secret detective" be dispatched to Ellis County to covertly discover the members of the gang and their nefarious plans. Williams told Pease that he could identify Bickerstaff regardless of any alias that he might be using. The governor passed the request on to General E. R. S. Canby, the state's new military commander, but nothing was done. After Gillian escaped, Bickerstaff left town riding south until he reached Navarro County where he established a new camp. The others in the gang vanished to parts unknown.[35]

Knowing when to run and knowing that lawmen and troopers would be on his trail soon, Bickerstaff and a few other gang members left the Corsicana area and slipped into Johnson County to hide. Once there, they robbed and tortured freedmen by using Ben's old trick of roasting their feet when the victims refused to hand over their valuables. The guerrillas renewed their acquaintance with the forty-year-old Josiah Thompson, Bickerstaff's old friend who sometimes rode with him, and with the former Confederate Cathey, who was the same disreputable scoundrel that he had always been.[36]

In the new killing field, Bickerstaff still used the alias of "Thomas." He and his men originally had some supporters in and around Alvarado, including the Mayfield family, relatives of Bickerstaff's mother. Alvarado was the oldest town in Johnson County. By 1860, it had a two-story Masonic Lodge that also served as a school. Typical of many rural Texas towns in the *antebellum* era, Alvarado had a private college operated by John C. Collier; four churches; more than a dozen businesses; and a population of 350. Local men would soon have to deal with Bickerstaff and his guerrillas.[37]

One particular man in Johnson County drew much of Bickerstaff's ire. John W. Powell was the minister of the Methodist Church in Alvarado. A native of England, Powell pastored in Arkansas, Louisiana, and East Texas before moving to Alvarado. Several times, Bickerstaff and Thompson threatened the good parson's life for preaching to and aiding the freedpeople of the community.[38]

Meanwhile, Bickerstaff told the county folk that he was a heroic Confederate, a believer in the Lost Cause, and a poor Civil War refugee whom the infernal Yankees had abused. But citizens of Alvarado noticed that "Mr. Thomas" was always heavily armed, constantly having his hands on his pistols. He was always alert, looking for possible personal enemies, be they lawmen, soldiers, or bounty hunters. He never mingled with other people, except for the one-time saddler Thompson.[39]

Many of the locals despised Thompson because he peddled whiskey. Off-and-on, he ran a saloon in town, thereby violating a local ordinance banning liquor. Thompson caused the town much heartache in the two years that he had lived in Alvarado. When authorities tried to enforce the ordinance banning the sale of spirits in town, Thompson threatened to "send all of them to hell," adding that he "had sent many a man there before."

Finally being overwhelmed by lawmen and run out of town, he threatened revenge. He plotted to burn the town to ashes and to kill the men who had opposed him, including his major nemesis Reverend Powell.[40] Little did Thompson know that the rest of his days on earth would be but few.

10 Killing the Bravest Man in the South, March-April, 1869

With Bickerstaff around (going by the alias "Thomas"), depredations began anew in Johnson County. In addition to his threats to kill Parson Powell, Bickerstaff made threats on the lives of E. M. Heath--Assistant Tax Assessor-Collector who was involved in the loss of county tax revenue less than two months earlier--Major Purdom, and Colonel Hoyl, all three former Confederate officers.[1]

For unknown reasons Bickerstaff now felt compelled to attack former Rebels in the county with the same viciousness as he did freedpeople and their white allies. Bickerstaff's decision to expand his reign of terror ultimately led to his demise. Still, the outlaw's primary target were those who society afforded the least protection: the freedpeople.

As they had done in Navarro, Bickerstaff and his band of thieves, who were drunk during most of their waking hours, visited plantations and farms when white owners were away, taking whatever they wished. They looted the homes of blacks, stealing food, clothing, arms, and anything else that could be carted away. They assaulted freedmen and raped freedwomen. Soon, blacks in the countryside "fled their homes in terror," hid in the woods, and became "entirely useless as laborers."[2]

Although many people of the county learned of "Thomas's" true identity, they were afraid to come forward. They feared certain death should they tell area authorities anything about the desperado. As days passed, Ben and his men became bolder. They came into Alvarado during the evening. Invariably, they got drunk, robbed people in open sight, and generally spread chaos. Local civilian authorities finally learned of Bickerstaff's true identity, but no officer was brave enough to confront him. No one even dared call him by his real name. To his face, he was still "Mr. Thomas." According to one source, "Thomas" and his men instituted "a carnival of robbery and other crimes."[3]

Concurrently, military headquarters made some changes in command. Captain Tolman's superiors relieved him of his post in Sulphur Springs so that he could devote more time to tracking desperadoes such as Bickerstaff and Bob Lee. Tolman had the continuing support of Colonel Pease. Although many renegades were still at large, Pease had nothing but praise for Tolman, Lieutenant Schreyer, and Lieutenant Gordon for their latest scouting patrols in the campaign to bring the felons to justice.[4]

Despite Bickerstaff's murderous career, he still had apologists, all of whom belonged to the Democratic Party that was struggling to regain control of Texas. Leaders of the party still regarded the assorted terrorist groups and the different gangs of outlaws as para-military arms of their group who could help undermine Reconstruction and hasten the day of renewed Democratic rule and the return the state to its *antebellum* days, complete with strong controls on the freedpeople. A Democratic delegate to the Texas constitutional convention, I. D. Evans, rose in March of 1869, to summarize the sins of white Republicans, their black allies, and the United States Army.[5]

Among other things, Evans denied that Texas had a "law and order" problem even though statistics proved that it did. Evans claimed that Republicans such as Governor E. M. Pease and military leaders such as General J. J. Reynolds were guilty of exaggeration, hoping to prolong military occupation. Republicans continued to whine, he said, about all the terrorist groups and all the outlaw gangs in Texas. Evans denied that such people caused trouble; rather, they acted only after extreme provocation.[6]

Evans admitted that men such as Cullen Baker and Bickerstaff were problematic but apologized for them nevertheless. He argued that the early Freedman's Bureau sub-agent in charge of Titus County, Brevet Lieutenant Colonel Samuel Starr, had incited the area's former slaves to near revolution and that Bickerstaff had acted only to protect the white community. Blacks made so many false claims of abuse, said Evans, that whites could take no more. Although no one likely believed Evans, especially with his sanctimonious and condescending attitude, his presentation made for good theater.[7]

While Evans was lying to the members of the constitutional

convention and apologizing for Bickerstaff, the desperado and some of his men, still roaming in the Alvarado countryside, were engaging in extortion, using former Rebel Cathey as an intermediary. Cathey called on local businessmen and civic leaders, threatening them with "fire and bloodshed" if they refused to pay protection money. Cathey said that only cash and coin would keep the Bickerstaff guerrillas from destroying them, their businesses, and their town. His actions and words leaving no doubt that he was a Bickerstaff man, Cathey threatened absolute "doom" to men who did not agree to pay the required shakedown money.[8]

The Bickerstaff gang's attacks on freedmen increased, the result being that yet more people were beaten and robbed. Conditions became so severe that the area's blacks went to the homes of their employers to complain that they could not work under such duress. As they had done before, many of them began spending most of their time in the woods, hiding from their oppressors. In a related development, Cathey approached a man whom Bickerstaff had earlier harassed. That man was the aged and respectable white minister Parson Powell, mentioned earlier, who taught the "Good News" to area blacks. Cathey told the minister that "he must die for no other offense than that of preaching the gospel to the ignorant [N]egroes of his community."[9]

According to a correspondent for the *Waco Semi-Weekly Register*, such conditions "struck terror into the hearts of the people." Their "farming operations" became completely "disorganized," their "lives threatened," and their town "doomed to the torch." The community trembled "under the threat of vengeance [from] this band of outlaws." Landowners "were compelled---for weeks with gun in hand---to keep untiring watch over their dependent families [sharecroppers], their property, and their own lives." During the crisis, "Cathey was in the confidence of the desperadoes," was their "unqualified friend, associated with them, kept them at his house, and whenever occasion offered threatened the people with the vengeance of Bickerstaff."[10]

The citizens of the county finally tired of Bickerstaff and his band's deadly antics. With their lives and property in the balance, they feared that immigration to their area would cease and that the local economy would enter a depression. The last straw came when Bickerstaff, Thompson, and Cathey burst into the county courthouse in Cleburne on March 29, 1869, and disrupted grand jury proceedings because the jury was meeting to hand down indictments against various gang members. Cathey made "wild and extravagant statements," telling the jurors that if they took action against Bickerstaff or any of his men, those jurors would not live long enough to even get home.[11]

The threats and hostility so unnerved the jurors that they immediately forgot about their duty, adjourned, and went directly home as quickly as possible. Although District Judge Norton had entered the jury room and remonstrated with the faint-hearted jurors, telling them that they must take action, they ignored him as they left. Then, the weak-kneed judge became afraid that he would become the next target of the Bickerstaff men. He fled in terror and went into hiding while the desperado and his band quietly slipped back into the Corsicana area.

As the *Cleburne Chronicle* reported, "the law could not be executed. The officers were cowed, [and] the grand jury [was] intimidated and went home with their work unfinished."[12]

Ironically, the Unionist Judge Norton had given aid to Texas officers in the Confederacy who were held at Camp Chase, Illinois, when he was exile at Mount Vernon, Ohio, during the war. It was entirely possible that Major Cathey, held for a time at Camp Chase, and Norton were acquainted. This was the way that the hardened Cathey showed his gratitude.

Meanwhile, folks in Navarro County managed to catch Bickerstaff and Thompson after they had robbed yet another black family, but both desperadoes escaped before lawmen could get them into a cell.[13]

After leaving Navarro County, Bickerstaff and Thompson were reinforced by other members of their band before committing new depredations in Wood and Van Zandt counties. They then entered Hunt County to collect more of their gang and to cause yet more mayhem in the black community and among the white Unionists. Some of Lee's men, and perhaps Lee himself, temporarily joined Bickerstaff, no doubt hoping for a little fun and a share of the loot. Yet the end was near, and Bickerstaff again knew when to run, for Chaffee and his troopers were closing.

The renegade again fled and moved his headquarters to a spot between Oquilla Creek and the Brazos River, near Peoria, in Hill County, about twenty-seven miles from Alvarado. Ben's wife was still living on the Bickerstaff farm in Hill County, which was within close proximity to her husband's new hideout.[14]

Along the Brazos, the guerrillas spent much time just hiding from the authorities, but, periodically, they raided into the countryside of both

Hill County and Johnson County. They did so in disguises since they did not want to be identified. But word leaked out about Bickerstaff's presence, and more of the area people learned his real identity. That made many folks even more afraid, for Bickerstaff's foul reputation was well known. When Ben learned that the county folk knew that he had returned, the desperado and his men forgot all thoughts of stealth.

Openly going into Alvarado Bickerstaff, always accompanied by Thompson, continued threatening to kill the town's officials and to burn the hamlet to the ground. The authorities were no match for the renegades who, for a time, did as they wished with no real opposition. Some nights, they or other gang members watched the homes of the most influential locals, hoping to catch them outside without protection to ambush and kill them.[15]

Concerned citizens in Alvarado finally decided that they must take action, for they had a "most desperate clan" to deal with. They appeared before the dismayed District Judge Norton, who had emerged from hiding and was again holding court in Cleburne. Next, they appeared before the Johnson County Grand Jury. The Alvarado contingent learned that all of Bickerstaff's deadly antics had intimidated both the jury and the judge.

Norton believed that he had only two safe choices. One was to inform the Johnson County bunch that there was a $1,000 reward for Bickerstaff, dead or alive. Second, the judge empowered Samuel Milliken, Parson Powell's partner in a mercantile store, as a sheriff's deputy and gave him a bench warrant that authorized him to summon a posse and to arrest Bickerstaff and his men, including the local extortionist and embezzler Cathey.[16] After issuing the warrant, the judge once again slipped away and went back into hiding. Because the terrified Norton could not or would not act, Johnson County residents feared for their lives and property once again. Their motives for ridding themselves of Bickerstaff were mounting.[17]

One source differed from the account presented above. That source claimed that since there was no resistance from authorities in Hill, Ellis, or Johnson counties, Bickerstaff and his band of terrorists became even bolder. In this account, Norton did not write out a bench warrant but simply wrote a note "informing [the citizens] that Governor Pease had by proclamation offered One Thousand Dollars for the apprehension of Bickerstaff."[18] Norton then told the delegation that they were authorized to make an arrest or to kill Bickerstaff in the attempt.[19]

Regardless of Norton's exact course, Bickerstaff learned of the judge's intent, and he immediately made his own plans to kill all involved in Norton's plot, including Milliken and Powell.[20] Leaving most of his men camped at an old dilapidated schoolhouse that had once also been the Masonic Lodge just outside town, Bickerstaff, accompanied only by Thompson, roared into Alvarado near sundown on Monday, April 5, 1869. They should have brought more men, but they apparently believed that they could "tree the town" (destroy the place) without the help of anyone else. Earlier, however, Chaffee, Tolman, and some of their men had followed the trail of Bickerstaff's band when they rode to join their leader, but the officers lost the trail in Johnson County. They then rode into Alvarado to contact the town's leaders.[21]

Knowing that it was likely that the marauders would commit more mayhem in Alvarado, Chaffee and Tolman, before they left on another scouting trip, warned town officials and civic leaders that bloodshed was likely unless they (Chaffee and Tolman) could find Bickerstaff and his men before they attacked the town. After the troopers left, a band of plucky civilians finally decided that they would confront Bickerstaff and Thompson even without military help.

Townsmen found volunteers for Samuel Milliken to deputize. They also laid plans to trick the desperadoes after they learned exactly when Bickerstaff planned to return to Alvarado. Ben had earlier told merchant Robert Moore, whom he had known in Titus County, that he would come late Monday afternoon, about 5:00 p.m., April 5, to pick up a barrel of flour.[22]

Bringing Thompson along as usual, Bickerstaff kept his appointment, intending not just to pick up his flour, but also to terrorize the citizens. Thompson rode ahead about eight to ten feet on a small gray horse, Bickerstaff behind. The two gunmen observed that the town was filled with people, mainly men. Then they saw merchants closing their shops and people fleeing the town's main street.

What the two villains could not see proved more dangerous, for all the men had secreted arms either on their persons or in their stores. They were ready to ambush the two brigands and send them to Old Scratch. Believing that the people were leaving because they were frightened, the desperadoes developed a false sense of security. As men joined, Bickerstaff and Thompson "gave vent to a lusty laugh" and raised their hats to salute the town. According to one source, Bickerstaff even boomed out, "Rats to your holes, damn you all!"[23]

After drawing their pistols, they rode to the store of Parson Powell and Milliken, intending to murder the two men because they had been two of the citizens who had earlier complained to Judge Norton. When the desperadoes reached Rogers's Shoeshop, firing began, the first volleys coming from Powell and Milliken's store.

Then, a fusillade of buckshot rained down on them from every business house in town.[24] One source felt that the townsmen were more anxious to kill Thompson than the despicable Bickerstaff because Thompson had lived in Alvarado for two years, had sold liquor illegally, and had threatened to kill most of the townsmenn and burn down the hamlet.[25]

After first firing from cover, gutsy merchants and other men from around the town and county---led by A. J. Barnes; Stephen Mills; Special Officer M. P. Hunnicutt (a future State Policeman and Texas Ranger); the deputized Samuel Milliken; Robert Moore, and David and John Myers---poured from the stores and appeared on the street, all well armed. Before the desperadoes even dismounted, quickly, with no remorse, the posse began delivering, at close quarters, lead in massive doses.

In the general mayhem, they gunned down Bickerstaff who fell from his horse after taking a shotgun blast to the face. Still alive but weltering in his own blood, the Texas terror lifted himself on one elbow and continued to fire his handgun to no effect while swearing that he would never surrender, never be taken alive.

At one point, a ball disabled Bickerstaff's right hand, his shooting hand. The rogue had to shift his handgun to his left. The change ruined the desperado's aim. His shots went wild amid cries of "finish him" and "shoot him again." Recognizing the gunman's new handicap, several men quickly rushed him, subdued him, and confiscated his weapons--three sixguns and two derringers.

Meanwhile, Thompson had taken buckshot pellets and rifle balls that stuck his chest, one penetrating his heart. Thus knocked out of his saddle, he was dead before he hit the ground (he left behind a destitute wife and six children, some of whom were later taken in by the townspeople).[26]

Eye-witnesses to the shoot-out confirmed many of the facts although there were some differences in testimony. Some witnesses later claimed that as Bickerstaff fell from his saddle, he was hit in the right hand, his gun hand. Switching his weapon to his left hand, he fired at random. One witness reported that a bullet from the outlaw's gun went up the chamber of Parson Powell's shotgun, knocking it from the preacher's hand.

Another witness said that the bullet simply grazed Powell's hand, forcing him to drop his gun. Clearly this was not a random shot but was, rather, intentionally aimed at one of Bickerstaff's most despised enemies, the Methodist preacher who believed in saving the souls of the freedmen and their women and children.[27] The good reverend undoubtedly felt equally sanctified in confronting the devil's minions on Earth and sending them back to hell where they belonged.

Mortally wounded, Bickerstaff lived for about two hours, all the while cursing Thompson for dying so quickly and for being no help at all in the fight. The posse members had fired twenty-six rounds that had pierced Ben's body. Several bullets and shotgun pellets had struck his legs, back,

After the Battle of Alvarado, Bickerstaff's best friend, Josiah Thompson, was buried in Alvarado's Balch Cemetery. Courtesy of Carol C. Taylor

chest, arms, and hands. Another shotgun round took out his right eye.[28] Lying in the street completely disabled, Bickerstaff asked for water, then for morphine and whiskey, all of which Alvarado's finest provided, a request that he often had denied to his own victims as they lay dying.[29]

Bickerstaff asked why he was shot, as if no one had reason to do so.

Benjamin Bickerstaff was buried in Alvarado's Balch Cemetery, but his wife came to claim the body, dug it up, and returned it to the Gray Rock Cemetery. Courtesy of Carol C. Taylor.

One man told him that his many evil deeds and his repeated threats delivered by Cathey had been the cause. When asked about the robbery of Heath and Cathey, Bickerstaff refused to confirm the plot. Many interpreted this as a cover-up for Heath and Cathey. Bickerstaff told the crowd that his saddlebags contained $15 and a Remington handgun and that he wished for Robert Moore to give the money and the gun to his wife. He asked the citizens not to abuse his wife, for she was a good woman. He said to tell her that he wanted her to go back to her people in Titus County.

Just before he died, Bickerstaff said that he regretted that Alvarado's men had given him no real chance in the fight, especially since there were so many of them. He added that he "came near getting [at least] one of you damned rascals anyhow." At the point of death, Bickerstaff exclaimed: "You have killed as brave a man as there is in the South."[30] Thus ended the life of another member of Northeast Texas's unholy triumvirate.

After Bickerstaff's death, the man who disarmed him gave Sheriff Heath the two Derringers and the watch that Bickerstaff had taken earlier when he had supposedly robbed Heath of Johnson County's tax money.[31] The bodies were left on the square until the next day. Photographs were made but have long since disappeared. An inquest was held to attest that the citizens of Alvarado acted in self-defense to protect lives and property from the madness of the Bickerstaff gang. The next day the bodies were buried in the northwest corner of the Alvarado Cemetery. No source has mentioned whether the two were buried outside the actual cemetery as was the Texas custom with outlaws and horse thieves.[32]

Meanwhile, Barnes and the Myers brothers led some of the posse to the old, dilapidated schoolhouse. They stormed the place and arrested several members of the gang who were still there, their number including men named Hatcher and Earhart. Taken to Waco under heavy guard, the men were turned over to military authorities. Also delivered to Waco was Bickerstaff's severed head to establish who he was and that he was, indeed, dead. Along with the head, the citizens of Alvarado sent thirteen affidavits attesting to the crimes of the guerrilla and his men. Judge Norton and H. H. Sneed, an attorney in Waxahachie, happily notified military authorities and Governor Pease that Bickerstaff and Thompson had breathed their last and that Texas had two less dangerous desperadoes.[33]

In the letter from Attorney Sneed to the governor, the citizens of Alvarado were depicted as honest citizens who feared for their lives and property. They wanted the governor, their children, and future posterity to know that they did not kill Bickerstaff and Thompson for the $1,000 reward but that they would gladly accept it. The community needed a new school. Further, they wanted everyone to understand that none of the participants would ever spend a cent of the money for personal gratification.[34]

In reporting Bickerstaff's death, the editor of the *Waxahachie Argus*, a poet at heart, waxed ecstatic, even if he reported some of the facts incorrectly, when giving some details about the deaths of Thompson and Bickerstaff. After saying that Bickerstaff was a "master associate" of Cullen Baker, the editor mentioned that Thompson had lived near Alvarado for about two years, that he seemed respectable at first, but that "he was seduced into a vicious career . . . by Bickerstaff." The poet continued:

> The good citizens of the village prepared themselves with shooting apparatus for the purpose of ridding their community of the greatest pests they had ever known . . . the men rode up to the horse rack and dismounted, and as soon as they had alighted, a shower of death-dealing leaden balls was directed at them. Thompson was killed instantly, and Bickerstaff was struck in three places. Notwithstanding his frightful and mortal wounds . . . he fired two well-aimed shots at his adversaries . . . When he was prostate upon the ground and his adversaries were gathered round, he exclaimed, 'You have killed as brave a man as there is in the South.' He was disposed to be communicative, but he failed to get any interested or attentive auditors. Thus passed from earth a man who had, doubtless, steeped himself in crimes as heinous and foul as are known in the annals of the country.[35]

Bickerstaff's stature was such that news of his death circulated in newspapers both throughout Texas and around the nation. Even in faraway Fort Smith, Arkansas, the *Fort Smith New Era* commented on his death. Though the editor got some of the details wrong, the *New Era* printed that both Bickerstaff and Thompson had been coming into Alvarado in the evening and had instituted a "carnival of robbery" and chaos. "Thompson was killed instantly, and Bickerstaff was struck in three places" and soon died.[36]

Closer to home, an Austin editor held that Bickerstaff would "occupy a bad eminence in the annals of crime in this state. He has spread terror in his pathway in whatever direction he has traveled . . . He was the equal of Cullen Baker."[37]

Staunch Democrats talked of arresting all the posse members and trying them for murder. That idea went nowhere because Judge Norton had empowered Milliken to act for the law, not against it. Shortly, someone contacted Bickerstaff's wife, called a handsome woman by some observers. She was living on Ben's land near the Bauble's Church neighborhood on Aquilla Creek in Hill County. Someone told her about the beheading. She hired a teamster to accompany her to Alvarado to claim what was left of his body which had been temporarily interred in Alvarado's cemetery. She came armed, intending to protect what was left of her husband's remains. Riding her horse near the teamster's wagon with a hand on her shotgun, and continuing to protect the body, she took the corpse to the Gray Rock Cemetery and put it in an unmarked grave.[38]

Bickerstaff and Baker's deaths, whom Orr had earlier sent to meet his maker, left only one member of Northeast Texas's unholy guerrilla triumvirate alive: Bob Lee---and he did not survive much longer. The $1,000 price on his head caused him many problems. But, first, the authorities went after two of his closest associates, the killers Bill Penn, only

Gray Rock Cemetery where Bickerstaff lies in an unmarked grave. Courtesy of Carol C. Taylor.

twenty-one years old, and a mysterious man known only as "Hayes." For a time they eluded lawmen by hiding in the Red River bottoms and alternately in White Rock in Hunt County. They also spent time in the Indian Nations and in Kentucky-Town in eastern Grayson County where Penn had relatives.[39]

Near the latter place, Penn made a terrible mistake. On the road north of Kentucky-Town, he encountered a young black man, Jerry Everheart. Penn stopped, cursed the youngster, and then murdered him by firing lead into his mouth and throat. As events proved, Penn had murdered one freedman too many. Jerry was the former slave and current employee of the white Everheart family, headed by United States Marshal Bill Everheart. When the marshal learned of Jerry's death, he took it hard, even though he had known and liked Penn when the desperado was but a child. Nevertheless, Bill Everheart decided that the young gun had to be stopped before he could murder yet more innocents. Marshal Everheart soon packed supplies and munitions for an extended trip; loaded his guns; saddled-up; and told his wife, "I won't be back 'till Bill Penn is dead."[40]

Once in the field, Marshal Everheart and two deputies learned that Penn and Hayes had been sighted near an old shack in the river bottoms north of Bonham in Fannin County. With the help of Grayson County Sheriff Benjamin Goode and a ten-man posse, the marshal and his deputies located the shack but found it empty. The lawmen picked up Penn's trail and followed it to Ladonia, a small hamlet in Fannin County. Continuing, the posse followed Penn and Hayes to the Honey Grove vicinity, thence to the mouth of the Boggy River in northeast Lamar County.[41]

On the night of April 20, 1869, Everheart and his posse located Penn and Hayes, who had been joined by the desperado William Beard. The lawmen surrounded the old log cabin and called for surrender. Instead, the desperadoes made a stand and "fought with desperation." With guns blazing, the renegades held off the posse for a time. Then, Penn burst from the shack, firing with Colt revolvers, one in each hand. He ran toward his horse, but the posse cut him down. Yet, in the time that the lawmen were occupied with Penn, Hayes and Beard escaped into the forest at the back of the cabin. Nevertheless, Everheart was satisfied. He came for Bill Penn, and he got him.[42]

After the gunplay, the marshal approached Penn, who was on the ground, still clinging to life and trying to talk. Perhaps remembering the man as a child, the marshal knelt down, trying to hear what Penn was saying.

Everheart did not notice that Penn still had a revolver in one hand. The young hotspur whispered to the marshal: "You got me, Bill," he said, just before he jerked his sixgun up and fired a round designed to blow Everheart's head off. But the young man was in the throes of pain, and his aim was poor. His ball only grazed Everheart's left ear and blew his hat off. The marshal grabbed the gun, sat back, and watched Penn die. Everheart then delivered Penn's dead body to his relatives in Kentucky-Town.[43] The marshal had squared accounts for freedman Jerry Everheart. Although Beard and Hayes got away, authorities later captured Beard, and Hayes soon died by his own hand in a successful suicide attempt.[44]

Shortly after Penn died, three unidentified bounty hunters rode into Pilot Grove, talked with locals, and learned that Bob Lee's hideout was in Wildcat Thicket. After they got directions to the area, what the hunters did bordered on insanity--they rode straight into the thicket in broad daylight and became lost in that extreme mistake of Mother Nature. Lee and his men picked them off one by one. No one could penetrate that thicket easily. Lee remained safe there.[45]

The authorities after Lee got a major break on May 22, 1869, when Henry Boren came to Pilot Grove and talked with Lieutenant Charles Campbell who commanded a small squad of troops who remained in the field searching for Lee and his men. Henry Boren was a loyal Nationalist. He was a Union man before and during the war. Rather than accept conscription, he dodged the Confederate authorities by hiding in first one area thicket and then another. He always managed to throw any pursuers off his trail. He had used Wildcat Thicket during the war and knew it well. He told Campbell that he would find Lee and kill him if a posse would support him.[46]

Boren had reasons to go after Lee because the felon had bedeviled him several times since 1865. Lee hated white Unionists as much as he hated freedmen. Early in 1869, for example, the two men had faced off during a county fair. At one point, each had a doubled-barreled shotgun cocked and pointed at the other. Lee had come to the fair astride a horse that had a large "K" on each of its flanks. Lee had stopped on the trail and used pokeberry juice to anoint his mount and to advertize his leadership in the area's terrorist group. Then, once at the fair, the "Man Eater," as Lee was often called, insulted Unionist Boren who refused to allow it; instead, he grabbed his shotgun. Surprised at Henry's sand, Lee had no intention of being one of the victims of a double slaying. He lowered his shotgun, backed away, mounted up, and rode away from trouble.[47]

Boren was not satisfied with standing down Lee because the desperado had killed several of Boren's friends, both white and black Unionists, hence the reason Boren met with Lieutenant Campbell. The officer could scarcely believe his luck. He sent three sergeants and military squad of eleven men to follow Boren who hoped to pick up Lee's trail near Pilot Grove. Lewis Peacock joined them on the trail, Peacock being the leading Unionist in the area and long a target of Lee's wrath. The contingent struck Lee's trail and zig-zagged with it for three days until they arrived at Wildcat Thicket. The date was May 24, 1869, and a cold fate was closing in on the "Man Eater."[48]

Boren and his posse avoided the fate of the three bounty hunters whom Lee and his men had killed. Instead of entering the thicket, the squad broke into smaller groups, and Boren showed them the two entrances to the mangled mass of nature. All remained quite, lest the men inside hear them. As fate would have it, Lee was not in the thicket. He had gone home the day before and spent the last night of his life with his family. But, after having breakfast at home the next morning, he rode back to the thicket to take food to what few men were within. He was almost in the mass when he encountered Boren, Peacock, and the military squad. Asked to surrender, Lee instead reached for his weapons, and the posse opened fire. Shot at least eight times, Lee saying not a word, without whimper or cry, slid from his saddle, dead by the time he hit the ground. Legend says that Henry Boren fired the first shot.[49]

In killing Lee, the authorities had accounted for the last of Northeast Texas's outlaw triumvirate. Lee joined Baker and Bickerstaff in Hell. Shortly before he died, the "Man Eater" had boasted of killing forty-two men after the Civil War, most being white and black Unionists. That he died of violence was perhaps fitting, for he had lived a violent, crime-drenched, blood-spilling life.[50]

Although the triumvirate was gone, loose ends remained. After the deaths of Bickerstaff and Thompson, the problems of the Johnson County folks did not immediately go away. They had to deal with the fate of Bickerstaff's friend William Cathey. Alvarado's authorities had arrested him with others of the gang who were at the old schoolhouse on the day that Bickerstaff was killed. Although he denied all charges, area authorities strongly believed that Cathey had been the brains behind the earlier supposed robbery of Sheriff Heath when he was on his way to Austin with Johnson County tax money. Cathey planned it all, they said, and he recruited Bickerstaff to carry out the scheme. Cathey wound up in the

Waco jail, as the one in Alvarado was most porous. Once he was locked up, remnants of the gang remained in contact with him, awaiting a chance to help him escape.[51]

A major question surfaced: Should the civil authorities or a military commission try Cathey? In the summer of 1869, a petition signed by more than 300 Johnson County residents "prayed" that the military allow the civil authorities jurisdiction. But, Cathey feared that a Johnson County jury would give him the maximum sentence because he had been such a hell-raiser and such a help to Bickerstaff while he lived. Cathey demanded a military trial, believing that an army tribunal might be more lenient than a local civilian jury. As well, his lawyer would be able to condemn the Army's high-handedness in taking jurisdiction. The lawyer hoped that targeting the Army might help Cathey win more support from former hard-core Rebels.[52]

The military trial began on November 8, 1869. After four days, the court adjourned until December 8 because several of the court's officials had to perform registration and election duties. Prior to the delay, Cathey's lawyer had claimed that Cathey was a loyal Union man who had been persecuted and "set up" by a "combination of bad men, constituting the Ku Klux Klan," a frightful prevarication. There was apparent jury-tampering, and several witnesses changed their testimony from one day to the next. The prosecutor's case appeared to be disappearing.[53]

Why did witnesses change their stories? Apparently, they reacted negatively because they objected to the military trying the case, their reaction being exactly what the defense wanted. Additionally, some of Bickerstaff's men made threats, and the witnesses may have altered their testimony for fear that their lives and property might be forfeit. Despite such developments, when the court reconvened, the prosecutor presented a chain of evidence that clearly demonstrated Cathey's guilt. Nevertheless, his attorney attempted to cloud the most important issues by painting the killers of Bickerstaff and Thompson as murderers who had join an illegal conspiracy. Then, in a bizarre twist, all arguments became moot when Cathey escaped before the trial was concluded.[54]

While Cathey's fate was playing out, military authorities captured one of Bickerstaff's men, H. B. Grissom, in mid-July of 1869. He was hiding in the Hunt County home of a friend, a Mr. Gillentine, and an informant relayed that information to the Post of Sulphur Springs; whereupon, the commander sent Sergeant Edgar Immel and two privates to arrest Grissom. The men soon returned with their quarry in tow.[55]

In February of 1870, military scouts picked up Cathey's trail and discovered that he had gone to Gray Rock in Titus County where Bickerstaff's parents harbored him. With another undesirable, John Colby, Cathey apparently remained determined to cause yet more mayhem. Led by Lieutenant C. G. Gibson, a squad of troopers rode to the Bickerstaff place, reaching there at 4:00 a.m. on February 18, 1870. They surrounded the house. At daybreak, they hailed the house, and Seaborne and Francis Bickerstaff came out. The troopers made a thorough search of the property but failed to turn up their prey. Bickerstaff's parents refused to give the troopers any information, likely because Cathey had been at their place and that they had aided and abetted him. Conversely, Cathey may have threatened them with death if they turned informers. Gibson reported about the negative aspect of the search, adding that he doubted if Cathey was even in the county. But, a short distance from Seaborne Bickerstaff's home, another squad arrested a man. He generally fit Cathey's description, and the squad charged him for the robbery of and the assault upon a freedman. Whoever that man was, he never made it to jail. He escaped on the trail and disappeared into the bush.[56]

Of more of immediate concern was that many of Bickerstaff's guerrillas were still roaming Johnson County. The timid District Judge Norton sounded the alarm. Writing Colonel John B. Johnson, who commanded the post of Waco, Norton said that the county residents remained in fear for their lives from a "number of desperate men of the Bickerstaff gang," Cathey and Colby supposedly being among their number. Norton asked the colonel to send a few soldiers to help local men "well disposed to the government and in favor of enforcing the laws."[57]

Relating to other developments, Colonel Johnson already had a squad from his Waco command ready to take the field and ride to Weatherford. Johnson asked the squad commander to make time to conduct a search in Johnson County to look for any desperadoes lurking there. The detachment did its job, found Colby near Cleburne, and arrested him; whereupon, part of the squad escorted him to Waco and tossed him into the guardhouse there, thus removing one of the old gang's leaders.[58]

Cathey escaped altogether. After breaking out of the jail in Waco, he disappeared for a time, only to turn up in Shreveport, Louisiana, in January of 1872. With him were Billy Gilliam and Ben Hatcher, two members of the old gang. None of the three were ever apprehended. They simply slipped from the pages of history, as did various others who had once been a part of the Reconstruction crime spree and terrorist campaign in Northeast Texas.[59]

Afterword

Even after the Northeast Texas criminal triumvirate of Bickerstaff, Baker, and Lee lay dead, and even after many of their men were either dead or on the run, the Lone Star State remained a dark and bloody ground. Other guerrilla leaders and their bands dealt misery to white Unionists and the freedpeople as did Klan-like terrorist groups that had set up shop in at least seventy-seven Texas counties. The Second Civil War, or the War of Reconstruction, continued as the former Confederates and their supporters in the Democratic Party vied with the Republicans for control of the state.

Many Republicans were encouraged by the outcome of state elections held in November of 1869. Radical Edmund J. Davis defeated conservative Republican A. J. Hamilton for the governorship, and Davis's supporters gained majorities in both the Texas House and Senate. In February of 1870, General Reynolds called the new legislature into session, and it applied for readmission into the Union. Readmission came in April. The Fifth Military District was dissolved, and troops of occupation withdrew from Texas.

In retrospect, the end of the occupation was the worst thing that could have happened. The national government abandoned the Texas Republicans--just as it abandoned the Republicans in all the Confederate states--to the tender mercies of the Democratic party and its para-military arms consisting of the many terrorist societies and guerrilla gangs. Such people were still willing to support the Democrats in return for a blank check regarding the murders and the robberies of white Unionists and the freedpeople. The War of Reconstruction simply continued.

The temporary successes in the early years of Reconstruction of men like Bickerstaff, Baker, Lee, and other of the Northeast Texas desperadoes taught lessons to the leading Democrats. Many of them continued to deny the existence of widespread violence in their state when, in fact, many of them supported (unofficially) such violence because it continued to undermine the Republicans, and it continued to hasten the day when the Democrats would return to power.

Davis coped with the Democrats' para-military arms as best he could. After mentioning that a "slow Civil War" was still ongoing in Texas, he led the effort to establish law and order by creating a new State Police Force, complete with the support of numerous "Special Policemen" recruited at the county level. The personnel of a newly raised state militia further supported the police when necessary.

Authorized by the legislature in July of 1870, the State Police appeared to have great success. In their first month of work, the new lawmen made 978 arrests, including 109 for murder and 130 for attempted murder. By 1872, arrests totaled 6,820 including 587 for murder, 760 for attempted murder, 1,748 for other felonies, and the remainder for lesser crimes.

Despite its success, the State Police were unpopular. First, blacks made up about 40 percent of the force, and that offended many whites, particularly the former Confederates. Second, it was controlled by the Republican administration; most Democrats opposed the force on that basis alone. During his term, violence and discord forced Governor Davis to declare martial law in five counties: Madison, Hill, Walker, Limestone, and Freestone. Although such action was necessary, Democrats condemned Davis and branded him as an autocrat. After the Democrats "redeemed" Texas by capturing the governor's chair and the legislature in the early 1870s, they repealed the law establishing the police.

Once the "Redeemers" controlled Texas, their party ceased to need the terrorist groups and the outlaw gangs who used the "excesses" of Reconstruction to justify their illegal activities. The Democrats created a new *status quo* and now wanted peace. With the State Police gone, redeemers re-instituted the Texas Rangers and used them to quell lawlessness.

By 1875, the Ranger crack-down on crime eliminated approximately 3,000 of the state's desperadoes. Most of the Klan-like terrorist organizations ceased to be, for such groups had accomplished their purpose: reinstall ex-Confederate Democratic rule and firmly reestablish white supremacy.

Under Democratic leadership, political stability returned to Texas, but the new leaders denied justice to the freedpeople and their white allies into the next century. Texas became part of the "Solid" South where conservative Democrat rule guaranteed that old Dixie would become the nation's number one problem politically, economically, and socially, as was pointed out during the New Deal Era by President Franklin D. Roosevelt. The real "Reconstruction" of the South, including Texas, did not come until the victories of the Civil Rights movement of the 1950s and 1960s. Finally, the rest of the nation tired of Southern violence and refused to let that violence stop needed racial reforms. But even now, Reconstruction remains incomplete.

Abbreviations used in the notes:

AG	Adjutant General
AAG	Assistant Adjutant General
AAAG	Acting Assistant Adjutant General
AGO	Adjutant General's Office
BRFAL	Bureau of Refugees, Freedmen, and Abandoned Lands
CAH	Center for American History, University of Texas at Austin Library
DT	Department of Texas
5MD	Fifth Military District
GPL	Archives, Greenville, Texas, W. Walworth Harrison Library
LR	Letters Received
LS	Letters Sent
MS	Unpublished Manuscript
NA	National Archives, Washington, D.C.
NHT	*New Handbook of Texas*
RG	Record Group
SWHQ	*Southwestern Historical Quarterly*
TAMC	Texas A&M University at Commerce Library
UTL	University of Texas at Austin Library
VC/UHA	Regional History Center, Victoria College/University of Houston at Victoria Library, Victoria, Texas
VF	Vertical File

NOTES

Introduction

[1]. *Waxahachie Argus*, Extra, April 6, 1869; *Clarksville Standard*, April 17, 1869; Traylor Russell and Robert T. Russell, *Some Die Twice* (Waco: Texian Press, 1979), 37; Ulvan T. Taylor, "Ben Bickerstaff," *Frontier Times* (October 1924), 10; Traylor Russell, *The History of Titus County* (2 Vols.; Waco: Library Binding Company, 1974), 2, 162-163; H. H. Sneed to Gov. Elisha Pease, April 12, 1869, E. Pease, GP, RG 301, Archives, TSL; David Minor, "Alvarado, Texas," *NHT*, 1, 136.

[2]. Judge Bernard Patterson, "Memoirs," Barry A. Crouch Collection, Regional History Center, VC/UHV; Sneed to Gov. E. Pease, April 12, 1869, E. Pease, GP, Archives, TSL;

Clarksville Standard, April 17, 1869; T. Russell and R. Russell, *Some Die Twice,* 37; T. Russell, *Titus County,* 2, 162-63; George G. Orren, "The History of Hopkins County" (M.A. Thesis, East Texas State Teachers College, 1938), 58-59; *Waxahachie Argus,* Extra, April 6, 1869; *Austin Daily Republican,* April 21, 1869.

[3].*Waxahachie Argus,* Extra, April 6, 1869; *Clarksville Standard,* April 17, 1869; *Austin Daily Republican,* April 21, 1869; Sneed to Gov. E. Pease, April 12, 1869, E. Pease, GP, Archives, TSL; T. Russell and R. Russell, *Some Die Twice,* 36-37; T. Russell, *Titus County,* 2, 162-63; U. T. Taylor, "Bickerstaff," *Frontier Times,* 10; T. Lindsay Baker, "Ben Bickerstaff Dead or Alive," *Cleburne Eagle-News,* November 3, 1988; Orren, "History of Hopkins County," 59.

[4].*Marshall Texas Republican,* August 4, 1865; *Clarksville Northern Standard,* July 8, 1865; Norman C. Russell, "The History of Titus County Since 1860" (M.A. thesis, East Texas State Teachers College, 1937), 32-33; James M. Smallwood, Barry A. Crouch, and Larry Peacock, *Murder and Mayhem: The War of Reconstruction in Texas* (College Station: University of Texas A&M Press, 2003), 27; June E. Tuck, *Civil War Shadows in Hopkins County, Texas* (Sulphur Springs: Wadsworth Publishing, 1993), 52-53.

[5].*Marshall Texas Republican,* August 4, 1865; *Clarksville Northern Standard,* July 8, 1865; N. Russell, "The History of Titus County Since 1860," 32-33; Smallwood, Crouch, and Peacock, *Murder and Mayhem,* 27; Tuck, *Civil War Shadows,* 52-53.

[6].James M. Smallwood, *Born in Dixie: The History of Smith County, Texas* (2 vols.; Austin: Eakin Press, 1999), 1, 237-238; Vicki Betts, *Smith County, Texas, in the Civil War* (Tyler: Smith County Historical Society, 1978), 76-78.

[7].Smallwood, *Born in Dixie,* 1, 237-238, 259-260; Betts, *Smith County in the Civil War,* 76-78; *Houston Tri-Weekly Telegraph,* June 7, 1865; *New York Times,* July 17, 1865; Ernest Wallace, *Texas in Turmoil* (Austin: Steck-Vaughn Company, 1965), 139-146.

[8].Kate Stone, *Brokenburn—The Journal of Kate Stone, 1861-1868,* ed. John Q. Anderson (Baton Rouge: Louisiana State University Press, 1955), 226-227.

[9].*Houston Tri-Weekly Telegraph,* June 7, 1865; *New York Times,* July 17, 1865; L. Roberts to Ashbel Smith, July 15, 1865, Ashbel Smith Papers, CAH, UTL; James M. Smallwood, *Time of Hope, Time of Despair: Black Texans During Reconstruction* (New York and London: Kennikat Press), 25; Wallace, *Texas in Turmoil,* 139-146.

[10].*Flake's Daily Bulletin* (Galveston), June 28, 1865; L. Roberts to A. Smith, July 15, 1865, A. Smith Papers, CAH, UTL; Smallwood, Crouch, and Peacock, *Murder and Mayhem,* 10.

[11].*Flake's Daily Bulletin,* June 28, 1865; Smallwood, *Time of Hope, Time of Despair,* 25; James Alex Baggett, "Gordon Granger," *NHT,* 3, 280; Granger's military career is discussed in some detail by Ezra J. Warner, *Generals in Blue* (Baton Rouge: Louisiana State University Press, 1964); and see James Sefton, *The United States Army and Reconstruction, 1865-1877* (Baton Rouge: Louisiana State University Press, 1967), 261-262.

[12].*Flake's Daily Bulletin,* June 28, 1865; Smallwood, *Time of Hope, Time of Despair,* 25; Sefton, *United States Army and Reconstruction,* 261-262.

[13].Claude Elliott, "The Freedmen's Bureau in Texas," *SWHQ* 56 (July 1952), 6. For a brief account of the Bureau in Texas, see Cecil Harper, Jr., "Freedmen's Bureau," *NHT,* 2, 1166-1167; for more depth, see Barry A. Crouch, *The Freedmen's Bureau and Black Texans* (Austin: University of Texas Press, 1992).

[14].Carl Moneyhon, *Texas After the Civil War: The Struggle of Reconstruction* (College Station: Texas A&M University Press, 2004), 35-36. For a brief account of Reconstruction, see Moneyhon, "Reconstruction," *NHT,* 5, 474-481.

[15].Smallwood, *Time of Hope, Time of Despair,* 128-133; Smallwood, *Born in Dixie,* 1, 260-263.

[16].Smallwood, *Time of Hope, Time of Despair*, 128-133; Smallwood, *Born in Dixie*, 1, 260-263.

[17].*Flake's Daily Bulletin*, October 4, 1865; *Houston Tri-Weekly Telegraph*, October 13, 1865; Smallwood, *Time of Hope, Time of Despair*, 128-133.

[18].For the Klan, see James M. Smallwood, "When the Klan Rode: White Terror in Reconstruction Texas," *Journal of the West* 25 (October 19865), 4-13; Smallwood, *Time of Hope, Time of Despair*, 29, 51, 53, 55, 61-62, 83-84, 92-93, 126-127, 132, 141-146, 152, 155-157.

[19].Smallwood, Crouch, and Peacock, *Murder and Mayhem*, 33. *Murder and Mayhem* chronicles the dastardly deeds of many of the desperadoes mentioned in the text.

[20].The best one-volume work on the causes of the Civil War is David Potter's Pulitzer Prize winning *The Impending Crisis, 1848-1861* (New York: Harper and Row, 1976). Potter examined all the sectional clashes from 1848 to 1861 and explained how each had slavery or its expansion as a cause. For a short summary that traces the origin of the Civil War to the eighteenth century and discusses how slavery always divided the nation, see James M. Smallwood's "The Predominate Cause of the Civil War Reconsidered: A Retrospective essay," *Lincoln Herald* 89 (Winter 1987), 152-160.

[21].*Cincinnati Commercial*, quoted in the *Montgomery Alabama State Journal*, January 30, 1869.

[22].For more on the violence in East-Northeast Texas during Reconstruction, see Gov. Andrew J. Hamilton to President Andrew Johnson, March 1, 1866, Andrew Johnson Papers, Archives, Manuscript Division, Library of Congress, Washington, D.C.; Bvt. Capt. Charles S. Roberts to AAG, August 12, November 12, 1867, Assistant Commissioner, Texas, LR, BRFAL, RG 105, NA; Capt. Samuel H. Starr to Lt. Charles E. Morse, AAAG, February 9, 1868, LR, DT, 5MD, RG 393, NA, copy also in Crouch Collection, Regional History Center, VC/UHV; Smallwood, "When the Klan Rode," *Journal of the West*, 4-13; also see Smallwood, *Time of Hope, Time of Despair*; Barrry A. Crouch and Donald E. Brice, *Cullen Montgomery Baker: Reconstruction Desperado* (Baton Rouge: Louisiana State University Press, 1997); Crouch, *Freedmen's Bureau and Black Texans*; William L. Richter, *The Army in Texas During Reconstruction, 1865-1870* (College Station: Texas A&M Press, 1987); William L. Richter, *Overreached on All Sides: Freedmen's Bureau Administrators in Texas, 1865-1868* (College Station: Texas A&M Press, 1991); Charles V. Keener, "Racial Turmoil in Texas, 1865-1871" (M. A. Thesis, North Texas State University, 1971); Rebecca A. Rosary, "Regression to Barbarism in Reconstruction Texas: An Analysis of White Violence against African- Americans from the Texas Freedmen's Bureau Records, 1865-1868 (M. A. Thesis, Southwest Texas State University, 1999).

[23].The most valuable study on Baker is Crouch and Donald Brice's *Cullen Baker*; the most thorough study of Bob Lee is Smallwood, Crouch, and Peacock, *Murder and Mayhem*.

Chapter 1

[1].United States Census, 1840, Jackson County, Alabama, Monroe County, Mississippi, manuscript returns; United States Census, 1850, 1860, Titus County, Texas, manuscript returns; T. Russell, *History of Titus County*, 2, 161; T. Russell and R. Russell, *Some Die Twice*, 33. And see, Titus County, Tax rolls, 1859, 1866; Carol Taylor, "Violence and Deception: The Outlaw Career of Ben Bickerstaff," paper presented to the East Texas Historical Association, September 15, 2005, 4[hereinafter cited as C. Taylor, ETHA, paper], VF, Randolph W. Farmer, "Ben Bickerstaff: An Apostle of Racial Hatred and Genocide in North Texas, 1865-1869," 1, VF, C. Taylor, "Bickerstaff notes," VF, copies in Taylor-Smallwood-Howell Collection, GPL. Also see Bob and Doris Bowman, *Historic*

Murders of East Texas: Book 3 (Lufkin: Best of East Texas Publishers, 2006), 55-56.

[2].United States Census, 1850, 1860, Titus County, Texas, manuscript returns; *Clarksville Northern Standard*, November 20, December 11, 1847; Cecil Harper, Jr., "Red River County," *NHT*, 5, 495-497; Nelson Denson, a former slave, described the Red River Raft as it existed in the 1860s. He said that "back in those days the Red River was nearly closed up by this timber raft, and the big boats couldn't get up the river at all. . . . The driftwood floating down the river stopped in the still waters and made a bunch of trees, and the dirt accumulated, and broom straws and willows and brush grew out of the rich dirt that covered the driftwood. The raft grew about a mile a year, and the oldest timber rotted and broke away, but this was not fast enough to keep the river clear." See statement of Nelson Denson, Federal Writers Project, "Texas Narratives," *A Folk History of Slavery in the United States from interviews with former slaves* (Washington, D.C.: Works Progress Administration, 1941), ms, housed in NA.

[3].United States Census, 1840, Jackson County, Alabama, Monroe County, Mississippi, manuscript returns; United States Census, 1850, 1860, Titus County, Texas, manuscript returns; T. Russell, *History of Titus County*, 2, 161; T. Russell and R. Russell, *Some Die Twice*, 33; *Clarksville Northern Standard*, December 22, 1860. And see, Titus County, Tax rolls, 1859, 1866; Farmer, "Ben Bickerstaff: An Apostle of Racial Hatred," 1, VF, C. Taylor, "Bickerstaff notes," VF, C. Taylor, "Ben Bickerstaff," ETHA, paper, 1, VF, copies in Taylor-Smallwood-Howell Collection, GPL. Also see B. and D. Bowman, *Historic Murders: Book 3*, 55-56. For the Masons in Texas, see William Preston Vaughan, "Freemasonry," *NHT*, 2, 1168-1169.

[4].Cecil Harper, Jr., "Titus County," *NHT*, 6, 507-509; also see John M. Ellis II, *The Way It Was: A Personal Memoir of Family Life in East Texas* (Waco: Texian Press, 1965).

[5].*Austin Daily Republican*, April 21, 1869; T. Russell and R. Russell, *Some Die Twice*, 33; B. And D. Bowman, *Historic Murders: Book 3*, 55; C. Taylor, "Ben Bickerstaff," ETHA paper, 3, VF, Taylor-Smallwood-Howell Collection, GPL.

[6].United States Census, 1860, Titus County, manuscript returns. The census reveals that Ben attended school during the previous year. He was twenty years old when the census was taken; thus he would have been beyond the traditional age of students in attendance at secondary schools in Titus County. Therefore, it seems likely that Ben took courses at one of the local academies or attended college for at least one session.

[7].Robert K. Peters, *"From Wilderness to War,"* in Robert Glover and Linda Cross, eds., *Tyler and Smith County, Texas: An Historical Survey* (Tyler: American Bicentennial Committee of Tyler- Smith County, 1976), 11-32; Smallwood, *Born in Dixie*, 1, 151. Also see, James M. Smallwood, "Slave Insurrections," *NHT*, 5, 1080-1081.

[8].*Houston Telegraph*, July 21, 1860; *Clarksville Northern Standard*, July 14, 1860; *Marshall Texas Republican*, August 4, 1860; *Tyler Reporter*, July 18, 1860, quoted in *Marshall Texas Republican*, August 11, 1860; Donald E. Reynolds, "Smith County and Its Neighbors During the Slave Insurrection Panic of 1860," *Chronicles of Smith County, Texas* 10 (Fall, 1971), 1-8. For more on the insurrection scare in Northeast Texas, see Norton, " Civil Disturbances in North Texas in 1859 and 1860," *SWHQ*, 317-341; Smallwood, "Slave Insurrections," *NHT*, 5, 1080-1081.

[9].Reynolds, "Slave Insurrection Panic of 1860," *Chronicles of Smith County, Texas*, 1-8; Norton, "Civil Disturbances in North Texas," *SWHQ*, 317-341; *Houston Telegraph*, July 21, 1860; *Clarksville Northern Standard*, July 14, 1860.

[10].*Austin Texas State Gazette*, August 11, 18, 25, 28, September 15, 1860; *Galveston Weekly News*, August 14, September 1, 1860; *Corsicana Navarro Express*, July 28, August 25, September 14, 1860; Alwyn Barr, *Black Texans—A History of Negroes in Texas, 1528-1971*

(Austin: Jenkins Publishing Company, 1973), 34; Reynolds, "Panic of 1860," *Chronicles of Smith County*, 1-8; *Marshall Texas Republican*, August 25, September 8, 1860.

[11]. Titus County, Texas, tax rolls, 1859, 1866, 1867; U. S. Census, 1860, Titus County, manuscript returns; C. Taylor, "Ben Bickerstaff," ETHA paper, 4, VF, Taylor-Smallwood-Howell Collection, GPL.

[12]. Randolph Campbell, *Gone to Texas: A History of the Lone Star State* (New York: Oxford University Press, 2003), 239; and see Potter, *Impending Crisis*.

[13]. Campbell, *Gone to Texas*, 239. And see, Ralph A. Wooster, "Civil War," *NHT*, 2, 121-126.

[14]. Campbell, *Gone to Texas*, 239; also see Walter L. Buenger and James Alex Baggett, "Constitutional Union Party," *NHT*, 2, 286-287.

[15]. See Bruce Levine, *Half Slave, Half Free: The Roots of the Civil War* (New York: Hill and Wang, 1992) and Potter, *Impending Crisis*.

[16]. Edward R. Maher, "Sam Houston and Secession," *SWHQ* 55 (April 1952), 452-453; Smallwood, *Born in Dixie*, 1, 162. And see Walter L. Buenger, "Secession," *NHT*, 5, 957-958.

[17]. Walter L. Buenger, *Secession and the Union in Texas* (Austin: University of Texas Press, 1984), 122-143.

[18]. Buenger, *Secession and the Union*, 142-143, 159-174.

[19]. Harper, "Titus County," *NHT*, 6, 507-509.

[20]. Confederate Muster Rolls, Eleventh Texas Cavalry, Archives, TSL; "Eleventh Texas Cavalry," ms, "Record of Events for Eleventh Texas Cavalry, October 1861-February 1864," ms, Confederate Research Center, Hill College, Hillsboro, Texas; Tuck, *Civil War Shadows*, 58; Farmer, "Ben Bickerstaff," 2, VF, Taylor-Smallwood-Howell Collection, GPL.

[21]. United States Department of War, *The War of the Rebellion: A Compilation of the Official Records of the Union and Confederate Armies* (128 vols; Washington, D.C.: Government Printing Office, 1880-1901), Series I, Vol. 4, 144-145.

[22]. Richard B. McCaslin, "Conditional Confederates: The Eleventh Texas Cavalry West of the Mississippi River," *Military History of the Southwest* 21 (Spring 1991), 91-95; Douglas Hale, "Rehearsal for Civil War: The Texas Cavalry in the Indian Territory, 1861," *The Chronicles of Oklahoma* 68 (Fall 1990), 232.

[23]. Confederate Muster Rolls, Eleventh Texas Cavalry, Archives, TSL; "Eleventh Texas Cavalry," ms, "Record of Events for Eleventh Texas Cavalry, October 1861-February 1864, ms, Confederate Research Center, Hill College, Hillsboro, Texas; Tuck, *Civil War Shadows*, 58; Farmer, "Ben Bickerstaff," 2, VF, Taylor-Smallwood-Howell Collection, GPL.

[24]. Department of War, *War of Rebellion*, Series I, Vol. 8, 5-11, 16-21.

[25]. Department of War, *War of Rebellion*, Series I, Vol. 8, 29-30.

[26]. Department of War, *War of the Rebellion*, Series I, Vol. 8, 11-14, 26; Hale, "The Texas Cavalry in the Indian Territory," *The Chronicles of Oklahoma*, 245-253.

[27]. Department of War, *War of the Rebellion*, Series I, Vol. 8, 26-27.

[28]. James McPherson, *Battle Cry of Freedom: The Civil War Era* (New York: Oxford University Press, 1988), 404-405.

[29]. *Confederate Veteran* (September 1911), 430; McCaslin, "Conditional Confederates," *Military History of the Southwest*, 96.

[30]. Department of War, *War of the Rebellion*, Series I, Vol. 16, Part 1, 931-949, 1109-1112; *Confederate Veteran* (September 1911), 430.

[31]. Department of War, *War of the Rebellion*, Series I, Vol, 20, Part 1, 932-33; *Dallas Herald*,

March 11, 1863. The *Dallas Herald* lists Bickerstaff as one of the wound men in Company I of the 11th Texas Cavalry.

32. T. Russell, *Titus County*, 2, 161; U. T. Taylor, "Ben Bickerstaff, the Noted Desperado," *Frontier Times*: 9; B. And D. Bowman, *Historic Murders: Book 3*, 56.

33. B. Patterson, "Memoirs," ms, James Patterson, "Recollections," ms, VF, in David Pickering-Judy Falls Collection, Archives, TAMC, copies also in the Barry A. Crouch Collection, VF, Regional History Center, VC/UHV; C. Taylor, "Ben Bicker staff," ETHA, paper, 3, VF, Taylor-Smallwood-Howell Collection, GPL.

34. B. Patterson, "Memoirs," ms, J. Patterson, "Recollections," ms, VF, in Pickering-Falls Collection, Archives, TAMC, copies also in the Crouch Collection, VF, Regional History Center, VC/UHV; C. Taylor, "Ben Bickerstaff," ETHA, paper, 3, VF, Taylor-Smallwood-Howell Collection, GPL.

35. Department of War, *War of the Rebellion*, Series II, Vol. 6, 568.

36. R. Scott Gartin, "11th Texas Cavalry, Titus County Guards: Company I," Internet: 11texascav.org/regiment/i_co.shtml; unidentified newspaper clippings, copies in Taylor-Smallwood-Howell Collection, GPL; B. and D. Bowman, *Historic Murders: Book 3*, 56. For more on punishment for abusing civilians, see *Fayetteville Arkansas Observer*, March 19, 1863.

Chapter 2

1. Gartin, "11th Texas Cavalry, Titus County Guards: Company I," Internet: 1texascav.org/regiment/i_co.shtml, unidentified newspaper clipping, VF, copies in Taylor-Smallwood-Howell Collection, GPL ; B. and D. Bowman, *Historic Murders: Book 3*, 56.

2. "Statement of J. F. Norman," "Statement of J. F. Smith," quoted by Tuck, *Civil War Shadows*, 156-157, 159-160; B. And D. Bowman, *Historic Murders: Book 3*, 3, 56.

3. "Statement of J. F. Norman," "Statement of J. F. Smith," quoted by Tuck, *Civil War Shadows*, 156-157, 159-160; B. and D. Bowman, *Historic Murders: Book 3*, 56.

4. Department of War, *War of the Rebellion*, Series II, Vol. 6, 1001-1003.

5. Department of War, *War of the Rebellion*, Series II, Vol. 6, 1003-1004.

6. Department of War, *War of the Rebellion*, Series II, Vol. 7, 1038-1040.

7. Department of War, *War of the Rebellion*, Series II, Vol. 7, 1038-1040.

8. Department of War, *War of the Rebellion*, Series II, Vol. 7, 654.

9. Department of War, *War of the Rebellion*, Series II, Vol. 7, 654.

10. Ben Bickerstaff, Confederate Service Record, NA; See U. T. Taylor, "Ben Bickerstaff," *Frontier Times*, 9-10.

11. U.T.Taylor, "Ben Bickerstaff," *Frontier Times*, 9-10; C. Taylor, "Ben Bickerstaff," ETHA, paper, 4, VF, C. Taylor, "Bickerstaff notes," VF, Taylor-Smallwood-Howell Collection, GPL; B. and D. Bowman, *Historic Murders: Book 3*, 56-57; and see Ben Bickerstaff, Confederate Service Record, NA.

12. C. Taylor, "Ben Bickerstaff," ETHA, paper 1-4, VF, C. Taylor, "Bickerstaff notes," VF, Taylor-Smallwood-Howell Collection, GPL; for the definitive work on Cullen Baker, see Crouch and Brice, *Cullen Baker*. Also see, Yvonne Vestal, *The Borderlands and Cullen Baker* (Atlanta, Texas: privately printed, 1978), 25. For a brief summary of Baker's misspent life, see James M. Smallwood, "Cullen Baker: The Swamp Fox of the Sulphur," *True West* 38 (October 1991), Pt. 1, 20-23, (November 1991), Pt. 2, 38-41.

13. C. Harper, "Cass County," *NHT*, 1, 1012-1015; for more on Cass County, see the older work by Thomas Clarence Richardson: *East Texas: Its History and Its Makers* (4 vols.; New York: Lewis Historical Publishing, 1940).

[14]. Barry A. Crouch, "Cullen Montgomery Baker," *NHT*, 1, 344; and see Crouch and Brice, *Cullen Baker*.

[15]. Barry A. Crouch, "Cullen Montgomery Baker," *NHT*, 1, 344; also see Crouch and Brice, *Cullen Baker*; for brief coverage, see Smallwood, "The Swamp Fox of the Sulphur," *True West*.

[16]. U. S. Census, 1860, Sebastian County, Arkansas, manuscript returns; William L. Richter, "'Oh God, Let Us Have Revenge': Ben Griffith and his Family during the Civil War and Reconstruction, *Arkansas Historical Quarterly* 57 (Autumn 1998), 258.

[17]. Jay Monaghan, *Civil War on the Wester Border, 1854-1865* (New York: Bonanza Books, 1955), 180; Department of War, *War of the Rebellion*, Series 1, Vol. 3: 121-125; Clement A. Evans, ed., *Louisiana and Arkansas in Confederate Military History* (17 vols.; 1899; reprint; Secaucus: Blue and Gray Press, 1988), 10, 51-53; Richter, "Ben Griffith," *Arkansas Historical Quarterly*, 259, 261-266.

[18]. Vestal, *The Borderlands and Cullen Baker*, 25; Smallwood, "Swamp Fox of the Sulphur" *True West*: Pt. 1, 20-23; C. Taylor "Ben Bickerstaff, ETHA, paper, 3, VF, Taylor-Smallwood-Howell Collection, GPL; Crouch and Brice, *Cullen Baker*, 49-50.

[19]. Crouch and Brice, *Cullen Baker*, 49-50; Vestal, *The Borderlands and Cullen Baker*, 25; Smallwood, "Swamp Fox of the Sulphur" *True West*, Pt. 1, 20-23, Pt. 2, 38-41; C. Taylor, "Ben Bickerstaff, ETHA, paper, 3, VF, Taylor-Smallwood-Howell Collection, GPL.

[20]. Crouch and Brice, *Cullen Baker*, 51.

[21]. Thomas Orr, *Life of the Notorious Desperadoe Cullen Baker, from his Childhood to his Death, with a Full Account of all the Murders He Committed* (Little Rock: privately printed, 1870), 17-18; Crouch and Brice, *Cullen Baker*, 51; B. and D. Bowman, *Historic Murders: Book 3*, 57.

[22]. See Daniel E. Sutherland, "Guerrillas: The Real War in Arkansas," *Arkansas Historical Quarterly* 52 (Autumn 1993), 257-285; Richter, "Ben Griffith," *Arkansas Historical Quarterly*, 267-269.

[23]. "Titus County," VF, Pickering-Falls Collection, Archives, TAMC; Harper, "Titus County," *NHT*, 6, 507-509; T. Russell and R. Russell, *Some Die Twice*, 34; T. Russell, *Titus County*, 2, 161-63; AG William Steele, *A List of Fugitives from Justice* (Austin: AGO, 1878), 112.

[24]. *Galveston Daily News*, March 7, 1865.

[25]. *Galveston Daily News*, June 21, 1865; Moneyhon, *Texas After the Civil War*, 7-8; Richter, *The Army in Texas During Reconstruction*, 14-16.

[26]. *Galveston Daily News*, August 10, 1865.

[27]. "Titus County," VF, Pickering-Falls Collection, Archives, TAMC; Harper, "Titus County," *NHT*, 6, 507-509; T. Russell and R. Russell, *Some Die Twice*, 34; T. Russell, *Titus County*, 2, 161-63; Traylor Russell, *Pioneers and Heroes of Titus County* (Waco: Library Binding Company, 1974), 15; AG Steele, *List of Fugitives*, 112; Ed Bartholomew, *Cullen Baker: Premier Texas Gunfighter* (Houston: Frontier Press, 1954), 36, 60; B. and M. Gilbert, "Hopkins County," *NHT*, 3, 694-695; U. T. Taylor, "Ben Bickerstaff," *Frontier Times*, 9; C. Taylor, "Bickerstaff notes," VF, copy in Taylor-Smallwood-Howell Collection, GPL.

[28]. T. Russell, *Heroes of Titus County*, 15; T. Russell and R. Russell, *Some Die Twice*, 34; C. Taylor, "Bickerstaff notes," VF, in Taylor-Smallwood-Howell Collection, GPL. For a brief account of the "Great Hanging" in Gainesville, see Smallwood, "Disaffection in Confederate Texas: The Great Hanging in Gainesville," *Civil War History* 22 (December 1976) and, for much more detail, see Richard B. McCaslin, *Tainted Breeze: The Great Hanging in Gainesville, Texas, 1862* (Baton Rouge: Louisiana State University Press, 1994).

29. U. S. Census, 1860, Hunt County, Texas, manuscript returns; Smallwood, Crouch, and Peacock, *Murder and Mayhem*, 31-32.
30. Lt. Anthony Bryan to AAAG Lt. J. P. Richardson, Sub-Assistant Commissioner, Sherman, LS, BRFAL, RG 105, NA.
31. Robert Lee, Confederate Service Record, NA; For Bob Lee's Civil War crimes, see John Gentry, interviewed by L. L. Bowman, July 22, 1931, in "Bob Lee," VF, L. L. Bowman Papers, Archives, TAMC; Gladys Ray, *Murder at the Corners* (San Antonio: Naylor, 1957), 2-5; Stewart Sifakis, *Compendium of the Confederate Armies: Texas* (New York: Facts on File, 1995), 61-63.
32. Lt. H. E. Scott, Post of Sherman, to AAAG Lt. Morse, March 12, 1868, LR, Box 5, DT, 5MD, RG 393, NA. Although Scott wrote Morse in March of 1868, his letter includes a summary of Bob Lee's activities, many of them criminal, from mid-1865 to 1868; G. W. King, interviewed by L. L. Bowman, July 22, 1931, in "Bob Lee," VF, L. L. Bowman Papers, Archives, TAMC.
33. Lt. Scott, Post of Sherman, to AAAG Lt. Morse, March 12, 1868, LR, Box 5, DT, 5MD, RG 393, NA; G. W. King, interviewed by L. L. Bowman, July 22, 1931, in "Bob Lee," VF, L. L. Bowman Papers, Archives, TAMC.
34. Lt. Scott to AAAG Lt. Morse, March 12, 1868, LR, Box 5, DT, 5MD, RG 393, NA.
35. Harrison, *History of Greenville and Hunt County*, 126-127; Pickering and Falls, *Brushmen and Vigilantes*, 15; and see Smallwood, Crouch, and Peacock, *Murder and Mayhem*.
36. "Titus County," VF, Pickering-Falls Collection, Archives, TAMC; Harper, "Titus County," *NHT*, 6, 507-509; T. Russell and R. Russell, *Some Die Twice*, 34; T. Russell, *Titus County*, 2, 161-63; T. Russell, *Pioneers and Heroes of Titus County*, 15; AG Steele, *A List of Fugitives*, 112; Bartholomew, *Cullen Baker*, 36, 60; N. Russell, "The History of Titus County Since 1860," 39-40; B. and M. Gilbert, "Hopkins County," *NHT*, 3, 694-695; Smallwood, Crouch, and Peacock, *Murder and Mayhem*, 46; U. T. Taylor, "Bickerstaff," *Frontier Times*, 9; B. and D. Bowman, *Historic Murders: Book 3*, 57; Farmer, "Bickerstaff," 4-5, VF, Taylor-Smallwood-Howell Collection, GPL.
37. L. L. Bowman, "Jernigan's Thicket," ms, VF, L. L. Bowman Papers, unsigned, untitled newspaper clipping in "Bob Lee," VF, "Backward Glances, Thicket was Outlaws Refuge," newspaper clipping, in "Bob Lee," VF, Pickering-Falls Collection, Archives, TAMC; Janice Jernigan Kiker, "William Jernigan, Founder of Commerce [Texas], *Commerce Journal*, October 31, 1982.
38. L. L. Bowman, "Jernigan's Thicket," ms, VF, L. L. Bowman Papers, unidentified newspaper clipping, "Backward Glances: Thicket was Outlaws Refuge" newspaper clipping in "Bob Lee," VF, Pickering-Falls Collection, Archives, TAMC; Kiker, "William Jernigan," *Commerce Journal*, October 31, 1982; for Howell's comments, see Alfred Howell to Morton Howell, May 14, 1854, in Morton Boyte Howell Collection, Archives, TAMC.
39. U. S. Census, 1860, 1870 Lamar County, manuscript returns, NA; Titus County Voter Registration List 1867, Titus County Courthouse; William Denning to Ron Brothers, n.d., copy in Taylor-Smallwood-Howell Collection, GPL; Denning may have speculated in land; according to the Van Zandt County Deed Book, he owned land there by 1867.
40. "Titus County," VF, Pickering-Falls Collection, Archives, TAMC; Harper, "Titus County," *NHT*, 6, 507-509; T. Russell and R. Russell, *Some Die Twice*, 34; T. Russell, *Titus County*, 2, 161-63; T. Russell, *Pioneers and Heroes of Titus County*, 15; Bartholomew, *Cullen Baker*, 36, 60; N. Russell, "The History of Titus County Since 1860," 39-40; B. and D. Bowman, *Historic Murders: Book 3*, 57; Gilbert and Gilbert, "Hopkins County," *NHT*, 3, 694-695; Smallwood, Crouch, and Peacock, *Murder and Mayhem*, 46; U. T. Taylor,

"Ben Bickerstaff," *Frontier Times*, 9.
[41].Tuck, Civil War Shadows, 58; B. and D. Bowman, *Historic Murders: Book 3*, 58.
[42].T. Russell and R. Russell, *Some Die Twice*, 7; John H. McLean, *Reminiscences of Rev. Jno. H. McLean, D. D.* (Dallas: Smith and Lamar, Publishers, n.d.), 274; U. T. Taylor, "Ben Bickerstaff," *Frontier Times*, 9-10; T. Russell, *Titus County*, 2: 94; and see Robert W. Teel, *Cullen Montgomery Baker: Champion of the Lost Cause* (Huntsville, Alabama: privately printed, 1995); B. and D. Bowman, *Historic Murders: Book 3*, 58.

Chapter 3

[1].See Eric Foner, *Reconstruction: America's Unfinished Revolution, 1863-1877* (New York: HarperCollins Publisher, 1988), 35-36.
[2].Foner, *Reconstruction*, 35-36.
[3].Glena R. Schroeder-Lein and Richard Zuczek, *Andrew Johnson: A Biographical Companion* (Sanata Barbara: ABC-CLIO, 2001), 239.
[43].For a brief review of Hamilton's career, see James A. Marten, "Andrew Jackson Hamilton," *NHT*, 3: 427-438. For depth, see John L. Waller, *Colossal Hamilton of Texas* (El Paso: Texas Western Press, 1968); also see Moneyhon, *Texas After the Civil War*.
[5].Campbell, *Gone to Texas*, 271; Schroeder-Lein and Zaczek, *Andrew Johnson*, 121-123.
[6].Moneyhon, *Texas After the Civil War*, 25-28.
[7].Campbell, *Gone to Texas*, 271-272; Moneyhon, *Texas After the Civil War*, 25-28.
[8].For a brief account of the Union League in Texas, see Moneyhon, "Union League," *NHT*, 6: 626.
[9].Campbell, *Gone to Texas*, 271-72; Moneyhon, *Texas After the Civil War*, 25-28.
[10].Richter, *The Army in Texas During Reconstruction*, 19. For a brief account of Custer's career, including his time in Texas, see Brian W. Dippie, "George Armstrong Custer," *NHT*, 2, 460; for more depth, see John M. Carroll, ed., *Custer in Texas: An Uninterrupted Narrative* (New York: Sol Lewis/ Liveright, 1975).
[11].See "Conditions of Affairs in Texas," U. S. House of Representatives, *Executive Documents*, Doc. no. 61, 39th Cong., 2 sess.; Capt. H. E. Scott, Post of Sherman, to AAAG Lt. Morse, March 12, 1868, LR, Box 5, DT, 5MD, RG 393, NA. And see Smallwood, Crouch, and Peacock, *Murder and Mayhem*, 40; B. and D. Bowman, *Historic Murders: Book 3*, 58-59.
[12].Mrs. L. E. Potts, Lamar County, to the President (Andrew Johnson), June 21, 1866, in "Condition of Affairs in Texas," U. S. House, *Executive Documents*, Doc. no. 61, 1-4. Also see, Smallwood, Crouch and Peacock, *Murder and Mayhem*, 44; Smallwood, *Time of Hope, Time of Despair*, 59, 132.
[13].Mrs. Potts to the President, June 21, 1866, in "Condition of Affairs in Texas," U. S. House, *Executive Documents*, Doc. no. 61, 1-4; Smallwood, Crouch, and Peacock, *Murder and Mayhem*, 44; Smallwood, *Time of Hope, Time of Despair*, 59, 132.
[14].A. Wright to Gov. Hamilton, January 22, 1866, Hamilton, GP, RG 301, Archives, TSL.
[15].Campbell, *Gone to Texas*, 272; Moneyhon, *Texas After the Civil War*, 38-48.
[16].For a Brief account of the Freedmen's Bureau, see Cecil Harper, Jr., "Freedmen's Bureau," *NHT*, 2, 1166-1167; for more detail, see Barry A. Crouch, *The Freedmen's Bureau and Black Texans*; also see, Richter's *The Army in Texas During Reconstruction* and *Freedmen's Bureau Administrators*; and see Smallwood, *Time of Hope, Time of Despair*. For details on advances in black education, see James M. Smallwood, "Early 'Freedom Schools': Black Self-Help and Education in Reconstruction Texas: A Case Study," *Negro History Bulletin* 41 (1978), 790-793 and James M. Smallwood, "Black Education in Reconstruction Texas: The Contributions of the Freedmen's Bureau and Benevolent

Societies," *East Texas Historical Journal* 19 (Fall 1981), 17-40.

17. Harper, "Freedmen's Bureau," *NHT*, 2, 1166-1167; Crouch, *The Freedmen's Bureau and Black Texans*; Richter, *The Army in Texas During Reconstruction*; Richter, *Freedmen's Bureau Administrators*; Smallwood, *Time of Hope, Time of Despair*. Crouch, Richter, and Smallwood have done a number of articles on the Freedmen's Bureau and black Texans; see the bibliography of this work.

18. Harper, "Freedmen's Bureau," *NHT*, 2, 1166-1167; Crouch, *The Freedmen's Bureau and Black Texans*; Richter, *The Army in Texas During Reconstruction*; Richter, *Freedmen's Bureau Administrators*; Smallwood, *Time of Hope, Time of Despair*.

19. Will Conine, *The Memories of Will Conine, [the] 1860s to the 1890s*, ed. Sharon E. Whitney (Waco: Texian Press, 1999), 20-22.

20. James Patterson to L. L. Bowman, July 16, 1931, VF, L. L. Bowman Papers, Archives, TAMC; Col. DeWitt Brown to AAAG Lt. Charles Vernou, "Monthly Report," July 30, 1868, Sub-Assistant Commissioner, Paris, LS, BRFAL, RG 105, NA.

21. Bvt. Capt. Roberts to AAAG Lt. J. P. Richardson, November 12, 1867, Sub-Assistant Commissioner, Clarksville, LS, Col. D. Brown to Bvt. Capt. Roberts, June 1, 1868, Sub-Assistant Commissioner, Paris, LS, BRFAL, RG 105, Lt. Scott, Post of Sherman, to AAAG Lt. Morse, March 12, 1868, LR, Box 5, DT, 5MD, RG 393, NA; Smallwood, Crouch, and Peacock, *Murder and Mayhem*, 46.

22. James B. Gillett, *Fugitive Justice: The Notebook of Texas Ranger Sergeant James B. Gillett* (Austin: State House Press, 1997), 66; C. Taylor, "notes on Guest," VF, Taylor-Smallwood-Howell Collection, GPL.

23. Capt. Charles Rand to AAAG Lt. J. Kirkman, April 19, 1867, Sub-Assistant Commissioner, Marshall, Texas, LS, BRFAL, RG 105, NA.

24. Kenneth W. Howell, "James Webb Throckmorton: The Life and Career of a Southern Frontier Politician, 1825-1894" (Ph.D. diss., Texas A&M University, 2005), *passim*; for a brief survey of Throckmorton's career, see David Minor, "James Webb Throckmorton," *NHT*, 6, 485-486.

25. Howell, "Throckmorton," *passim*; Minor, "James Webb Throckmorton," *NHT*, 6, 485-486.

26. Roger A. Griffin, "Elisha Marshall Pease," *NHT*, 5, 112-113; for more on Pease's life and public career, see Griffin's "Connecticut Yankee in Texas: A Biography of Elisha Marshall Pensee" (Ph.D. diss., University of Texas, 1973) and James T. DeShields's *They Sat in High Places: The Presidents and Governors of Texas* (San Antonio: Naylor, 1940). Also see Kenneth E. Hendrickson, Jr., *The Chief Executives of Texas: From Stephen F. Austin to John B. Connally, Jr.* (College Station: University of Texas A&M Press, 1995).

27. Texas Secretary of State, Election returns for 1866, State Papers, RG 307, Archives, TSL. For more on the Black Codes see Smallwood, Time of Hope, Time of Despair, 54-59, 64, 123-124, 130-131; for briefer accounts, see Moneyhon, "Black Codes," *NHT*, 1, 562 and Barry A. Crouch, "'All the Vile Passions': The Texas Black Code of 1866," *SWHQ* 97 (1993), 13-34.

28. Smallwood, *Time of Hope, Time of Despair*, 54-59, 64, 123-124, 130-131; Crouch, "Texas Black Code of 1866," SWHQ, 13-34; Bartholomew, *Cullen Baker*, 44.

29. *New York Times*, September 29, 1866.

30. T. Russell, *Titus County*, 2: 162; T. Russell, *Pioneers of Titus County*, 15.

31. Gillett, *Frontier Justice*, 104.

32. Robert K. Smith, quoting Judge Albert Latimer, to Gen. J. B. Kiddoo, October 30, 1866, Texas Assistant Commissioner, LR, BRFAL, RG 105, NA.

33. R. Smith, quoting Judge Latimer, to Gen. Kiddoo, October 30, 1866, Texas Assistant

Commissioner, LR, BRFAL, RG 105, NA.

Chapter 4

[1]. U. S. Census, Morgan County, Illinois, manuscript returns, 1850; Crouch and Brice, *Cullen Baker*, 70-71.

[2]. Lt. William G. Kirkman to Lt. Adam C. Malloy, Sub-Assistant Commissioner, Marshall, September 26, 1867, Lt. W. Kirkman to Ira A. Clapp, August 20, 1867, LS, BRFAL, RG 105, NA; Crouch and Brice, *Cullen Baker*, 73-76.

[3]. Lt. W. Kirkman to Lt. Malloy, Sub-Assistant Commissioner, Marshall, September 26, 1867, Lt. W. Kirkman to Ira A. Clapp, August 20, 1867, LS, BRFAL, RG 105, NA; Crouch and Brice, *Cullen Baker*, 73-76.

[4]. Lt. W. Kirkman to Maj. Gen. Charles Griffin, Assistant Commissioner, Texas, July 9, 1867, Lt. W. Kirkman to Lt. James S. Kirkman, July 25, 1867, Lt. W. Kirkman to Lt. Malloy, September 26, 1867, Lt. W. Kirkman to Clapp, August 20, 1867, Lt. W. Kirkman to AAAG Lt. Richardson, November 13, 1867, Sub-Assistant Commissioner, Boston, LS, BRFAL, RG 105, NA; Crouch and Brice, *Cullen Baker*, 73-76.

[5]. Lt. W. Kirkman to Maj. Gen. Griffin, Assistant Commissioner, Texas, July 9, 1867, Lt. W. Kirkman to Lt. J. S. Kirkman, July 25, 1867, Lt. W. Kirkman to Lt. Malloy, September 26, 1867, LS, Lt. W. Kirkman to Clapp, August 20, 1867, Lt. W. Kirkman to AAAG Lt. Richardson, November, 13, 1867, Sub-Assistant Commissioner, Boston, LS, BRFAL, RG 105, NA; Crouch and Brice, *Cullen Baker*, 73-76.

[6]. Smallwood, "When the Klan Rode," *Journal of the West*, 4-13; John E. Thompson to Gov. Hamilton, October 8, 1865, D. J. Baldwin to Gov. Hamilton, n.d., Hamilton, GP, RG 301, Archives, TSL.

[7]. *New Orleans Tribune*, September 1, 1866; Smallwood, "When the Klan Rode," *Journal of the West*, 4-13; Although he greatly undercounted the number of Klan groups in Texas (he did not claim to have an exhaustive list), see Allen Trelease, *White Terror: The Ku Klux Klan Conspiracy and Southern Reconstruction* (New York: Harper & Row, 1971), xlviii, 419-420, *et passim*. Whereas Trelease identified Klan groups in seventeen Texas counties, researcher Barbara Clayton Barnhill found Klan organizations in seventy-seven counties. See her "Lone Star Conspiracy: Racial Violence and the Ku Klux Klan Terror in Post-Civil War Texas" (M. A. thesis, Oklahoma State University, 1979).

[8]. See "Conditions of Affairs in Texas," U. S. House, *House Executive Documents*, doc. no. 61, 39th Congress, 2d sess.; *New Orleans Tribunes*, September 1, 1866; Smallwood, "When the Klan Rode, *Journal of the West*, 4-13; Trelease, *White Terror*, xlviii, 419-420, *et passim*.

[9]. See "Conditions of Affairs in Texas," U. S. House, *House Executive Documents*, doc. no. 61, 39th Cong., 2d sess.; *New Orleans Tribune*, September 1, 1866; Smallwood, "When the Klan Rode," *Journal of the West*, 4-13; Trelease, *White Terror*, xlviii, 419-20, *et passim*; see also James Marten, "What is to Become of the Negro?' White Reaction to Emancipation in Texas," *Mid-America* 73 (April-July 1991), 115-133; William L. Richter, "The Revolver Rules the Day: Colonel DeWitt Brown and the Freedmen's Bureau in Paris, Texas," *SWHQ* 93 (January 1990), 319.

[10]. Statement of Lee Pierce, Federal Writers Project, "Texas Narratives," *A Folk History of Slavery*, NA; N. Russell, "The History of Titus County Since 1860," 37; *New York Daily Tribune*, September 18, 1868; Trelease, *White Terror*, 138; C. Taylor, "Bickerstaff notes," VF, Taylor-Smallwood-Howell Collection, GPL.

[11]. Orren, "The History of Hopkins County," 62-63; "A. J. Hurdle," VF, Northeast Texas Genealogy Committee, GPL.

12. "A. J. Hurdle," VF, Northeast Texas Genealogy Committee, GPL; Orren, "The History of Hopkins County," 62-63.
13. Amanda Sartin to Gov. Throckmorton, September 5, 1866, Throckmorton, GP, RG 301, Archives, TSL.
14. Capt. Rand to AAAG Lt. J. Kirkman, April 19, 1867, Sub-Assistant Commissioner, Marshall, LS, BRFAL, RG 105, NA.
15. Capt. Rand to AAAG Lt. J. Kirkman, April 19, 1867, Sub-Assistant Commissioner, Marshall, LS, BRFAL, RG 105, NA.
16. T. Russell, *Titus County*, 2: 162; T. Russell and R. Russell, *Some Die Twice*, 35; Bartholomew, *Cullen Baker*, 60; B. and D. Bowman, *Historic Murders: Book 3*, 59; U. T. Taylor, "Ben Bickerstaff," *Frontier Times*, 9-10.
17. Lt. Latimer to AAAG Lt. J. Kirkman, May 21, 1867, Sub-Assistant Commissioner, LS, Clarksville, LS, BRFAL, RG 105, NA.
18. Lt. A. Latimer to AAAG Lt. J. Kirkman, May 21, 1867, Sub-Assistant Commissioner, LS, Clarksville, LS, BRFAL, RG 105, NA.
19. Col. William Sinclair, to AAAG Lt. J. Kirkman, July 2, 1867, Texas, Texas Assistant Commissioner, LR, BRFAL, RG 105, NA.
20. Col. Sinclair to AAAG Lt. J. Kirkman, July 2, 1867, Texas Assistant Commissioner, LR, BRFAL, RG 105, NA.
21. Col. Sinclair to AAAG Lt. J. Kirkman, July 2, 1867, Texas Assistant Commissioner, LR, BRFAL, RG 105, NA; *Flake's Semi-Weekly Bulletin*, July 24, 1867. Both the *Bulletin* and Sinclair reported the same event independently.
22. Lt. John S. Williamson to Lt. W. Kirkman, August 3, 1867, Sub-Assistant Commissioner, Boston, LR, BRFAL, RG 105, NA; *Paris Vindicator*, quoted in *Marshall Texas Republican*, September 14, 1867.
23. Lt. Moses Wiley to Maj. Samuel H. Starr, October 13, 1867, Maj. Starr to AAAG Lt. H. A. Swartwout, October 18, 1867, Lt. Wiley to Mount Pleasant Post Adjutant, October 20, 1867, Maj. Starr to AAAG Lt. Morse, November 8, 1867, LR , Box 15, DT, 5MD, RG 393, NA; Richter, "'Oh God, Let Us Have Revenge," *Arkansas Historical Quarterly*, 269-270; Crouch and Brice, *Cullen Baker*, 80-85.
24. Lt. Wiley to Maj. Starr, October 13, 1867, Maj. Starr to AAAG Lt. Swartwout, October 18, 1867, Lt. Wiley to Mount Pleasant Post Adjutant, October 20, 1867, Maj. Starr to AAAG Lt. Morse, November 8, 1867, LR, Box 15, DT, 5MD, RG 393, NA.
25. Lt. Wiley to Maj. Starr, October 13, 1867, Maj. Starr to AAAG Lt, Swartwout, October 18, 1867, Lt. Wiley to Mount Pleasant Post Adjutant, October 20, 1867, Maj. Starr to AAAG Lt. Morse, November 8, 1867, LR, Box 15, DT, 5MD, RG 393, NA; Crouch and Brice, *Cullen Baker*, 85-88.
26. Crouch and Brice, *Cullen Baker*, 83-89; T. Russell, *Titus County*, 2: 162; T. Russell and R. Russell, *Some Die Twice*, 75; Bartholomew, *Cullen Backer*, 60; *San Antonio Express*, October 28, 1867.
27. C. Taylor, "Ben Bickerstaff," ETHA, paper, 5, VF, copy in Taylor-Smallwood-Howell Collection, GPL; T. Russell and R. Russell, *Some Die Twice*, 34; "Titus County," VF, Pickering-Falls Collection, Archives, TAMC; T. Russell, *Pioneers of Titus County*, 15; N. Russell, "History of Titus County Since 1860," 39-40; Smallwood, Crouch, and Peacock, *Murder and Mayhem*, 46; Harper, "Titus County," *NHT*, 6, 507-509; U. T. Taylor, "Ben Bickerstaff, *Frontier Times*, 9-10; Bartholomew, *Cullen Baker*, 60.
28. "Titus County," VF, Pickering-Falls Collection, Archives, TAMC Library; Harper, "Titus County," *NHT*, 6, 507-509; T. Russell and R. Russell, *Some Die Twice*, 34; T. Russell, *Titus County*, 2, 161-163; T. Russell, *Pioneers of Tutus County*, 15; Bartholomew,

Cullen Baker, 60; N. Russell, "History of Titus County Since 1860," 39-40; Bob and Michelle Gilbert, "Hopkins County," *NHT*, 3, 694-695; Smallwood, Crouch, and Peacock, *Murder and Mayhem*, 46; U. T. Taylor, "Ben Bickerstaff," *Frontier Times*, 9; C. Taylor, "Ben Bickerstaff," ETHA, paper, 5, VF, Taylor-Smallwood-Howell Collection, GPL.

[29].Col. Samuel H. Starr to AAAG Lt. Morse, January 15, 1868, LS, Box 15, DT, 5MD, RG 393, Col. Starr to AAAG Lt. Morse, February 14, 1868, Sub-Assistant Commissioner, Mount Pleasant, LS, BRFAL, RG 105, NA; T. Russell, *Titus County*, 2, 94-95.

[30].T. Russell, *Titus County*, 2: 94-95; C. Taylor, "Bickerstaff notes," VF, copy in Taylor-Smallwood-Howell Collection, GPL; Col. Starr to AAAG Lt. Morse, February 14, 1868, Sub-Assistant Commissioner, Mount Pleasant, LS, BRFAL, RG 105, NA.

[31].Col. Starr to AAAG Lt. Morse, January 15, 1868, LS, Box 15, DT, 5MD, RG, 393, NA.

[32].Col. Starr to AAAG Lt. J. Richardson, "Monthly Report," February 29, 1868, LS, BRFAL, RG 105, NA.

[33].Col. Starr to AAAG J. Richardson, March 5, 1868, Sub-Assistant Commissioner, Mount Pleasant, LS, BRFAL, RG 105, NA; Smallwood, Crouch, and Peacock, *Murder and Mayhem*, 45.

[34].Smallwood, Crouch, and Peacock, *Murder and Mayhem*, 45; Col. Starr to AAAG Lt. J. Richardson, March 5, 1868, Sub-Assistant Commissioner, Mount Pleasant, LS, BRFAL, RG 105, NA.

[35].Col. Starr to AAAG Lt. J. Richardson, March 5, 1868, Sub-Assistant Commissioner, Mount Pleasant, LS, BRFAL, RG 105, NA.

[36].Crouch and Brice, *Cullen Baker*, 83-89; T. Russell, *Titus County*, 2, 162; T. Russell and R. Russell, *Some Die Twice*, 75; Bartholomew, *Cullen Baker*, 60.

[37].Capt. Rand to Col. Starr, Commanding, Post of Mount Pleasant, March 4, 1868, LS, BRFAL, RG 105, NA.

[38].Col. D. Brown to AAAG Lt. Richardson, "Monthly Report," April 30, 1868, Sub-Assistant Commissioner, Paris, LS, BRFAL, RG 105, NA.

Chapter 5

[1].Campbell, *Gone to Texas*, 275; and see Moneyhon, "Reconstruction," *NHT*, 5, 474-481.

[2].Campbell, *Gone to Texas*, 275; and see Moneyhon, "Reconstruction" *NHT*, 5, 474-481.

[3].Campbell, *Gone to Texas*, 275-76; Moneyhon, "Reconstruction" *NHT*, 5, 474-481.

[4].Campbell, *Gone to Texas*, 276; Moneyhon, "Reconstruction" *NHT*, 5, 474-481.

[5].Capt. Rand to AAAG, February 1, 1868, May 10, 1868, Sub-Assistant Commissioner, Clarksville, LS, BRFAL, RG 105, NA.

[6].Col. D. Brown to AAAG Lt. Roberts, June 1, 1868, Col. D. Brown to AAAG Lt. Charles Vernou, June 8, 1868, Col. D. Brown to M. L. Armstrong, June 10, 1868, Sub-Assistant Commissioner, Paris, LS, BRFAL, RG 105, NA; and see Crouch and Brice, *Cullen Baker*, 113-115 and Richter, "'Colonel DeWitt Brown," *SWHQ*, 329.

[7].Col. D. Brown to Armstrong, June 10, 1868, Sub-Assistant Commissioner, Paris, LS, BRFAL, RG 105, NA.

[8].Col. D. Brown to Armstrong, June 10, 1868, Sub-Assistant Commissioner, Paris, LS, BRFAL, RG 105, NA.

[9].Lt. Charles Vaughn to AAAG Lt. Vernou, "Monthly Report," June 30, 1868, "Monthly Report," August 1, 1868, Sub-Assistant Commissioner, Waco, LS, BRFAL, RG 105, NA; *New York Times*, August 31, 1868.

[10].Lt. Vaughn to AAAG Lt. Vernou, "Monthly Report," June 30, 1868, "Monthly Report," August 1, 1868, Sub-Assistant Commissioner, Waco, LS, BRFAL, RG 105, NA; *New York*

Times, August 31, 1868.

11. Lt. Vaughn to AAAG Lt. Vernou, "Monthly Report," August 1, 1868, Sub-Assistant Commissioner, Waco, LS, BRFAL, RG 105, NA.

12. Claude Elliot, "Constitutional Convention of 1868-1869," *NHT*, 2, 284; William L. Richter, *The ABC-Clio Companion to American Reconstruction, 1862-1877* (Santa Barbara: ABC-Clio, Inc., 1996), 217-219; Howell, "Throckmorton," 376-378.

13. Texas Secretary of State, Election Returns for Constitutional Convention, 1868, State Papers, RG 307, Archives, TSL; Elliot, "Constitutional Convention of 1868-1869," *NHT*, 2, 284; Richter, *The ABC-Clio Companion to American Reconstruction*, 217-19; Howell, "Throckmorton," 376-378.

14. Elliott, "Constitutional Convention of 1868-1869," *NHT*, 2, 284.

15. Elliott, "Constitutional Convention of 1868-1869," *NHT*, 2, 284; for broader coverage of the convention see Carl Moneyhon, *Republicanism in Reconstruction Texas* (Austin: University of Texas Press, 1980); for a contemporary study see John Sayles, *The Constitutions of the State of Texas* (St. Paul, Minnesota: West Publishing, 1872).

16. For more on Ruby, see James M. Smallwood, "G. T. Ruby: Galveston's Black Carpetbagger in Reconstruction Texas," *Houston Review* 5 (Winter 1983), 24-33; for brief coverage of his career, see Merline Pitre, "George Thompson Ruby," *NHT*, 5, 705-706.

17. Smallwood, "G. T. Ruby," *Houston Review*, 24-33; Pitre, "Ruby," *NHT*, 5, 705-706.

18. See Appendix for the complete report of Caldwell's committee.

19. For a brief summary of Caldwell's political career, see Charles Christopher Jackson, "Colbert Caldwell," *NHT*, 1, 894.

20. S. S. McKay, "Constitution of 1869," *NHT*, 2, 289; Elliott, "Constitutional Convention of 1868-1869," *NHT*, 2, 284; and see Moneyhon, *Republicanism in Reconstruction Texas* and Sayles, *Constitutions of Texas*; also see, Betty J. Sandlin, "The Texas Constitutional Convention of 1868-1869" (Ph. D. diss., Texas Tech University, 1970).

21. Joe Easley to M. L. Armstrong, July 17, 1868, LR, copy in Assistant Commissioner, Texas, BRFAL, RG 105, NA.

22. Easley to Armstrong, July 17, 1868, LR, copy in Assistant Commissioner, Texas, BRFAL, RG 105, NA.

23. Easley to Armstrong, July 17, 1868, LR, copy in Assistant Commissioner, Texas, BRFAL, RG 105, NA.

24. Easley to Armstrong, July 17, 1868, LR, copy in Assistant Commissioner, Texas, BRFAL, RG 105, NA.

25. Lt. Vaughn to AAAG Lt. Vernou, "Monthly Report," July 30, 1868, LS, BRFAL, RG 105, NA; *Galveston Daily News*, July 4, 1868; for Joe Easley's statement, see *Austin Daily Republican*, August 4, 1868. Even the faraway *New York Times* covered the nefarious doings in Navarro County in its August 31, 1868, issue.

26. Easley to Armstrong, July 17, 1868, copy in Assistant Commissioner, Texas, LR, BRFAL, RG 105, NA.

27. Easley to Armstrong, July 17, 1868, copy in Assistant Commissioner, Texas, LR, BRFAL, RG 105, NA.

28. Easley to Armstrong, July 17, 1868, copy in Assistant Commissioner, Texas, BRFAL, RG 105, NA.

29. Easley to Armstrong, July 17, 1868, copy in Assistant Commissioner, Texas, LR, BRFAL, RG 105, NA.

30. Easley to Armstrong, July 17, 1868, copy in Assistant Commissioner, Texas, LR, BRFAL, RG 105, NA.

31. Easley to Armstrong, July 27, 1868, copy in Assistant Commissioner, Texas, LR,

BRFAL, RG 105, NA.

[32].*Austin Daily Republican*, August 1, 4, 1868; *Marshall Texas Republican*, August 7, 1868; *San Antonio Express*, August 13, 1868; Easley to Armstrong, July 17, 1868, Assistant Commissioner, Texas, LR, BRFAL, RG 105, NA; Trelease, *White Terror*, 106; Tuck, *Civil War Shadows*, 58; *New York Times*, August 31, 1868.

[33]. Easley to Armstrong, July 17, 1868, LR, Assistant Commissioner, Texas, LR, BRFAL, RG 105, NA; *New York Times*, August 31, 1868; *Austin Daily Republican*, August 1, 4, 1868; *Marshall Texas Republican*, August 7, 1868; Trelease, *White Terror*, 106; *San Antonio Express*, August 13, 1868; Tuck, *Civil War Shadows*, 58.

[34]. Easley to Armstrong, July 17, 1868, LR, Assistant Commissioner, Texas, LR, BRFAL, RG 105, NA; *New York Times*, August 31, 1868; *Austin Daily Republican*, August 1, 4, 1868; *Marshall Texas Republican*, August 7, 1868; Trelease, *White Terror*, 106. For more on Bickerstaff's capture of the train and for discussion of criminals and outlaw gangs, see Carl C. Rister, "Outlaws and Vigilantes of the Southern Plains, 1865-1885," *The Mississippi Valley Historical Review* 19 (March 1933), 537-554.

[35]. Col. D. Brown to Armstrong, July 19, 1868, Sub-Assistant Commissioner, Paris, LS; Easley to Armstrong, July 17, 1868, LR, Assistant Commissioner, Texas, BRFAL, RG 105, NA.

[36]. *McKinney Messenger*, quoted in *San Antonio Express*, July 30, 1868.

[37]. Capt. T. M. K. Smith to AAAG Lt. Vernou, "Monthly Report," July 31, 1868, Sub-Assistant Commissioner, Marshall, LS, BRFAL, RG 105, NA.

[38]. Capt. Rand to AAAG Lt. Richardson, July 21, 28, 1868, "Monthly Report," July 31, 1868, Sub-Assistant Commissioner, Clarksville, LS, BRFAL, RG 105, NA; Richter, "Oh God, Let Us Have Revenge," *Arkansas Historical Quarterly*, 273-274; Richter, *Freedmen's Bureau Administrators*, 281.

[39]. Capt. Rand to AAAG Lt. Richardson, July 21, 28, 1868, "Monthly Report," July 31, 1868, Sub-Assistant Commissioner, Clarksville, LS, BRFAL, RG 105, NA; Richter, "'Oh God, Let Us Have Revenge,"*Arkansas Historical Quarterly*, 273-274; Richter, *Freedmen's Bureau Administrators*, 281.

[40]. Capt. Rand to AAAG Lt. Richardson, July 21, 28, 1868, "Monthly Report," July 31, 1868, Sub-Assistant Commissioner, Clarksville, LS, BRFAL, RG 105, NA; Richter, "Oh God, Let Us Have Revenge," *Arkansas Historical Quarterly*, 273-274; Richter, *Freedmen's Bureau Administrators*, 281.

[41]. Capt. Rand to AAAG Lt. Richardson, July 21, 28, 1868, "Monthly Report," July 31, 1868, Sub-Assistant Commissioner, Clarksville, LS, BRFAL, RG 105, NA; Richter, "'Oh God, Let Us Have Revenge,' *Arkansas Historical Quarterly*, 273-74; Richter, *Freedmen's Bureau Administrators*, 281.

[42]. *Flake's Bulletin*, n.d., quoted by Bartholomew, *Cullen Baker*, 73.

[43]. Capt. Rand to AAAG Lt. Richardson, July 21, 28, 1868, "Monthly Report," July 31, 1868, Sub-Assistant Commissioner, Clarksville, LS, BRFAL, RG 105, NA; Richter, "Oh God, Let Us Have Revenge," *Arkansas Historical Quarterly*, 273-274.

[44]. Capt. Rand to AAAG Lt. Richardson, July 21, 31, August 2, 1868, Sub-Assistant Commissioner, Clarksville, LS, BRFAL, RG 105, NA.; for a brief treatment of Rand's travail, see Crouch and Brice, *Cullen Baker*, 114-115.

[45]. Capt. Rand to AAAG Lt. Richardson, July 21, 31, August 2, 1868, Sub-Assistant Commissioner, Clarksville, LS, BRFAL, RG 105, NA.

[46]. Capt. Rand to AAAG Lt. Richardson, July 21, 31, August 2, 1868, Sub-Assistant Commissioner, Clarksville, LS, BRFAL, RG 105, NA.

[47]. Capt. Rand to AAAG Lt. Richardson, July 21, 31, August 2, 1868, Sub-Assistant

Commissioner, Clarksville, LS, BRFAL, RG 105, NA.
⁴⁸.Capt. Rand to AAAG Richardson, August 2, 15, 30, 1868, Sub-Assistant Commissioner, Clarksville, LS, BRFAL, RG 105, NA.
⁴⁹.Judge A. B. Norton to Gov. E. Pease, September 24, 1868, E. Pease, GP, RG 301, Archives, TSL; and see *Flake's Bulletin*, September 29, 1868.
⁵⁰.Judge Norton to Gov. E. Pease, September 24, 1868, Pease, GP, RG 301, Archives, TSL; and see *Flake's Bulletin*. September 29, 1868.
⁵¹.Col. Brown to AAAG Lt. Morse, September 2, 5, 1868, Sub-Assistant Commissioner, Paris, LS, BRFAL, RG 105, NA; Richter, "The Revolver Rules the Day," *SWHQ*, 319.
⁵².*Clarksville Standard*, August 15, 1868; Col. A. G. Malloy to AAAG Capt. Roberts, December 3, 1868, LR, Box 14, DT, 5MD, RG 393, NA; Special Orders No. 64, October 30, No. 67, November 19, No. 69, November 30, 1868, BRFAL, RG 105, NA; Richter, *Freedmen's Bureau Administrators*, 280; Richter, "The Revolver Rules the Day," *SWHQ*, 319-320.

Chapter 6
¹.See *New York Times*, September 29, 1868.
².*Clarksville Standard*, August 15, 1868; and see, *Marshall Texas Republican*, August 21, 1868; N. Russell, "Titus County Since 1860," 39. For a brief summation of DeMorse's career, see Earnest Wallace, "Charles DeMorse," *NHT*, 2, 591-592.
³.*Marshall Texas Republican*, August 21, 1868.
⁴.*Paris Vindicator*, n.d., quoted in *Marshall Texas Republican*, September 4, 1868.
⁵.*Flake's Daily Bulletin*, September 26, 1868.
⁶.*Flake's Daily Bulletin*, September 26, 1868; Gen. Reynolds, Special Order no. 16, August 27, 1868, LS, Box 6, DT, 5MD, RG 393, NA; various newspapers printed Reynolds's reward; see, for example, *Marshall Texas Republican*, September 11, 1868; also see Sefton, *The United States Army During Reconstruction*, 191.
⁷.Marion County Judge to Gov. E. Pease, August 19, 1868, quoted in Tuck, *Civil War Shadows*, 197-198.
⁸.Marion County Judge to Gov. E. Pease, August 19, 1868, quoted in Tuck, *Civil War Shadows*, 197-198.
⁹.Marion County Judge to Gov. E. Pease, August 19, 1868, quoted in Tuck, *Civil War Shadows*, 197-198.
¹⁰.Capt. Thomas M. Tolman to AAAG, August 15, 1868, Gen. Reynolds to Secretary of War, September 3, 1868, LR, Box 16, DT, 5MD, RG 393, NA.
¹¹.Gladys St. Clair, *A History of Hopkins County* (Waco: Texian Press, 1965), 32; Orren, "History of Hopkins County," 49-50; Tuck, *Civil War Shadows*, 56.
¹².Tuck, *Civil War Shadows*, 64, 194.
¹³.J. K. Milam, "Personal Journal," quoted by Tuck, *Civil War Shadows*, 56.
¹⁴.J. K. Milam, "Personal Journal," quoted by Tuck, *Civil War Shadows*, 56. Tuck adds details on Grisom's death on her page 60.
¹⁵.Capt. Tolman to AAAG Lt. Morse, August 14, 15, 1868, LS, Gen. Reynolds to Secretary of War, with endorsements, September 3, 1868, LR, Box 16, DT, 5MD, RG 393, NA; John W. Hunter, "Killing of John Vaden at Fort McKavett," *Frontier Times*, 2 (November 1924), 16.
¹⁶.Capt. Tolman to AAAG Lt. Morse, August 14, 15, 1868, LS, Gen. Reynolds to Secretary of War, with endorsements, September 3, 1868, LR, Box 16, DT, 5MD, RG 393, NA; Hunter, "Killing of Vaden," *Frontier Times*, 16; Tuck, *Civil War Shadows*, 67.
¹⁷.Capt. Tolman to AAAG Lt. Morse, August 14, 1868, LS, Gen. Reynolds to Secretary of

War, September 3, 1868, LS, Box 16, DT, 5MD, RG 393, NA.

[18].Capt. Tolman to AAAG Lt. Morse, August 14, 15, LS, Box 16, DT, 5MD, RG 393, NA; Tuck, *Civil War Shadows*, 67.

[19].Hunter, "Killing of Vaden," *Frontier Times*, 16; Tuck, *Civil War Shadows*, 56, 60-61.

[20].Hunter, "Killing of Vaden," *Frontier Times*, 16; Tuck, Civil War Shadows, 56, 60-61.

[21].Tuck, *Civil War Shadows*, 56, 60-61; *Marshall Texas Republican*, August 27, 1868; *New York Times*, August 31, 1868; *Austin Daily Republican*, August 4, 1868.

[22].Tuck, *Civil War Shadows*, 56, 60-61; *Marshall Texas Republican*, August 27, 1868; *New York Times*, August 31, 1868; *Austin Daily Republican*, August 4, 1868.

[23].*Marshall Texas Republican*, August 7, 1868; *New York Times*, August 31, 1868; *Austin Daily Republican*, August 4, 1868; *Galveston Daily News*, July 4, 1868; Lt. Gregory Barrett to AAAG Lt. Vernou, August 1, 1868, Sub-Assistant Commissioner, Tyler, LS, BRFAL, RG 105, NA; Smallwood, *Time of Hope, Time of Despair*, 144-145; Orren, "History of Hopkins County," 55.

[24].Milam, "Personal Journal," quoted in Tuck, *Civil War Shadows*, 57.

[25].Capt. Tolman to AAAG Lt. Morse, August 15, 1868, Lt. Vernou to AAAG Lt. Morse, September 3, 1868, AAAG to Lt. J. H. Sands, September 16, 1868, LR, Gen. Reynolds to Secretary of War, September 3, 1868, LS, Box 16, DT, 5MD, RG 393, NA; T. Russell, *Titus County*, 2, 161-162; T. Russell and R. Russell, *Some Die Twice*, 34-35.

[26].Capt. Tolman to AAAG Lt. Morse, August 15, 1868, Lt. Vernou to AAAG Lt. Morse, September 3, 1868, LS, Box 16, DT, 5MD, RG 393.

[27].Capt. Tolman to AAAG Lt. Morse, August 15, 1868, LR, Box 16, DT, 5MD, RG 393, NA; Tuck, *Civil War Shadows*, 194.

[28].Capt. Tolman to AAAG Lt. Morse, August 15, 1868, LR, Box 16, DT, 5MD, RG 393, NA; Tuck, *Civil War Shadows*, 194.

[29].For an in-depth account of Chaffee's career, see William Giles Carter, *Life of Lieutenant General Chaffee* (Chicago: University of Chicago Press, 1917); for an overview that highlights his Texas years, see H. Allen Anderson, "Adna Romanza Chaffee," *NHT*, 2, 24-25.

[30].Gen. Reynolds to Secretary of War, September 3, 1868, LS, Capt. Tolman to AAAG, August 15, 1868, [?] to AAAG Lt. Louis v. Cariarc, January 14, 1869, Gen. Reynolds to Bvt. Maj. Chaffee, September 1, 1868, LR, Box 16, DT, 5MD, RG 393, NA; and see Crouch and Brice, *Cullen Baker*, 97, 118-119; Smallwood, Crouch, and Peacock, *Murder and Mayhem*, 75.

[31].Gen. Reynolds to Secretary of War, September 3, 1868, LR, Box 16, DT, 5MD, RG 393, and see file 849M18868, AGO, RG 94, NA.

[32].Gen. Reynolds, Special Order no. 16, August 27, 1868, LS, Box 6, DT, 5MD, RG 393, NA. Various newspapers printed Reynolds's reward offer: as an example, see *Marshall Texas Republican*, September 11, 1868. And see File 849M18868, AGO, RG 94, NA. Also see Sefton, *The United States Army During Reconstruction*, 191; and see Crouch and Brice, *Cullen Baker*.

[33].Gen. Reynolds to Secretary of War, September 3, 1868, [?] to AAG, December 24, 1868, LS, Box 16, DT, 5MD, RG 393, NA; Sefton, *The U. S. Army and Reconstruction*, 191.

[34].Capt. W. B. Pease to AAAG Lt. Morse, September 10, 1868, Capt. Tolman to AAAG Lt. Morse, August 15, 1868, LR, [?] to AAG, December 24, 1868, [?] to AAAG Lt. Caziarc, January 14, 1869, LR, Gen. Reynolds to Secretary at War, September 3, 1868, endorsements attached, LS, Box 16, DT, 5MD, RG 393, NA; Sefton, *The U. S. Army and Reconstruction*, 191.

[35].Texas Legislature, *Report of the Special Committee on Lawlessness and Violence in Texas*

(Austin: Texas Legislature, 1868); Col. Sinclair to AAAG Lt. Roberts, August 18, 1868, Assistant Commissioner, Texas, LR, BRFAL, RG 105, NA. The late Barry A. Crouch explained the political importance of violence directed toward the freedpeople and the white Unionists. Crouch held that such violence disrupted the entire state and kept Republicans from properly organizing and made social stability impossible to achieve. In other words, the violence was most responsible for Democratic victories after 1869.

[36]. T. Russell, *Titus County*, 2, 161-62; T. Russell and R. Russell, *Some Die Twice*, 34; T. Russell, *Pioneers of Titus County*, 15; Orren, "The History of Hopkins County," 35.

[37]. T. Russell and R. Russell, *Some Die Twice*, 34.

[38]. U. T. Taylor, "Ben Bickerstaff," *Frontier Times*, 9; T. Russell and R. Russell, *Some Die Twice*, 35; Tuck, *Civil War Shadows*, 58-59.

[39]. T. Russell, *Titus County*, 2, 162.

[40]. Gen. Reynolds to AG United States, October 2, 1868, LR, AGO, RG 94, NA; Sefton, *The U. S. Army During Reconstruction*, 192.

Chapter 7

[1]. Lt. J. H. Sands to AAAG Lt. Morse, September 9, 1868, Lt. Vernou to AAAG Lt. Morse, September 3, 1868, LR, Box 6, DT, 5MD, RG 393, NA.

[2]. Lt. Sands to AAAG Lt. Morse, September 9, 1868, Lt. Vernou to AAAG Lt. Morse, September 3, 1868, LR, Box 6, DT, 5MD, RG 393, NA.

[3]. Lt. Sands to AAAG Lt. Morse, September 9, 1868, Lt. Vernou to AAAG Lt. Morse, September 3, 1868, LR, Box 6, DT, 5MD, RG 393, NA.

[4]. Lt. Vernou to AAAG Lt. Morse, September 3, 1868, Lt. Sands to AAAG Lt. Morse, September 9, 1868, LR, Box 6, DT, 5MD, RG 393, NA.

[5]. Lt. Vernou to AAAG Lt. Morse, September 3, 1868, LR, Lt. Sands to AAAG Lt. Morse, September 9, 1868, LR, Box 6, DT, 5MD, RG 393, NA.

[6]. Lt. Sands to AAAG Lt. Morse, September 9, 1868, LR, Box 6, DT, 5MD, RG 393, NA.

[7]. Lt. Sands to AAAG Lt. Morse, September 9, 1868, AAAG Lt. Morse to Lt. Sands, September 16, 1868, LS, Lt. Vernou to AAAG Lt. Morse, September 3, 1868, LR, Box 6, DT, 5MD, RG 393, NA.

[8]. Lt. Vernou to AAAG Lt. Morse, September 3, 1868, Lt. Sands to AAAG Lt. Morse, September 9, 1868, LR, AAAG Lt. Morse to Lt. Sands, September 16, 1868, LS, Box 6, DT, 5MD, RG 393, NA.

[9]. Lt. Sands to AAAG Lt. Morse, September 9, 1868, LR, AAAG Lt. Morse to Lt. Sands, September 16, 1868, LS, Lt. Vernou to AAAG Lt. Morse, September 3, 1868, LR, Box 6, DT, 5MD, RG 393, NA.

[10]. Lt. Sands to AAAG Lt. Morse, September 9, 1868, LR, Box 6, DT, 5MD, RG 393, NA.

[11]. *Paris Vindicator*, n.d., quoted by the *Marshall Texas Republican*, August 28, September 4, 1868.

[12]. Col. D. Brown to AAAG Bvt. Capt. C. S. Roberts, September 30, 1868, Sub-Assistant Commissioner, Paris, LS, BRFAL, RG 105, NA.

[13]. Col. D. Brown to AAAG Bvt. Capt. C. S. Roberts, September 30, 1868, Sub-Assistant Commissioner, Paris, LS, BRFAL, RG 105, NA.

[14]. Col. D. Brown to AAAG Lt. Morse, September 5, 1868, October 28, 1868, Sub-Assistant Commissioner, Paris, LS, BRFAL, RG 105, NA.

[15]. M. L. Armstrong to Gen. Reynolds, October 28, 1868, copy in Sub-Assistant Commissioner, Paris, LS, BRFAL, RG 105, NA.

[16]. Col. D. Brown to AAAG Lt. Morris, September 5, 1868, October 28, 1868, Col. D.

Brown to AAAG Capt. Roberts, September 30, 1868, Sub-Assistant Commissioner, Paris, LS, BRFAL, RG 105, NA.

[17].Hunter, "Killing of Vaden," *Frontier Times*, 16-17; Tuck, *Civil War Shadows*, 62.

[18].Hunter, "Killing of Vaden," *Frontier Times*, 16-17; Tuck, *Civil War Shadows*, 62.

[19].Hunter, "Killing of Vaden," *Frontier Times*, 17; Tuck, *Civil War Shadows*, 62-63.

[20].Col. Sinclair to AAAG Bvt. Capt. Roberts, August 18, 1868, LR, Box 5, DT, 5MD, RG 393, NA; and see Texas Legislature, *Report of the Special Committee on Lawlessness and Violence in Texas*.

[21].Capt. Tolman to AAAG Lt. Morse, August 15, 1868, [?] to AAG, December 24, 1868, [?] to AAAG Lt. Caziarc, January 14, 1869, LR, Box 6, DT, 5MD, RG 393, NA; Richter, "Oh God, Let Us Have Revenge," 275; Richter, *The Army in Texas*, 146-147. Papers relating to Tolman's court martial are in the files of the Office of the Judge Advocate General, "General Courts Martial, 1812-1938," 728, Box 1577, RG 153, NA.

[22].J. H. Fowler to Gov. E. Pease, September 29, 1868, E. Pease, GP, LS, RG 301, Archives, TSL.

[23].J. H. Fowler to Gov. E. Pease, September 29, 1868, E. Pease, GP, LS, RG 301, Archives, TSL.

[24].Gen. Reynolds to Secretary of War, September 18, 1868, Lt. Sweeney to AAAG Bvt. Capt. Roberts, November 3, 1868, copies in AGO, RG 94, NA.

[25].Capt. Chaffee to AAAG Lt. Morse, September 21, 1868, cited in Tuck, *Civil War Shadows*, 207.

[26].Capt. Chaffee to AAAG Lt. Morse, September 21, 1868, cited in Tuck, *Civil War Shadows*, 207.

[27].Col. W. Pease to AAAG Lt. Morse, October 2, 1868, citied in Tuck, *Civil War Shadows*, 209-210.

[28].T. Russell, *History of Titus County*, 2, 48-49.

[29].Col. W. Pease to AAAG Lt. Morse, October 3, 1868, LR, Box 13, DT, 5MD, RG 393, NA; and see G. W. King, interviewed by L. L. Bowman, July 22, 1931, in "Bob Lee," VF, L. L. Bowman Papers, Archives, TAMC.

[30].Col. W. Pease to AAAG Lt. Morse, October 3, 1868, LR, Box 13, DT, 5MD, RG 393, NA; and see G. W. King, interviewed by L. L. Bowman, July 22, 1931, in "Bob Lee," VF, L. L. Bowman Papers, Archives, TAMC.

[31].Col. W. Pease to AAAG Lt. Morse, October 3, 1868, LR, Box 13, DT, 5MD, RG 393, NA; and see King, interviewed by L. L. Bowman, July 22, 1931, in "Bob Lee," VF, L. L. Bowman Papers, Archives, TAMC; "Greenville Guards" muster roll, with commits by C. Taylor, Taylor-Smallwood-Howell Collection, GPL.

[32].Col. W. Pease to AAAG Lt. Morse, October 3, 1868, LR, Box 13, DT, 5MD, RG 393, NA; and see King, interviewed by L. L. Bowman, July 22, 1931, in "Bob Lee," VF, L. L. Bowman Papers, Archives, TAMC.

[33].Col. W. Pease to AAAG Lt. Morse, October 3, 1868, LR, Box 13, DT, 5MD, RG 393, NA.

[34].Col. W. Pease to AAAG Lt. Morse, October 3, 1868, LR, Box 13, DT, 5MD, RG 393, NA.

[35].Col. W. Pease to AAAG Lt. Morse, October 3, 1868, LR, Box 13, DT, 5MD, RG 393, NA.

[36].Col. W. Pease to AAAG Lt. Morse, October 3, 1868, LR, Box 13, DT, 5MD, RG 393, NA.

[37]36.Col. W. Pease to AAAG Lt. Morse, October 3, 1868, LR, Box 13, DT, 5MD, RG 393, NA.

38. Col. W. Pease to AAAG Lt. Morse, October 3, 1868, LR, Box 13, DT, 5MD, RG 393, NA; King interviewed by L. L. Bowman, July 22, 1931, in "Bob Lee," VF, L. L. Bowman Papers, Archives, TAMC.

Chapter 8

1. Bvt. Maj. James Curtis to AAAG, September 19, 1868, Lt. H. Sweeney to AAAG, November 2, 1868, copies in AGO, RG 94, DT, 5MD, RG 393, NA; Dan Campbell and B. W. Gray to Gov. E. Pease, May 1, 1868, E. Pease, GP, RG 301, Archives, TSL.
2. Bvt. Maj. Curtis to AAAG, September 19, 1868, Lt. Sweeney to AAAG, November 2, 1868, copies in AGO, RG 94, DT, 5MD, RG 393, NA; Campbell and Gray to Gov. E. Pease, May 1, 1868, E. Pease, GP, RG 301, Archives, TSL.
3. Bvt. Maj. Curtis to AAAG, September 19, 1868, Lt. Sweeney to AAAG, November 2, 1868, copies in AGO, RG 94, NA; Campbell and Gray to Gov. E. Pease, May 1, 1868, E. Pease, GP, RG 301, Archives, TSL; *San Antonio Express*, December 25, 1868, January 1, 1869; *New York Times*, October 25, 1868; Richter, *Freedmen's Bureau Administrators*, 284-285; Trelease, *White Terror*, 137-148; Gen. Reynolds, General Order no. 14, October 12, 1868, DT, 5MD, RG 393, NA.
4. Bvt. Maj. Curtis to AAAG, September 19, 1868, Lt. Sweeney to AAAG, October 12, 26, November 2, 1868, copies in AGO, RG 94, NA; *San Antonio Express*, December 25, 1868; *New York Times*, October 25, 1868; Richter, *Freedmen's Bureau Administrators*, 285; Trelease, *White Terror*, 137-148.
5. Bvt. Maj. Curtis to AAAG, September 19, 1868, Lt. Sweeney to AAAG, October 12, 26, November 2, 1868, copies in AGO, RG 94, NA; *San Antonio Express*, December 25, 1868; *New York Times*, October 25, 1868; Richter, *Freedmen's Bureau Administrators*, 285; Trelease, *White Terror*, 137-148.
6. Statement of Lee Pierce, "Texas Narratives," *Folk History of Slavery*, NA.
7. Statement of Pierce, "Texas Narratives," *Folk History of Slavery*, NA.
8. T. Russell and R. Russell, *Some Die Twice*, 36-37; *Waco Register*, n.d., quoted by *Austin Weekly Republican*, April 21, 1869; *Waxahachie Argus*, Extra, April 6, 1869; Col. W. Pease to AAAG Lt. Morris, December 14, 1868, LR, micro-film copy, DT, 5MD, RG 393, NA.
9. James M. Smallwood, "The Freedmen's Bureau Reconsidered: Local Agents and the Black Community," *Texana* 11 (1973), 309-320; Crouch and Brice, *Cullen Baker*, 122-124.
10. Smallwood, "Freedmen's Bureau Reconsidered," *Texana*, 309-320; Crouch and Brice, *Cullen Baker*, 123-124.
11. Smallwood, "Freedmen's Bureau Reconsidered," *Texana*, 318-320; Crouch and Brice, *Cullen Baker*, 123-124.
12. Col. W. Pease to AAAG Lt. Morse, October 2, 3, 1868, LR, Box 13, DT, 5MD, RG 393, NA.
13. Col. W. Pease to AAAG Lt. Morse, October 2, 3, 1868, LR, Box 13, DT, 5MD, RG 393, NA.
14. Col. W. Pease to AAAG Lt. Morse, October 2, 3, 1868, LR, Box 13, DT, 5MD, RG 393, NA; Col. W. Pease to AAAG Lt. Vernou, November 10, 1868, Sub-Assistant Commissioner, Sulphur Springs, LS, BRFAL, RG 105, NA.
15. Col. W. Pease to AAAG Lt. Vernou, November 10, 1868, Sub-Assistant Commissioner, Sulphur Springs, LS, BRFAL, RG 105, NA.
16. Col. W. Pease to AAAG Lt. Vernou, November 10, 1868, Sub-Assistant Commissioner, Sulphur Springs, LS, BRFAL, RG 105, NA.
17. Col. W. Pease to AAAG Lt. Morse, October 2, 1868, Box 13, DT, 5MD, RG 393, NA.

[18].Col. W. Pease, Special Order No. 27, October 21, 1868, Post of Sulphur Springs, quoted in Tuck, *Civil War Shadows*, 224.
[19].Col. W. Pease, General Order No. 9, October 26, 1868, Post of Sulphur Springs, quoted in Tuck, *Civil War Shadows*, 228.
[20].Gen. Reynolds to AG, U. S. Army, October 22, 1868, typescript copy in Traylor Russell, *Carpetbaggers, Scalawags & Others* (Waco: Texan Press, 1973), 57-58.
[21].Gen. Reynolds to AG, U. S. Army, October 22, 1868, typescript copy in T. Russell, *Carpetbaggers, Scalawags & Others*, 57-58.
[22].Gen. Reynolds to AG, U. S. Army, October 22, 1868, typescript copy in T. Russell, *Carpetbaggers, Scalawags & Others*, 57-58.
[23].Bvt. Maj. Chaffee to AAAG Lt. Morse, October 20, 1868, Lt. C. G. Gordon to AAAG Lt. Morse, October 29, 1868, "Guard Report, Post of Sulphur Springs," December 31, 1868, LR, Box 14, DT, 5MD, RG 393, NA; C. Taylor, "Ben Bickerstaff," ETHA, paper, 5, VF, copy in Taylor-Smallwood-Howell Collection, GPL.
[24].Bvt. Maj. Chaffee to AAAG Lt. Morse, October 20, 1868, Lt. Gordon to AAAG Lt. Morse, October 29, 18668, "Guard Report, Post of Sulphur Springs," December 31, 1868," LR, Box 14, DT, 5MD, RG 393, NA; C. Taylor, "Ben Bickerstaff," ETHA, paper, 9, VF, copy in Taylor-Smallwood-Howell Collection, GPL.
[25].Col. W. Pease, Special Order No. 25, October 17, 1868, Post of Sulphur Springs, Col. W. Pease to AAAG Lt. Morse, October 22, 1868, quoted in Tuck, *Civil War Shadows*, 222, 225.
[26].Bvt. Maj. Chaffee to AAAG Lt. Morse, October 20, 1868, Lt. Gordon to AAAG Lt. Morse, October 29, 1868, Box 17, DT, 5MD, RG 393, NA.
[27].Bvt. Maj. Chaffee to AAAG Lt. Morse, October 30, 1868, Box 17, DT, 5MD, RG 393, NA.
[28].Office of Civil Affairs, "Abstract of Crimes," DT, 5MD, RG393, NA; Orr, *Cullen Baker*, 43;
Crouch and Brice, *Cullen Baker*, 133-134.
[29].Office of Civil Affairs, "Abstract of Crimes," DT, 5MD, RG 393, NA; Orr, *Cullen Baker*, 43; *Harrison Flag*, January 28, 1869; Crouch and Brice, *Cullen Baker*, 133-134.
[30].Lt. Sweeney to AAAG Capt. Roberts, November 23, 1868, Sub-Assistant Commissioner, Jefferson, LS, BRFAL, RG 105 [copy also in AGO, RG 94, NA], Lt. Malloy to AAAG Capt. Roberts, December 3, 1868, LS, Capt. James Brown to "Commander of the Post of Sulphur Springs," December 3, 1868, "Register of LS," DT, 5MD, RG 393, NA; Smallwood, "Swamp Fox of the Sulphur," Pt. 2, 41; Crouch and Brice, *Cullen Baker*, 134-136.
[31].Judge H. S. Crossland to AAAG Lt. Louis Caziarc, March 4, 1869, LR, Box 12, DT, 5MD, RG 393, NA.
[32].Capt. Tolman to Lt. J. M. Burns, Adjutant, Post of Sulphur Springs, November 5, 1868, LR, Box 13, DT, 5MD, RG 393, NA.
[33].Capt. Tolman to Lt. Burns, Adjutant, Post of Sulphur Springs, November 5, 1868, LR, Box 13, DT, 5MD, RG 393, NA.
[34].Smallwood, *Time of Hope, Time of Despair*, 144-145; and see Crouch and Brice, *Cullen Baker*.
[35].H. C. Mack, *Texas: Information for Emigrants* (Franklin, Tennessee: Haynes & Figures Publishers, 1869), 141-143.
[36].Tuck, *Civil War Shadows*, 194.
[37].T. Russell and R. Russell, *Some Die Twice*, 36; T. Russell, *Titus County*, 2, 162; *Waco Register*, n.d., quoted in *Austin Weekly Republican*, April 21, 1869; Col. W. Pease to AAAG

Lt. Morris, December 14, 1868, LR, micro-film copy, DT, 5MD, RG 393, NA.

38. T. Russell and R. Russell, *Some Die Twice*, 36; T. Russell, *Titus County*, 2, 162; *Waco Register*, n.d., quoted by *Austin Weekly Republican*, April 21, 1869; Col. W. Pease to AAAG Lt. Morris, December 14, 1868, LR, micro-film copy, DT, 5MD, RG 393, NA.

39. Col. W Pease to AAAG Lt. Morse, December 14, 1868, Sub-Assistant Commissioner, Sulphur Springs, LS, BRFAL, RG 105, NA.

40. *San Antonio Express*, December 18, 1868.

41. *San Antonio Express*, December 18, 1868.

42. Lt. Burns to Adjutant Lt. Josiah Chance, Post of Sulphur Springs, November 23, 1868, Col. W. Pease to AAAG Lt. Morse, December 16, 1868, cited in Tuck, *Civil War Shadows*, 235-236.

43. Lt. Burns to Adjutant Lt. Chance, Post of Sulphur Springs, November 23, 1868, Col. W. Pease to AAAG Lt. Morse, December 16, 1868, cited in Tuck, *Civil War Shadows*, 235-236, 246-248.

44. Lt. Burns to Adjutant Lt. Chance, Post of Sulphur Springs, November 23, 1868, Col. W. Pease to AAAG Lt. Morse, December 16, 1868, cited in Tuck, *Civil War Shadows*, 235-236, 246-248.

45. Lt. Burns to Adjutant Lt. Chance, Post of Sulphur Springs, November 23, 1868, Col. W. Pease to AAAG Lt. Morse, December 16, 1868, cited in Tuck, *Civil War Shadows*, 235-236, 246-248.

46. Lt. Burns to Adjutant Lt. Chance, Capt. Tolman to Lt. Chance, Post of Sulphur Springs, November 23, 24, 1868, Col. W. Pease to AAAG Lt. Morse, December 16, 1868, LS, cited in Tuck, *Civil War Shadows*, 235-238, 246-248.

47. Capt. Toman to Adjutant Lt. Chance, Post of Sulphur Springs, November 24, 1868, LS, cited in Tuck, *Civil War Shadows*, 237-238.

48. Capt. Tolman to Adjutant Lt. Chance, Post of Sulphur Springs, November 24, 1868, LS, cited in Tuck, *Civil War Shadows*, 237-238.

49. Capt. Tolman to Adjutant Lt. Chance, Post of Sulphur Springs, November 24, 1868, LS, cited in Tuck, *Civil War Shadows*, 237-238.

50. Capt. Tolman to Adjutant Lt. Chance, Post of Sulphur Springs, November 24, 1868, LS, cited in Tuck, *Civil War Shadows*, 237-238.

51. Capt. Tolman to Adjutant Lt. Chance, Post of Sulphur Springs, November 24, 1868, LS, cited in Tuck, *Civil War Shadows*, 237-238.

52. Capt. Tolman to Adjutant Lt. Chance, Post of Sulphur Springs, November 24, 1868, LS, cited in Tuck, *Civil War Shadows*, 237-238.

53. Col. W. Pease to AAAG Lt. Morse, December 16, 1868, LS, Post of Sulphur Springs, LS, cited in Tuck, *Civil War Shadows*, 246-248.

54. Col. W. Pease to AAAG Lt. Morse, December 16, 1868, Post of Sulphur Springs, LS, cited in Tuck, *Civil War Shadows*, 246-248.

55. Col. W. Pease to AAAG Lt. Morse, December 16, 1868, Post of Sulphur Springs, LS, cited in Tuck, *Civil War Shadows*, 246-248.

56. Rebecca A. Rosary, "Wantonly Maltreated and Slain, Simply because They are Free: White violence Perpetrated against Black Women in Reconstruction Texas, 1865-1868," ms, Taylor-Smallwood-Howell Collection, GPL; Col. W. Pease to AAAG Lt. Morse, December 14, 1868, LR, microfilm copy, DT, 5MD, RG 393, NA.

57. Lt. H. E. Scott to Maj. Chaffee, December 24, 1868, Post of Sulphur Springs, cited in Tuck, *Civil War Shadows*, 249.

58. Post of Sulphur Springs, "Post Guard Report," January 15, 1869, cited in Tuck, *Civil War Shadows*, 255-256.

Chapter 9

[1]. Lt. Sweeney to AAAG Capt. Roberts, November 23, 1868, Sub-Assistant Commissioner, Jefferson, LS, copy in AGO, RG 94, NA; Lt. Malloy to AAAG Capt. Roberts, December 3, 1868, LS, Capt. Brown to "Commander of the Post of Sulphur Springs," December 3, 1868, "Register of LS," DT, 5MD, RG 393, NA; *Waco Register*, n.d., quoted by *Austin Weekly Republican*, April 21, 1869; *Waxahachie Argus* Extra, April 6, 1869.

[2]. "Bickerstaff, Ben," VF, Archives, TSL.

[3]. The most thorough account of the months leading up to the death of the Swamp Fox belongs to Crouch and Brice, *Cullen Baker*, 131-160.

[4]. Marvin D. Evans, comp., *The Orrs of Miller County, Arkansas* (Fort Worth: privately published, 1951), 29-31, 33; Crouch and Brice, *Cullen Baker*, 60-61. For a brief account of the clash between Baker and Orr, see Smallwood, "Swamp Fox," *True West*.

[5]. Thomas Orr, *The Life and Times of Cullen Baker* (Little Rock: Price and Barton, 1870), 22-23; Bartholomew, *Cullen Baker*, 52; Crouch and Brice, *Cullen Baker*, 61-63. And see, Smallwood, "Swamp Fox," *True West*, Pt. 2: 38.

[6]. Orr, *Life of Baker*, 23.

[7]. Orr, *Life of Baker*, 23-24; Crouch and Brice, *Cullen Baker*, 62-63.

[8]. Orr, *Life of Baker*, 23-24; Crouch and Brice, *Cullen Baker*, 63.

[9]. *Marshall Texas Republican*, January 15, 1869; *Flake's Daily Bulletin*, January 20, 1869; Orr, *Life of Baker*, 47; Crouch and Brice, *Cullen Baker*, 147-148.

[10]. Orr, *Life of Baker*, 47; Crouch and Brice, *Cullen Baker*, 147-148; *Flake's Daily Bulletin*, January 20, 1869.

[11]. *Cleburne Chronicle*, January 23, 1869; *Waco Semi-Weekly Register*, February 5, 1870; Judge Norton to Gov. E. Pease, April 8, 1869, E. Pease, GP, RG 301, Archives, TSL.

[12]. *Cleburne Chronicle*, January 23, 1869, Judge Norton to Gov. E. Pease, April 8, 1869, E. Pease, GP, RG 301, Archives, TSL; Pam Jetsel, "Prominent Pioneer E. M. Heath dead in 1902," *Cleburne Times-Review & Democrat*, December 7, 2003; *Waco Semi-Weekly Register*, February 5, 1870.

[13]. Judge Norton to Gov. E. Pease, April 18, 1869, E. Pease, GP, RG 301, Archives, TSL.

[14]. Justin M. Sanders, "Anthony Benning Norton, *NHT*, 4: 1049.

[15]. Sanders, "Norton," *NHT*, 4: 1049.

[16]. Campbell, *Grass-Roots Reconstruction in Texas*, 80-81.

[17]. Judge Norton to Gov. E. Pease, April 18, 1869, E. Pease, GP, RG 301, Archives, TSL; *Cleburne Chronicle*, January 23, 1869; H. P. Gammed, *Laws of Texas*, 1822-1897 (Austin: H. P. Gammell Book Company, 1898), vol. 6, 83; Texas Legislature, *Special Laws of the Twelfth Legislature of the State of Texas* (Austin: Twelfth Legislature, 1869), 585; Jetsel, "Heath," *Cleburne Times-Review & Democrat*, December 7, 2003 ; *Waco Semi-Weekly Register*, February 5, 1870.

[18]. James M. McCaffrey, *This Band of Heroes: Cranbury's Texas Brigade, CSA* (Austin: Eakin Press, 1985), 14-16, 19, 22-24, 37, 46. Department of War, *War of the Rebellion*, Series 1, Vol. 20, pt. 1, 48. For more on the brutal treatment prisoners received after their surrender, see Smallwood, *Born in Dixie*, 1, 255-257. The guards purposely exposed Cathey and the others to smallpox, no doubt hoping that many would die.

[19]. Jetsel, "Heath," *Cleburne Times-Review & Democrat*, December 7, 2003.

[20]. Jetsel, "Heath," *Cleburne Times-Review & Democrat*, December 7, 2003.

[21]. Campbell to H-TEXAS @H-NET.MSU.EDU, Tuesday 20 August 2002, 8:13 P.M.

[22]. Judge Norton to Gov. E. Pease, April 18, 1869, E. Pease, GP, RG 301, Archives, TSL.

[23]. Capt. Charles Steelhammar, Post of Canton, to AAAG Lt. Caziaic, January 6, 1869, LS, Lt. John Little to Capt. Steelhammar, January 4, 1869, LS, Box 8, DT, 5MD, RG 393, NA;

Judge Norton to Gov. E. Pease, April 18, 1869, E. Pease, GP, RG 301, Archives, TSL.
[24].Capt. Steelhammar, Post of Canton, to AAAG Lt. Caziaic, January 6, 1869, LS, Lt. Little to Capt. Steelhammar, January 4, 1869, LS, Box 8, DT, 5MD, RG 393, NA ; Judge Norton to Gov. E. Pease, April 18, 1869, E. Pease, GP, RG 301, Archives, TSL.
[25].Maj. Chaffee to Capt. C. S. Nelson, Post of Canton, March 29, 1869, LS, Box 8, DT, 5MD, RG 393, NA; Judge Norton to Gov. E. Pease, April 18, 1869, E. Pease, GP, RG 301, Archives, TSL.
[26].Judge Norton to Gov. E. Pease, April 18, 1869, E. Pease, GP RG 301, Archives, TSL.
[27].*San Antonio Express*, February 16, 17, 1869; Judge Norton to Gov. E. Pease, April 18, 1869, E. Pease, GP, RG 301, Archives, TSL.
[28].*New York Times*, February 1, 1869; Gillett, *Frontier Justice*, 112.
[29].Thad Sitton and James H. Conrad, *Freedom Colonies: Independent Black Texans in the Time of Jim Crow* (Austin: University of Texas Press, 2005.), 197. Freedom colonies or black towns developed during Reconstruction times in Texas as a safeguard against outlaws such as Bickerstaff, Baker, and Lee. Usually located in the woods or on the outskirts of white towns, freedom colonies allowed freedmen to speak without fear and to develop a society somewhat free from pressures and threats of post-Civil War whites.
[30].Judge H. S. Crossland to AAAG Lt. Caziarc, March 4, 1869, LR, Box 12, DT, 5MD, RG 393, NA.
[31].Sheriff Peter Williams to Gov. E. Pease, March 18, 1869, LR, copy in Box 15, DT, 5MD, RG 393, NA.
[32].Edna Davis Hawkins, *et al*, *The History of Ellis County, Texas* (Waco: Texian Press, 1972), 154.
[33].Sheriff Williams to Gov. E. Pease, March 18, 1869, LR, copy in Box 15, DT, 5MD, RG 393, NA; Gov. E. Pease to Gen. E. R. S. Canby, March 23, 1869, E. Pease, GP, RG 301, Archives, TSL.
[34].Sheriff Williams to Gov. E. Pease, March 18, 1869, LR, copy in Box 15, DT, 5MD, RG 393, NA.
[35].Gov. E. Pease to Gen. Canby, March 23, 1869, E. Pease, GP, RG 301, Archives, TSL; Sheriff Williams to Gov. E. Pease, March 18, 1869, copy in Box 15, DT, 5MD, RG 393, NA.
[36].*Marshall Texas Republican*, April 30, 1869; T. Russell, *Titus County*, 2, 162; *Austin Daily Republican*, April 21, 1869.
[37].Macus Phelan, *A History of the Expansion of Methodism in Texas, 1867-1902: Being a Continuation of the History of Early Methodism in Texas* (Dallas: Mathis, Van Nort, & Company, 1937), 448.
[38].Phelan, *A History of the Expansion of Methodism*, p. 448.
[39].*Marshall Texas Republican*, April 30, 1869; *Austin Daily Republican*, April 21, 1869; T. Russell, *Titus County*, 2, 162; Orren, "History of Hopkins County," 58.
[40].*Marshall Texas Republican*, April 30, 1869; *Austin Daily Republican*, April 21, 1869; T. Russell, *Titus County*, 2, 162; Orren, "History of Hopkins County," 58.

Chapter 10
[1].Mollie Gallop Bradbury and others, *History of Johnson County, Texas* (Dallas: Curtis Media Corporation, 1985), 71.
[2].*Marshall Texas Republican*, April 30, 1869; *Austin Daily Republican*, April 21, 1869; T. Russell, *Titus County*, 2: 162; Orren, "History of Hopkins County," 58.
[3].*Waxahachie Argus* Extra, April 6, 1869; T. Russell, *Titus County*, 2, 162; Orren, "History of Hopkins County," 58.

4. Col. W. Pease, General Order No. 2, February 24, 1869, Post of Sulphur Springs, Box 17, DT, 5MD, RG 393, NA.
5. *Marshall Texas Republican*, March 12, 1869.
6. *Marshall Texas Republican*, March 12, 1869.
7. *Marshall Texas Republican*, March 12, 1869.
8. *Waco Semi-Weekly Register*, February 5, 1870.
9. *Waco Semi-Weekly Register*, February 5, 1870.
10. *Waco Simi-Weekly* Register, February 5, 1870; *Austin Daily Republican*, April 21, 1869.
11. *Cleburne Chronicle*, April 17, 1869; *Marshall Texas Republican*, April 30, 1869; *Austin Daily Republican*, April 21, 1869.
12. *Cleburne Chronicle*, April 17, 1869; *Marshall Texas Republican*, April 30, 1869; *Austin Daily Republican*, April 21, 1869.
13. *Marshall Texas Republican*, April 30, 1869; *Austin Daily Republican*, April 21, 1869; *Waco Semi-Weekly Register*, February 5, 1870; *Cleburne Chronicle*, April 17, 1869; [?] to AAAG Lt. Caziarc, December 24, 1868, [?] to AAAG Lt. Caziarc, January 14, 1869, LR, Box 17, DT, 5MD, RG 393, NA; Smallwood, *Time of Hope, Time of Despair*, 144-145.
14. H. H. Sneed to Gov. E. Pease, April 12, 1869, E. Pease, GP, RG 301, Archives, TSL; *Marshall Texas Republican*, April 30, 1869.
15. Sneed to Gov. E. Pease, April 12, 1869, E. Pease, GP, RG 301, Archives, TSL; *Marshall Texas Republican*, April 30, 1869; *Waxahachie Argus*, Extra, April 6, 1869; Smallwood, *Time of Hope, Time of Despair*, 144-146.
16. Sneed to Gov. E. Pease, April 12, 1868, Pease, GP, RG 301, Archives, TSL; *Marshall Texas Republican*, April 30, 1869; *Cleburne Chronicle*, April 10, 17, 1869.
17. Sneed to Gov. E. Pease, April 12, 1868, Pease, GP, RG 301, Archives, TSL; *Marshall Texas Republican*, April 30, 1869; *Austin Daily Republican*, April 21, 1869; *Waco Semi-Weekly Register*, February 5, 1870; *Cleburne Chronicle*, April 10, 17, 1869.
18. "Bickerstaff, Ben," VF, Archives, TSL.
19. "Bickerstaff, Ben," VF, Archives, TSL.
20. "Bickerstaff, Ben," VF, Archives, TSL.
21. Sneed to Gov. E. Pease, April 12, 1869, E. Pease, GP, RG 301, Archives, TSL; Smallwood, *Time of Hope, Time of Despair*, 144-146; [?] to AAAG Lt. Caziarc, December 24, 1868, [?] to AAAG Lt. Caziarc, January 4, 1869, LR, Box 17, DT, 5MD, RG 393, Lt. Gregory Barrett to AAAG Lt. Vernou, "Monthly Report," August 1, 1868, Sub-Assistant Commissioner, Tyler, LS, BRFAL, RG 105 NA; *Marshall Texas Republican*, April 30, 1869; *Waxahachie Argus*, Extra, April 6, 1869.
22. Sneed to Gov. E. Pease, April 12, 1869, E. Pease, GP, RG 301, Archives, TSL; *Waxahachie Argus*, Extra, April 6, 1869; T. Russell and R. Russell, *Some Die Twice*, 37; U. T. Taylor, "Ben Bickerstaff," *Frontier Times*, 10.
23. *Cleburne Chronicle*, April 10, 1969; T. Russell and R. Russell, *Some Die Twice*, 37; U. T. Taylor, "Ben Bickerstaff," *Frontier Times*, 10; T. Russell, *Titus County*, 2, 162-63; *Clarksville Standard*, April 17, 1869; Sneed to Gov. E. Pease, April 12, 1869, E. Pease, GP, RG 301, Archives, TSL; *Waxahachie Argus*, Extra, April 6, 1869.
24. Judge Patterson, "Memoirs," Crouch Collection, Regional History Center, VC/UHV; Sneed to Gov. E. Pease, April 12, 1869, E. Pease, GP, RG 301, Archives, TSL; *Clarksville Standard*, April 17, 1869; T. Russell and R. Russell, *Some Die Twice*, 37; T. Russell, *Titus County*, 2, 162-163; Orren, "History of Hopkins County," 58-59; *Waxahachie Argus*, Extra, April 6, 1869; *Austin Daily Republican*, April 21, 1869 Bradbury, *History of Johnson County*, 71.
25. Bradbury, *History of Johnson County*, 71.

[26].*Cleburne Chronicle*, April 10, 1869; *San Antonio Express*, April 16, 1869; *Waxahachie Argus*, Extra, April 6, 1869; *Clarksville Standard*, April 17, 1869; Sneed to Gov. E. Pease, April 12, 1869, E. Pease, GP, RG 301, Archives, TSL.

[27].Bradbury, *History of Johnson County*, 71; *A Memorial and Biographical History of Johnson and Hill Counties, Texas: Containing the Early History of This Important Section of the Great State of Texas, Together with glimpses of Its Future Prospects, also Biographical Mention of Many of the Pioneers and prominent Citizens of the Present Time, and Full-Page portraits of Some of the Most Eminent Men of This Section* [no author listed] (Chicago: Lewis Publishing Company, 1892), 112.

[28].Bradbury, *History of Johnson County*, 71.

[29].*Waxahachie Argus*, Extra, April 6, 1869; *Clarksville Standard*, April 17, 1869; *Austin Daily Republican*, April 21, 1869; Sneed to Gov. E. Pease, April 12, 1869, E. Pease, GP, RG 301, Archives, TSL; T. Russell and R. Russell, *Some Die Twice*, 36-37; T. Russell, *Titus County*, 2, 162-163; U. T. Taylor, "Ben Bickerstaff," *Frontier Times*, 10.

[30].*Cleburne Chronicle*, April 10, 1869; *Waxahachie Argus*, Extra, April 6, 1869; *Clarksville Standard*, April 17, 1869; *Austin Daily Republican*, April 21, 1869; Sneed to Gov. E. Pease, April 12, 1869, E. Pease, GP, RG 301, Archives, TSL; T. Russell and R. Russell, *Some Die Twice*, 36-37; T. Russell, *Titus County*, 2, 162-63; U. T. Taylor, "Ben Bickerstaff," *Frontier Times*, 10; T. Lindsay Baker, "Ben Bickerstaff Dead or Alive," *Cleburne Eagle-News*, November 3, 1988; Orren, "History of Hopkins County," 59.

[31].Jetsel, "Pioneer E. M. Heath," *Cleburne Times-Review*, December 7, 2003.

[32].Bradbury, *History of Johnson County*, 71.

[33].Sneed to Gov. E. Pease, April 12, 1869, E. Pease, GP, RG 301, Archives, TSL; H. P. Hunnicutt to AAAG, April 7, 1869, LR, Box 12, Judge Norton to AAAG, April 7, 1869, Judge Norton to Gov. E. Pease, April 7, 1869, copy in LR, Box 10, DT, 5MD, RG 393, NA. *Marshall Texas Republican*, April 30, 1869. For the fate of Bickerstaff's head, see Stephen Mills, Samuel Milken, *et al* to Capt. J. B. Johnson, April 30, 1869, LR, Capt. Johnson, "receipt for Bickerstaff's head," LS, Box 16, DT, 5MD, RG 393, NA.

[34]."Bickerstaff, Ben," FV, Archives, TSL.

[35].*Waxahachie Argus*, Extra, April 6, 1869.

[36].*Fort Smith New Era*, April 21, 1869, copy in Carl Coke Rister Papers, Box 10, Southwest Collection, Archives, Texas Tech University, Lubbock, Texas.

[37].*Austin Daily Republican*, April 21, 1869.

[38].Orren, "History of Hopkins County," 60; Capt. Johnson to AAAG Lt. Morse, June 10, 1869, H. H. Sneed to Capt. Johnson, June 7, 1869, LR, Box 1, DT, 5MD, RG 393, NA. There is still some controversy surrounding the fate of Bickerstaff's body. Some people continue to believe that he was buried in the Alvarado Cemetery and remains there, but from the best sources we have, we believe that Ben's wife came to Alvarado, dug up the body, pitched it in a wagon, and hauled it back to Gray Rock for re-interment there.

[39].G. E. Ramey to H. W. Torbett, April 1, 1869, copy in Box 16, DT, 5MD, RG 393, NA; Smallwood, Crouch, and Peacock, *Murder and Mayhem*, 106.

[40].Joe W. Chumbley, "Brief Biography of Bill Penn," in *Kentucky-Town and Its Baptist Church* (Houston: D. Armstrong, 1975), two unnumbered pages. None of the pages of Chumbley's book are numbered; Smallwood, Crouch, and Peacock, *Murder and Mayhem*, 106-107.

[41].Deputy Sheriff John Hunter, W. A. Salman, *et al* to Capt. George E. Head, Post of Greenville, April 23, 1869, LR, Box 16, DT, 5MD, RG 393, NA; Chumbley, "Penn Biography," *Kentucky-Town*, two unnumbered pages.

[42].Hunter, Salman, *et al* to Capt. Head, Post of Greenville, April 23, 1869, LR, Box 16, DT,

5MD, RG 393, NA; Chumbley, "Penn Biography," *Kentucky-Town*, two unnumbered pages.
[43].Hunter, Salman, *et al* to Capt. Head, Post of Greenville, April 23, 1869, LR, Box 16, DT, 5MD, RG 393, NA; Chumbley, "Penn Biography," *Kentucky-Town*, two unnumbered pages.
[44].Hunter, Salman, *et al*, to Capt. Head, Post of Greenville, April 23, 1869, LR, Box 16, DT, 5MD, RG 393, NA; Chumbley, "Penn Biography," *Kentucky-Town*, two unnumbered pages.
[45].G. B. Ray, *Murder at the Corners* (San Antonio: Naylor, 1957), 66-68; James Stephen Peters, *Mace Bowman: Texas Feudist, Western Lawman* (N.p.: Privately printed, 1996), 46-47.
[46].G. W. King, interviewed by L. L. Bowman, Mrs. W. C. Lee, interviewed by L. L. Bowman, July 22, 1931, in "Bob Lee," VF, L. L. Bowman Papers, Archives, TAMC; Lt. Charles Campbell, Post of Pilot Grove, to AAAG Lt. H. Corbett, May 30, 1869, LR, Box 16, DT, 5MD, RG393, NA.
[47].W. R. Adams, interviewed by L. L. Bowman, summer of 1931, in "Bob Lee," VF, L. L. Bowman Papers, Archives, TAMC; Smallwood, Crouch, and Peacock, *Murder and Mayhem*, 61.
[48].Lt. Campbell, Post of Pilot Grove, to AAAG Lt. H. Corbett, May 30, 1869, LR, Box 16, DT, 5MD, RG 393, NA; G. W. King, interviewed by L. L. Bowman, Mrs. W. C. Lee, interviewed by L. L. Bowman, July 22, 1931, in "Bob Lee," VF, L. L. Bowman Papers, Archives, TAMC; Ray, *Murder at the Corners*, 68-71; Smallwood, Crouch, and Peacock, *Murder and Mayhem*, 109-110.
[49].Lt. Campbell, Post of Pilot Grove, to AAAG Lt. H. Corbett, May 30, 1869, LR, Box 16, DT, 5MD, RG 393, NA; G. W. King, interviewed by L. L. Bowman, Mrs. W. C. Lee, interviewed by L. L. Bowman, July 22, 1931, in "Bob Lee," VF, L. L. Bowman Papers, Archives, TAMC; Ray, *Murder at the Corners*, 68-71; Smallwood, Crouch, and Peacock, *Murder and Mayhem*, 110-111.
[50].G. W. King, interviewed by L. L. Bowman, Mrs. W. C. Lee, interviewed by L. L. Bowman, July 22, 1931, in "Bob Lee," VF, Archives, TAMC; Smallwood, Crouch, and Peacock, *Murder and Mayhem*, 111.
[51].*Cleburne Chronicle*, April 10, 1869; *Waco Semi-Weekly Register*, February 5, 1870; Williams to AAAG, June 5, 1869, Register of LR, Judge Advocate General (prosecutor) William Rupert to AAAG Lt. Morse, January 1, 1870, Box 30, DT, 5MD, RG 393, NA; Gov. E. Pease to Gen. Reynolds, August 27, 1869, E. Pease, GP, RG 301, Archives, TSL.
[52].*Cleburne Chronicle*, April 10, 1869; *Waco Semi-Weekly Register*, February 5, 1870; Williams to AAAG, June 5, 1869, Register of LR, Judge Advocate General (prosecutor) Rupert to AAAG Lt. Morse, January 1, 1870, Box 30, DT, 5MD, RG 393, NA.
[53].*Cleburne Chronicle*, April 10, 1869; *Waco Semi-Weekly Register*, February 5, 1870; Williams to AAAG, June 5, 1869, Register of LR, Judge Advocate General (prosecutor) Rupert to AAAG Lt. Morse, January 1, 1870, Box 30, DT, 5MD, RG 393, NA; E. Pease to Gen. Reynolds, August 27, 1869, Pease, GP, RG 301, Archives, TSL.
[54].Rupert to AAAG Lt. Morse, January 1, 1870, Box 30, DT, 5MD, RG 393, NA.
[55].Special Order No. 21, July 16, 1869, Sergeant Immel, "Report," Post of Sulphur Springs, Box 18, DT, 5MD, RG 393, NA.
[56].Lt. Col. J. B. Johnson, Post of Waco, to AAAG Lt. Morse, February 14, 1870, Capt. Jacob Wagner to AAAG Lt. Morse, March 1, 1870, Maj. W. W. Webb, Post of Jefferson, to AAAG Lt. Morse, March 2, 1870, LR, Box 34, Lt. C. G. Gibson to Capt. Wagner, LR, Box 27, DT, 5MD, RG 393, NA.

[57]. Judge Norton to Col. John B. Johnson, April 9, 1870, LR, Box 27, DT, 5MD, RG 393, NA.
[58]. Judge Norton to Col. Johnson, April 9, 1870, Capt. A. K. Arnold to AAAG (and secretary of civil affairs) Lt. Morse, April 13, 1870, LR, DT, 5MD, RG 393, NA.
[59]. George A. O'Brien to AG, United States, January 20, 1872, Crouch Collection, VC/UHV.

APPENDIX 1

MAJOR GENERAL GEORGE ARMSTRONG CUSTER'S TESTIMONY BEFORE CONGRESS RELATING TO THE CONDITIONS AND VIOLENCE IN TEXAS

The following is an excerpt from the "Report of the Joint Committee on Reconstruction at the First Session Thirty-Ninth Congress." In the selection Major General Custer reports that many white Texans refused to accept the results of the Civil War and continued to commit atrocities against the freed people and white Unionists. Custer's testimony is based upon his personal observations while stationed in Texas between September 1865 and February 1866.

WASHINGTON, March 10, 1866.
Major General George A. Custer sworn and examined.
 By Mr. Williams:

  Question: State whether you have been in any part of the States lately in rebellion. If so, in what part and in what capacity?
  Answer: I have been in Texas and western Louisiana, in command of cavalry. I was lately in command of all the cavalry in the former State, and previous to that in command of a division of cavalry in western Louisiana. I also commanded the central district of Texas.
  Question: When did you go to Texas and when did you leave there?
  Answer. I went to Texas in the early part of September last from Western Louisiana. I went to western Louisiana in June. I left Texas about the middle of February.
  Question. State if you have been in different parts of Texas, and what opportunities you have had to ascertain in the views and feelings of the people of that State.
  Answer. I have been over a considerable portion of the State, the eastern, southeastern, and central portions. And, in addition to this, I have, in my official capacity as commander of cavalry, sent detachments of troops to many of the points not visited by myself. In sending out these detachments of cavalry I have instructed the commanding officers to ascertain the condition of affairs as regards the sentiments and disposition of the people towards the general government, and to report to me on their return. In this way I have had facilities for ascertaining the true condition of the people, their present disposition and sentiments, to a greater extent than almost any other officer in the service.
  Question. State from your own personal knowledge, and from such information as you have received from subordinate officers, what are the present temper and disposition of the people of Texas in regard to the power and authority of the United States?
  Answer. I do not regard the disposition of the majority of the people towards the general government as at all friendly. To use their own words, they "accept the situation," but I think their motives are entirely selfish; and they acknowledge that it is from a desire to obtain the benefits of the government, rather than to give the government any support. The feeling of the people there towards the government is far more hostile and antagonistic than it was three or six months ago. They affirm, as a reason for this, that they are kept in

the condition they are now in, and are denied the exercise of their former power. They are particularly dissatisfied with the action of the government in not permitting them to reoccupy those places in congress, which they voluntarily relinquished five years ago, and to uphold which course they have been fighting during the past five years.

Question. What proportion of the people, where you have been, are new or have been during the war, faithful to the Union?

Answer. In Texas it would hardly be possible to find a man who has been strictly faithful to the Union, and remained in the State, during the war. They forced all who were truly Union men to leave the State. Those who did not were murdered. The people of the north have no conception of the number of murders that have been committed in that State during and since the war. A great many of the Union men who were compelled to leave the State have returned since the return of the United States troops to the State. There are men in the State who claim to be loyal and yet have remained, during the war, unmolested; but, upon investigation, it will be found that their loyalty is not unimpeachable, and that they have, to a certain degree, sympathized and acted with the rebels to a greater or less extent.

Question. What would the condition of the loyal men in Texas now, in case the military protection now afforded were withdrawn from the State?

Answer. I would not consider it safe for a loyal man to remain in Texas now, at least in that portion I have visited, after the troops were withdrawn. I have within my possession letters from prominent Union men in the State, saying that if the troops were to be withdrawn they wished to be informed of, it for the purpose of making arrangements to leave when the troops did; that it would be unsafe and unwise for them to remain after the troops were withdrawn. Even now there is no friendly feeling, and very little intercourse, between the loyal and disloyal portion of the inhabitants. The feeling of hostility towards loyal men is carried to such an extent that a loyal man engaged in business receives no patronage except from loyal men.

Question. What do the disloyal people desire upon that subject; are they willing to have the troops remain, or anxious to have them withdrawn?

Answer. They are very anxious to have them withdraw. They say there is no longer any necessity for them, if any necessity ever existed, and that it is an imposition upon the people for the government to keep them there. And this assertion, that there was no necessity for the troops, have been made ever since I first entered the State.

Question. State, as fully as you are able, what were the condition, sentiments, and disposition of the people of Texas towards the general government at the time you went into the State, and what they are now. And if any change has occurred, give your opinion as to the reason of that change.

Answer. When I entered the State last summer I found the condition of the people, as regards their sentiments and intentions towards the general government, to be as satisfactory as any loyal man could wish, so far as it was observable. They made use of no expressions hostile to the government, or against government officials, or against the policy of the government. On the contrary, they regarded the result of the war as final —no appeal to be made from it—and were willing to conform to any conditions the general government might see fit to impose. And I am confident that, especially their leaders, those who had born a prominent part in the rebellion, were in the expectation of being dealt with in accordance with the extreme provisions of law. Those of them possessing much property believed their property would be confiscated, and they also thought that at least the leaders would be tried and executed for treason. So long as the policy of the government towards the southern States seemed undeveloped or unknown, the most submissive feeling was everywhere prevalent. Those who had been engaged in rebellion, particularly those who had born a prominent part, realized, without being told, that they had forfeited every right, even to that of life. They regarded the course of the government as magnanimous in the extreme, and far more generous than they had reason to expect. After it was seen what policy was to be pursued towards the leaders, and towards the southern States generally, they assumed a more defiant position, assailed the government, assailed the measures of the government, denounced the system of provisional governments which had been established in the south, were opposed to the location of troops their midst, and were opposed to the location of agents of the Freedmen's Bureau. And this feeling continued to grow and manifest itself more strongly, day by day. I think their opposition to the government and disloyalty is as openly visible and as plainly manifest now as it was in 1861. I am speaking of the majority. Of course, there are exceptions. There are men who have born a prominent part in the war, but who fairly accept the situation in good faith, and do not do so from any selfish motive, but from a sincere desire and purpose to sustain the government. If necessary, I could name honorable exceptions, of men who have, since the surrender of the rebel armies, labored energetically in support of the government and of government measures, notwithstanding the fact that during the war they were foremost as its opposers. This class adhere strictly to the terms and conditions of their oath of allegiance, and as conscientious men regard their oath as binding to the fullest degree. The majority, or at least a large proportion, of those who have taken the oath of allegiance to the general government, do not hesitate to assert that they do not regard it as binding, but maintain, for some unknown reason, that the oath has been forced upon them, and was taken only with a view of obtaining protection under it.

Question. State your opinion as to whether or not the lenient policy, which has been pursued towards the rebels, has been beneficial to that country, or otherwise.

Answer. In my opinion it has been very detrimental, not only to that portion of the country, but to the entire country, and more immediately to the interests of the Union and Union men in the south. It has certainly produced one result not intended nor contemplated. It has led the people of the south to forget the enormity of the crime they committed by engaging in rebellion, and they are not endeavoring to school themselves to the belief that they are the party aggrieved, and the general government the aggressor. To such an extent have they succeeded in thus educating themselves, that I have no doubt, had they the power, they would arraign the government for suppressing the rebellion.

Question. Is there as much freedom among the Union men now in the expression of their views there as there was at the time you went there? And if not, what is the reason for it?

Answer. In many parts of Texas Union men dare not express their sentiments as regards loyalty to the general government. Their lives would be endangered by so doing. Union men are being murdered there to this day; at least murders were occurring constantly before I left and I think were on the increase.

Question. Do you know of any cases in which Union men were murdered, and the reasons why they were murdered?

Answer. Except that it did not fall under my own personal observation, I have as positive information as a man can have of what he does not actually witness. I have within my reach written documents from prominent Union men in the State informing me of the murders of Union men for no other reason than that they were Union men, and had fought in defense of their country. I know one instance of a man who was murdered about two weeks prior to my departure from the State, within twenty miles of Austin, the capital of the State. During the war a Texas regiment of cavalry of Union soldiers was organized, composed for the most part of refugees. They were not, I think, organized in the State, but in New Orleans, during General Butler's command there. Since the close of the war this regiment has been mustered out, and the men long returned to their homes. I have learned, officially and otherwise, of the murder of several of these men. I was informed by Governor Hamilton of the murder of six of them in one county. Three days before I came away I received the flag I have in my hand, sent to me by a Union lady from Texas. The large flag from which this was made was raised over the house of her husband. A committee of citizens waited on him and told him to take it down. He refused, and they shot him, intending to kill him. He escaped, however, with his life, but suffered the loss of an eye. The name of this loyal man is F.W. Sumner, of whom mention has been made in some of our northern papers. I believe this transpired about three weeks before I left the State. The circumstances, as I have related them, were reported to me officially by an officer of my command whom I had sent to that part of the State with a detachment of cavalry. Several similar instances have been reported to me. In one case a man raised a Union flag over his house; was ordered by a committee of citizens to take it down; he refused, and was killed. In Fannin county, Texas, I learn from written reports of Union citizens, some of whom participated in the meeting, and also from the official report of the officer who was sent there to restore order, that the Union citizens met for the purpose of listening to union addresses from loyal men. They formed a procession and marched down one of the streets with a flag at the head of the procession. The disloyal portion of the inhabitants collected together, and being armed, dispersed the meeting, took possession of the flag, dragged it through the streets, tore it in pieces, and gave notice that no Union sentiments could be proclaimed there. A party of cavalry was sent there of the purpose of arresting the leaders, but they escaped. The facts, however, are as I have stated. I have the written report of the officer in command, also a written statement of some of the Union citizens who participated in the meeting. I reported the facts to Governor Hamilton at the time.

Question. Were you there when the election in that State took place?

Answer. I was.

Question. What feeling was prevalent at the time of the election as between those who were Union men and those who were rebels as candidates for office?

Answer. The two parties, loyal and disloyal, had each their candidates. In Travis County, where the Union party have usually been stronger than in almost any other county in the State, except the German settlements, the disloyal party elected their candidates by a vote of about three to one. Some of the most prominent Union men in the State were candidates for the convention in the county; but they were defeated by a large majority. Candidates generally before the convention seemed to base their claims upon the extent to which they had opposed the government during the war, and the extent to which they at that time opposed measures that had been adopted by the government in reference to the southern States. A large number of members came to the convention before having taken the amnesty oath, or having received special pardons. The secretary of the convention took his seat wearing the uniform he had worn in the rebel service.

Question. To what convention do you refer?

Answer. I refer to the convention which was called by Governor Hamilton for the purpose of reorganizing the State.

Question. Have you any knowledge of an organization in that State, secret or otherwise, for the purpose of opposing or thwarting the action of the government of the United States?

Answer. It was reported to me frequently that such organizations did exist, and I have no doubt in my own mind that they have existed in the northern part of the State. I was so thoroughly convinced of the fact that I sent a considerable force into that section of the State to disperse them. The fact that such organizations did exist was confirmed by the statements, written and oral, of loyal men, and by the reports of officers sent there on duty.

Question. What feeling do they evince in Texas towards officers and soldiers of the United States?

Answer. Where the soldiers are in sufficient numbers to control the section of country in which they are located the people are very respectful to them and to their officers, because they are unable to adopt any other course; but officers or soldiers traveling in small parties through the State are insulted wherever they meet any considerable number of citizens. In leaving the State it was necessary that I should travel one hundred and twenty-five or one hundred and fifty miles overland before reaching railroad communication, and wherever a number of the citizens were met, either at hotels or on the cars or steamboats, their conversation was generally of the most insulting character, being abusive of the federal government and of its measures, and strongly opposed to the army. Such conversations are generally not directed to the persons for whose ears they are intended. By this course, they aim to prevent loyal men from remaining in their midst.

Question. What do the people desire there as to the recognition of the State by the federal government? Do they expect to desire the reception of their senators and representatives into Congress?

Answer. The division of opinion is very clearly marked upon that question. The entire disloyal portion of the inhabitants are very anxious that the State should be immediately restored to its former rights and privileges in the Union; that it should be represented in Congress and in the other branches of the government; while the loyal portion of the inhabitants are equally anxious that the general government should continue to maintain its present control over the State. In this they say is their only safety, in which opinion I most heartily concur.

Question. Do the disloyal people expect that when the State is restored and its representatives received into Congress the troops will immediately be withdrawn from the State, and they be left to take care of themselves?

Answer. They think both these events will occur together; that the troops are only being kept there while the State is under a provisional government. They are convinced that the present governor, who thoroughly appreciates the condition and wants of his State, is strongly opposed to the removal of the troops. They are equally well satisfied that if permitted to elect or choose a governor, one will be selected who will favor and urge the withdrawal of the federal troops.

Question. What, in your judgment, would have been the effect as to the development of Union feeling and strength in that Sate if there had been, up to this time, a military government preserved there adequate for the protection of the Union people in the expression and advocacy of their Union views and feelings?

Answer. I think that, while at present the Union men are entirely without influence and are forced to remain silent, in that case, they would have been the predominant or ruling party, because, there as everywhere, there is a large portion of the inhabitants who try to attach themselves to those who are in power, or to those who have most authority. As it is now, the Union men have little or no voice in controlling the local affairs of the State. I think that a great many men who, at the close of the war, were anxious to be known as Union men, and to act with the Union party, have been deterred from so doing by the influence and strength of the disloyal portion of the inhabitants. Had military rule prevailed, I am confident that the strength of the loyal party would have steadily increased, while the opposing party would have undergone a corresponding decrease, until, in course of time, treason would become unpopular, and traitors would not be chosen as officeholders. There is no disguising the fact that loyalty at the south has become a byword and a reproach to those who have the courage to profess it.

Question. Can you give any opinion, from what you have seen and heard in Texas, as to what the people there would do if they were to obtain the power or ascendancy in that country, and could have entirely their own way?

Answer. I think, in the first place, non but those who had been most prominent as leaders in the rebellion would be appointed or elected to office; this no one will deny. If they were allowed to legislate upon the question they would be opposed to paying their share of the national debt unless the rebel debt was incorporated with it. Indemnification would be claimed and insisted upon for all losses sustained by rebel property-holders during the war; while a system of laws regulating labor would be passed which would virtually place the freedmen under the entire control of their former owners. Had they the power, neither northern men or freedmen would be permitted to acquire property in the south.

Question. Suppose the general government were to be involved in a foreign war with Great Britain or France, what course, in your opinion, would these rebels take; would they fight for the flag, be neutral, or join the enemy?

Answer. That question frequently comes up in conversation in the south, and there is a division of opinion. I could scarcely decide which way a majority would go, whether it would be for or against the flag. I think, though, that the most sensible, and certainly all those inclined at all to be loyal, would fight for the flag. The original secessionists would undoubtedly fight against it.

Question. Suppose an opportunity was offered to a majority of the people in Texas to secede without war, do you suppose they would prefer to stay in the Union or go out?

Answer. I think they would prefer to go out.

Question. State what you know as to the operations or necessity of the Freedmen's Bureau, or some other agency of a similar nature in that State.

Answer. I have paid considerable attention to the action of the Freedmen's Bureau in various parts of the State; at least such parts as were embraced within the limits of my command, and I am firmly of the opinion that unless the present bureau or some substitute is maintained for an indefinite period, great wrongs and an immense amount of oppression would be entailed upon the freedmen. As it exists there at present, the bureau is totally unable to do all that might be done or that is required to be done.

Question. What feelings do these people, or a majority of them, evince at this time towards the freedmen?

Answer. There is a very strong feeling of hostility towards the freedmen as a general thing. There are exceptions, of course; but the great mass of the people there seem to look upon the freedman as being connected with, or as being the cause of, their present condition, and they do not hesitate to improve every opportunity to inflict injuries upon him in order, seemingly, to punish him for this. This feeling exists to a certain extent, and is often manifested in their courts. I might illustrate it by stating what I know to be true, that since the establishment of the provisional government in Texas the grand juries throughout the State have found upwards of five hundred indictments of murder against disloyal men, and yet in not a single case has there been a conviction, while in one judicial district, embracing seven counties, adjoining Travis county, the judge, in making to the governor his report of the last session of court held by him, stated that fourteen Negroes had been tried within his jurisdiction for various slight offences; that the fourteen had all been convicted and sentenced to various terms in the State prison. And to show you the manner in which justice is meted out in their course towards the freedmen, one was tried and convicted of stealing one bushel of sweet potatoes, and sentenced to the penitentiary for two years. Another for stealing an equally small amount was sentenced for the same period. Then, to show you their hostility further, it is of weekly, if not of daily, occurrences that freedmen are murdered. Their bodies are found in different parts of the country, and sometimes it is not known who the perpetrators are; but when that is known no action is taken against them. I believe a white man has never been hung for murder in Texas, although it is the law. Cases have occurred of white men meeting freedmen they never saw before, and murdering them merely from this feeling of hostility to them as a class.

Question. What are the views and feelings of the freedmen in Texas, as well as you could ascertain them, towards the government?

Answer. They are loyal without a single exception, so far as my experience goes. They were always our friends, both in time of war and since active hostilities have ceased.

Question. Have they any apprehension or understanding of the condition of things in that country?

Answer. They have, to a certain extent. They realize, as all Union men in the State do, that their only safety and protection lies in the general government; and they realize, too, that if the troops are withdrawn, they will be still more exposed than they are now.

Question. What would be the condition of the colored population in Texas, if the people were left to do with them just as they pleased?

Answer. I think a system of laws would be passed, which, while it would not give to former owners the right to transfer freedmen without their consent to another owner, they would still have as much control over their labor as they had before slavery was abolished. And I think, too, they would inaugurate a system of oppression that would be equally as bad as slavery itself.

Question. What do those who have been rebels say as to the education of the freedmen, and the extension to them of the right of becoming property-holders in the State?

Answer. They are opposed to allowing them to possess land; they are fearful that by so doing they will eventually lose control over them. They rather look upon the idea of educating them as an absurdity; and while you will find exceptional cases of southern men doing all they can to advance the freedmen intellectually, you will, in a majority of cases, find them opposed to the principle of schools for freedmen.

Question. What is the prevailing opinion there as to whether the Negro will or will not work without physical compulsion?

Answer. The expressed opinion is, that he will not work without physical compulsion. I hardly think a majority of them are sincere when they say this, because they have demonstrated to a great extent that the freedmen will work as well, if not better, in some cases, by giving him an interest in the proceeds of his labor, than by the former method. There are many cases where it is impossible to make them labor; but it is not to be wondered at when we consider what a great change has taken place in their condition. I frequently visited quite a number of plantations in Texas, and saw the freedmen at work in the cotton-fields. As a general thing, they did well; and, in many instances, picked more cotton than they had done in former years, because the owners of the cotton paid them so much per hundredweight. I believe three or four hundred pounds is a very good day's work for a hand in picking cotton; but I have known hands paid fifty cents per hundred weight, gathering six hundred in a day. One reason or difficulty in the arrangements for labor in many cases, as I am informed, occurs from the disinclination of the planter to contract with those whom he formerly owned. He does not like the idea of relinquishing his former claim, and the difficulty in these cases is not because the freedmen are unwilling to contract, but the unwillingness is on the part of the planter. In many cases, however, the freedmen are unwilling. To confirm the opinion that the fault lies to a certain extent with the contractor or former owner, northern men, who have engaged in business in the south since the surrender of the rebel armies, have had little or no difficulty with the labor question. As a general thing, the freedmen are anxious to acquire the title to land, and cultivate it for their own interest.

Question. Have these freedmen any knowledge of the political questions and discussions of the day?

Answer. They manifest a great interest in the discussions that are going on, and are very anxious as to what the result will be, particularly as regards them.

Question. Do the freedmen have anything to say in reference to, or do they expect to exercise the right of suffrage at any time?

Answer. They are very quiet as regards that question. They do not seem as anxious about that as they are whether the general government will continue the control as it does now, or whether the affairs of the State will be placed entirely in the hands of the State authorities. They seem to be very anxious, indeed, to acquire education, and those who are working under contract and have not an opportunity to attend schools have purchased books and are acquiring such information as they can under the tuition of those who are more advanced. And in this manner many have made remarkable progress.

Question. Suppose the federal government were to withdraw all interference in the affairs of the State, into whose hand would the political power of that country go?

Answer. It would be at once transferred into the hands of the most prominent rebels. Of the truth of this I do not entertain a doubt.

Question. Do you think that any out-spoken Union man could be elected to Congress in Texas?

Answer. I do not think that any man but one who had born a prominent part in the war, or one who had distinguished himself in his opposition to the federal government, could be elected-certainly no loyal man could. Some months ago they were willing to make a sacrifice of their opinions, for the time being, if no so doing—by sending a man who would be accepted—they could regain their former place in the Union; but they do not seem to think now that even that is necessary, and in case of an election I think they would select a man of their choice, and that man would be disloyal.

Question. How long were you in the State of Louisiana?

Answer. I went to Louisiana about the middle of June, and left the first of September.

Question. State what you found to be the condition of things in that State.

Answer. The condition of affairs at that time in Louisiana was more encouraging than the present condition is in Texas, for the reason I have stated, that at that time they were uncertain what policy the government would pursue towards them. They seemed to feel that they deserved punishment, and to expect it. The only question was, which of them would be punished; and they were conducting themselves remarkably well at that time. But that feeling was undergoing a gradual change before I left the State. In our march from Alexandria, on the Red River, through western Louisiana and eastern Texas, I found that the feeling towards the government was by no means friendly. At that time there were very few Union men there, and they were not allowed to remain at their homes. They had been generally driven away during the war and had not returned. The freedmen were not permitted to contract. In many cases their former owners would not contract with them, nor would they allow them to leave the plantation to contract with other planters. I think as many as a dozen instances were brought to my notice where freedmen had been fired upon and wounded in their attempts to leave their former owners to contract with other planters, and at the same time they could not contract with their former owners. I marched through a portion of the country, which, up to that time, had not been occupied by our troops. And as my command marched along, at every encampment the freedmen would flock to my headquarters in large numbers in order to ascertain and understand their precise condition, as to whether they had the right to contract with other parties, saying their former owners had told them they had no right to-do so. The hostility of the citizens was so observable—it became so manifest that in several instances when we encamped they would fell trees across our road two or three miles in advance of us during the night in order to impede and delay our march.

Question. Suppose the colored population in Texas were allowed to vote; what would be the effect, in your judgment, upon the whites and upon the blacks? What course would they probably take? Would they co-operate and act together with Union men, or would they be controlled by their old masters?

Answer. I think the vast majority of them would co-operate with Union men. There might be exceptional cases in which the freedmen would be under the control of their employers to such an extent that the employer would control their votes; but, as a general thing, I believe the freedmen would consult their own interest in casting their votes, and judging from their conduct during the past war, their votes would always be cast in favor of loyalty and union.

Question. Have they generally the necessary intelligence to distinguish between Union men and rebels, and between those who would be friendly to their interests and those who would oppose their interest?

Answer. As far as my experience goes they could discern more quickly who are their friends and who are their enemies than many of the white inhabitants or than our soldiers or officers could-probably because they have better opportunities for ascertaining. For the same reason we always relied on them during active operations in the field for information, and their information was always correct, or far more correct than that we derived from the whites that were disloyal.

Question. During the war did you find in your operations Negroes who were unwilling to assist the federal government, or who attempted to mislead or do you have any injury?

Answer. I have had many opportunities of judging of that, by having command of cavalry, and generally being in advance of the army, in search of information as to the strength, position, and intentions of the enemy. It was necessary to inquire of the inhabitants of the country through which we marched, and I cannot call to mind an instance of a Negro misleading us or giving us false information. It was in fact very seldom that I inquired of any but Negroes, because the whites could not be relied upon; being unfriendly, they would mislead us, if the opportunity offered; but the Negroes were always friendly, and gave us all the information in their power. As far as knowledge of roads and people were concerned, they seemed to be more correct and better informed than the whites. I never found a Negro who was not thoroughly loyal and friendly to the Union army. They were willing to do anything to aid them. At the battle of Trevilian Station, I was ordered with my command to move by a by-road and attack the enemy in the rear. No man in my command knew the road, and no white man in that portion of the country would have been willing to give me the information. A Negro guided me to the point I desired to reach. And this occurred in a large number of cases within my experience. I could not repeat the number of cases. I almost invariably had Negro guides, and I never hesitated to place the most implicit confidence in them. They would sometimes ride or walk miles to give us information which they thought might be valuable to us, such as of the position of the enemy's forces, or of their trains, which we might desire to capture. They would count the guns and troops as they passed a certain point, and they would give us the number with remarkable accuracy.

Question. What, in your judgment, is the best policy for the government to pursue in reference to those parts of the south as to which you have testified?

Answer. I do not regard the people in that portion of the southern country in which I have been as in a proper condition, or as manifesting a proper state of feeling, to be restored to their former rights and privileges under the general government. And I do not think they have been sufficiently taught the enormity of the crime they have committed by rebelling against the government. I think the government ought to maintain control of those States that were in rebellion until it is thoroughly satisfied that a loyal sentiment prevails in at least a majority of the inhabitants-that certainly does not exist now; and when allowed representation, none but loyal men should be admitted as representatives. Five years ago the southern people voluntarily abandoned their rights and privileges as States in the Union, and with their rights and privileges they forfeited their share in the general government. Having waged a bloody and determined war for four years to carry out their designs against the government, and having failed up to the present time to manifest a penitent spirit for the great crime committed against the nation, or to give a proper and sufficient guarantee of good conduct, I cannot but give it as my opinion, that just regard for our nation safety in time to come, our obligation to foster and encourage throughout the southern States a proper regard and affection for the national authority, as well as to give support to those who are and have been loyal, imperatively demand that the government should maintain its present control of the States lately in rebellion until satisfied that they may, without detriment, be intrusted with their former rights and privileges.

APPENDIX 2

REPORT ON THE CONDITIONS OF AFFAIRS IN TEXAS, 1865-1866

The Secretary of War, Edwin Stanton, submitted the following report to the United States House of Representatives during the Second Session of the Thirty-Ninth Congress. Contained in the report were two significant letters. In the first letter, Mrs. L. E. Potts wrote to President Johnson informing him of the volatile conditions in Texas and requesting federal protection for the freedpeople living in the Northeast Texas region. Potts's letter revealed the dire circumstances that loyal citizens faced in the Lone Star State. Also important is Major General H. G. Wright's correspondence to Brevet Lieutenant Colonel George Lee. In his letter, Wright confirms Potts's report of widespread violence in the northeastern counties of Texas and recommends that additional Federal cavalry troops be garrisoned in the region. Wright's correspondence highlighted that the military did not have enough men to properly protect the freedpeople and loyal citizens residing in the state. A shortage of troops would continue to be a problem for both the Freedmen's Bureau as well as the U.S. Army throughout the entire process of Reconstruction.

HOUSE OF REPRESENTATIVES,
39TH Congress, 2nd Session
Ex. Doc. No. 61.

CONDITION OF AFFAIRS IN TEXAS

LETTER
from
THE SECRETARY OF WAR,
relative to
The condition of affairs in Texas, in reply to a resolution of January 14, 1867

January 30, 1867 -- Referred to the Committee on Resconstruction and ordered to be printed.

War Department
Washington City, January 29, 1867
Sir: In compliance with a resolution of the House of Representative of January 14, 1867, I have the honor to send herewith two communications by Major General Wright, dated repectively November 20, 1865, and July 21, 1866, relative to the condition of affairs in Texas, being the only ones on the sjubject from that officer on file in this department.
Very respectfully, your obident servant.

EDWIN M. STANTON,
Secretary of War

Hon. S. Colfax,
Speaker of the House of Representatives

Headquarters Department of Texas
Galveston, November 20, 1865

Major: It seems to me important, both for public and private interests, that the United States district court for the district of Texas be re-established with as little delay as practicable; and I have the honor to bring the subject to the attention of the major general commanding the military division with a view to its being presented to the government, in case he thinks proper to do so.

Cases are constantly arising which are properly referable to the district United States court, and which call for prompt adjustment; and as they often involve nice points of law I have not the means for properly deciding them, even if I conceived myself authorized to entertain them. I hope, therefore, that the views of the authorities may permit of the speedy re-establishment of the court referred to.

Very respectfully, your obedient servant,

H. G. Wright
Major General Commanding

Major George Lee,
A.A.G., Headquarters Mil. Dir. of the Gulf, New Orleans, La.
(Indorsement)

Headquarters Military Division of the Gulf.
New Orleans, November 27, 1895

Respectfully forwarded through the Adjutant General of the army to the proper authority, urgently requesting that the United States district courts be re-established in Texas at as early a day as practicable

P. H. Sheridan
Major General U.S. A. Commanding.

Paris, Lamar County, Texas

Dear Sir: In addressing you I do not address you as the Chief Magistrate only but as the father of our beloved country, one to whom we all look more or less for protection, but most especially the poor negroes. I wish that my poor pen could tell you of their persecutions here. They are now just out of slavery only a few months, and their masters are so angry to have to lose them that they are trying to persecute them back into slavery. It is not considered a crime here to kill a negro; they are often run down by bloodhounds and shot because they do not do precisely as the white man says. I have been at Nashville, Tennessee, all the winter, and I am being constantly reminded of the difference in their condition here and there. There have never been any federal troops in here, and everything savors of rebellion. I wish that we could have a few soldiers here just for a while, to let these rebels know that they have been whipped. The confederacy have ruined mine and my children's property. In 1858 I took my two children and went to California, with the hope of restoring the health of my daughter, who was in a deep decline, and in 1861 I was ready to return home, when the rebellion broke out, and fearing that my son, a youth only thirteen years of age, might be forced into the war, I remained there until peace. We left a large estate here, which they confiscated and destroyed all that they could. The land is all that is left to us. They stripped it of all the timber and destroyed my houses; had my notes and claims turned over to the confederate receiver, who has them yet. But it is not to my wrongs that i wish to call your attention, but, for humanity's sake, I implore you to send protection, in some form, to these suffering freedmen. Your good heart and wise head know best what to do. I have stated only facts; the negroes need protection here. When they work they scarcely ever get any pay; and what are they to do? I am a plain woman, from your own State, and hope this appeal may not be made in vain. I have never had the pleasure of your acquaintance, but as a Tennessee woman I am proud of you; and as President I approve your course, and hope that bright laurels may forever crown your brow. Nothing more at present, but subscribe myself,

Respectfully yours, &c.,

Mrs. L. E. Potts

Respectfully referred to Major General O.O. Howard, Commissioner, by order of the President.

R. Morrow, *Secretary.*

WAR DEPARTMENT, BUREAU OF REFUGEES,
FREEDMEN, AND ABANDONED LANDS,

Washington, July 2, 1866

Respectfully referred to Brevet Major General Kiddoo, assistant commissioner of Texas, with instructions to make requisitions for sufficient force to visit Paris, Lamar county, Texas, to make investigation of the within statements and if necessary give the protection required.

Parties guilty of murder and other outrages upon freedmen and refugees must be brought to justice.

O.O. Howard,
Major General, Commissioner

Washington, July 2, 1866

Respectfully forwarded to Lieutenant General Grant, United States army, whose attention is called to indorsement within, with request for his approval and return to this office.

O.O. Howard
Major General, Commissioner

Headquarters Army United States
July 6, 1866

Respectfully referred to Major General P. H. Sheridan, commanding military division of the Gulf, through Major General Howard, Commissioner Bureau Refugees, Freedmen, and Abandoned Lands, with directions to furnish, upon applications of agents of the Freedmen's Bureau, such assistance as the means at his command will permit, either for the protection of refugees, freemen, and Union men, or to enforce punishment for crimes.

By command of Lieutenant General Grant.

George K. Leet,
Assistant Adjutant General

WAR DEPARTMENT, BUREAU REFUGEES, &C.,
Washington, July 6, 1866

Respectfully referred to Berevet Major General J. B. Kiddoo, assistant commissioner, whose attention is invited to the indorsement of Lieutenant General U. S. Grant upon the within envelope, and the indorsement from this office upon the enclosed papers.

General Kiddo will take immediate action in this matter.
By order of Major General O.O. Howard, Commissioner.

A. P. Ketchum,
Brevet Major and Acting Assistant Adjutant General.

HEADQUARTERS BUREAU OF REFUGEES,
FREEDMAN, AND ABANDONED LANDS,
July 20, 1866.

Respectfully transmitted to Major General Sheridan, through headquarters department of Texas.

J.B. Kiddoo,
Brevet Major General, Assistant Commissioner.

HEADQUARTERS DEPARTMENT OF TEXAS,
Galveston, July 21, 1866

Respectfully forwarded and attention invited to my letter of this date upon the subject of further disposition of troops in this department.

H.G. Wright,
Major General Commanding.

HEADQUARTERS DEPARTMENT OF TEXAS,
Galveston, Texas, July 21, 1866

COLONEL: I send to-day an application from Mrs. L. E. Potts, of Paris, Lamar county, Texas, to the President, for troops to be sent to that locality for the protection of the people, and particularly of the freedmen, whom she represents to be subject to much ill treatment on the part of their former masters. This application is referred from headquarters of the army to General Sheridan, through the commissioner of the Freedmen's Bureau, but it was inadvertently, no doubt, sent to General Kiddoo, who refers it to General Sheridan through these headquarters.

I get frequent complaints from the northeastern section of the State regarding the condition of that part of the country, of the barbarities practiced towards refugees and freedmen, but owing to the want of force for the purpose, nothing could be done in the matter. The troops we have are already widely distributed, generally in one-company posts, and in some instances in detachments of four or five men, with large commands at San Antonio and Austin, which latter are held ready for any case of emergency. But as the remainder of the 17th United States infantry will soon be here, thus giving an important increase of force, I would ask the attention of the major general commanding to the distribution to be made of it.

The 1st battalion of the 17th infantry, which is at preset a mere skeleton of three companies, it held at the point awaiting assignment. The 2d battalion of two small companies is at San Antonio. The 3d, which is fully organized, is distributed in this section of the State at posts of one company, except at Galveston, where there are two companies. On the arrival of the remainder, now on the way, the three battalions will be filled to their maximum nearly.

I think that the northeastern and northern portion of the State should be garrisoned; but as infantry seems to be of comparatively little use for such service, I would suggest that on the arrival of the remainder of the 2d battalion at San Antonio, the 4th cavalry, or at any rate eight companies of it, be sent into the section and be distributed in one-company posts, generally.

This recommendation is made, of course, on the supposition that the present policy of maintaining garrisons in the interior of the State is to be continued for some time to come, otherwise a very different disposition of troops should be made by assigning them to posts on the frontiers with a view to their protection from the Indians.

Very respectfully, your obedient servant.

H. G. WRIGHT
Major General Commanding

Brevet Lieutenant Colonel GEORGE LEE,
   Asst. Adj't Gen., Mil. Div. of the Gulf, New Orleans, La.

HEADQUARTERS MILITARY DIVISION OF THE GULF,
New Orleans, Louisiana, August 3, 1867

Respectfully forwarded to Brevet Major General Rawlins, chief of staff, United Sates army, inviting attention to the within letter of Major General Wright.

P.H. SHERIDAN
Major General U.S.A., Commanding.

APPENDIX 3

REPORT OF SPECIAL COMMITTEE ON LAWLESSNESS AND VIOLENCE IN TEXAS

Edmund J. Davis, President of the Texas Constitutional Convention of 1868-1869, submitted the following report to the United States Senate during the Second Session of the Fortieth Congress in July 1868. The convention created a special committee to examine and to compile statistics on the violence taking place in the state between 1865 and 1868. The committee's final report reveals that freedpeople and white Unionists were the primary victims of criminal activities taking place within the state. It should be noted that the committee members believed that their findings represented a significant undercount of the actual violence taking place in Texas.

LETTER
OF THE
PRESIDENT OF CONSTITUTIONAL CONVENTION OF TEXAS

COMMUNICATING

The report of special committee on lawlessness and violence in that State.

July 20, 1868.-Referred to the Committee on the Judiciary and ordered to be printed.

Austin, Texas, July 8, 1868.

Sir: By direction of the reconstruction convention, I have the honor to enclose the report of the committee of this convention on "Lawlessness and violence."

Very respectfully, your obedient servant,

EDWIN J. DAVIS,
President of Convention.

Hon. B.F. Wade,
    President of the Senate of the United States.

REPORT OF SPECIAL COMMITTEE ON LAWLESSNESS AND VIOLENCE IN TEXAS.

Committee Room, Austin, Texas, June 30, 1868.

Sir: The committee on lawlessness and violence respectfully submit the following report:

    We have had access to the following sources of information, viz: 1. The records of the state department, particularly the official reports of the clerks of the district courts. These reports are, however very meager, inasmuch as they represent only about 40 counties, and take notice of only those offences for which indictments have been found. 2. The records of the office of the Freedmen's Bureau. These records are likewise very imperfect, as they give information from only about 60 counties, and do not supply accounts of all the outrages committed in those counties. And 3. The sworn statements of competent and reliable witnesses in different sections of the State. These are also incomplete, for they were made from memory; neither are they as numerous as they should be. We have found no little difficulty in getting gentlemen to testify before us. Many are unwilling, and others are afraid of assassination should they do so, and hence very few have responded to the summons of the committee. We do not, therefore, offer this report as a complete exhibit of crime in Texas. We feel confident that it represents a very imperfect view of the actual violence and disorder in the State.

In collecting the statistics here presented we have carefully excluded every record that did not bear the marks of veracity. In compiling the number of homicides, for example, we have included only such cases are either officially reported or distinctly mentioned or remembered by affiants; and we have ventured no statement which is not fully warranted by facts. It is claimed for the report, therefore, that it is faithful and true.

In our statistics we have not embraced assaults with intent to kill, rapes, robberies, whipping of freedmen, and other outrages, many of which are found to be most cruel and wanton; such a summation would impose an almost endless task. We have directed our investigations to the homicides committed during the period of time intervening between the close of the rebellion and the 1st of June, 1868; and, from the three sources of information mentioned, we present the following statistics of homicides in Texas:

	Whites.	Freedmen.	Total.
Killed in 1865	39	38	77
Killed in 1866	70	72	142
Killed in 1867	166	165	331
Killed in 1868	171	133	304
Year unknown	24	21	45
Of unknown race	...	...	40
Total	470	429	939

Making a grand total of 939 homicides committed in Texas since the conclusion of the war, June, 1865, to June 1, 1868, including a few cases casually reported in the present month. This gives an average of 313 per year.

Of these 939 homicides there were, by whites, 464 whites, 373 freedmen—833; by freedmen, 10 whites, 48 freedmen—58; and by parties whose race is unknown, 48.

Now, incomplete as they are, these figures tell a frightful story of blood. They represent stubborn facts, which cannot be suppressed by denials or by denouncing them as fabricated for political effect; and whoever attempts it is not only unfaithful to history, not only an apologist for crime, but may be justly charged as an accessory to the wickedness itself, as encouraging and abetting murderers, and as equally guilty with them. We cannot shut our eyes upon these appalling scenes of bloodshed; and, instead of attempting to conceal them, it becomes us to face them honestly, and address ourselves to the duty of discovering the cause and locating the responsibility of this slaughter of our fellow citizens.

Many of these homicides have doubtless been committed for purposes of plunder and robbery. The facts and the testimony show that many of our highways are infested by bandits, who will take life for a horse, or a pistol, or a purse. These desperadoes, with very few exceptions, were either confederate officers or soldiers, or bushwhackers, during the late war, and now constitute one of the legitimate entailments of secession and rebellion. It is also true that many of these homicides have resulted from private quarrels; there is such bad blood in the land. But this wholesale killing cannot be accounted for by either or both of the causes named. The figures themselves shed some light on this subject. During the last three years, according to the reports consulted, 373 freedmen have been killed by whites, whilst only 10 whites have been killed by freedmen. Now it cannot be that all those colored people, or any considerable number of them, were murdered for their money; their extreme poverty forbids the supposition. Neither can it be that many of them were slain in personal altercations with whites, for in that event, there should have been as many whites killed by freedmen as freedmen by whites, the freedmen being, it is said, generally as well armed as the whites. This great disparity between the numbers of the two races killed, the one by the other, shows conclusively that the "war of faces" is all on the part of the white against the blacks. The evidence in our possession also shows that a very large of the whites murdered were Union men, and that the criminals, with remarkably few exceptions, were and are disloyal to the government.

We are hence directed to the hostility of feeling entertained by ex-rebels against loyal men of both races for the discovery of the cause of a large portion of these outrages. Men naturally hate those whom they have wronged. And we are authorized by facts to affirm, that multitudes who participated in the rebellion, disappointed and saddened by their defeat, are now intensely embittered against the freedmen on account of their emancipation and enfranchisement, and on account of their devotion to the republican party, and against the loyal whites for their persistent adhesion to the Union; that they are determined to resist by every means promising success the establishment of a free republican State government; that it is their purpose even by desperate measures to create such a state of alarm and terror among Union men and freedmen as to compel them to abandon the advocacy of impartial suffrage or fly from the State; and that this feeling of animosity prompts and inspire them to many of these murders, unrestrained as it is by any fear of retribution.

There is absolute freedom of speech in very few localities in Texas. Union men dare not generally avow their political convictions. In many places they can hold public meetings only when supported by troops or armed men; and in many others they dare not hold them at all. In several instances their assemblies have been broken up and fired upon, and their speakers ordered to desist. The dominant rebel element will not tolerate free discussion.

We have been challenged to produce cases of Union men and freedmen being persecuted for their loyalty. We now do so. Judge Black was a republican; he was murdered in 1867, in Uvalde County, by a rebel. Milton Biggs was a Union man, and had been appointed county judge of Blanco County; he was murdered in 1867, while plowing in his field, before he could qualify. Judge Christian, a loyal man of Bell County, was pursued into Missouri and murdered by a party of rebels. Mr. Wade and seven other gentlemen were killed in Lamar County last year for their unionism. Four men were recently murdered in the county of Hunt, and six in Bell County, for their loyalty. Within the present month the county judge and the district clerk of Hunt County have been driven from their homes and compelled to fly or their lives, because of their unyielding attachment to the government. Hundreds of loyal men, to our knowledge, are at this time forsaking their homes in Texas, fleeing from the assassin, forced away by rebel intolerance. And we here put it to record that honorable members of this convention are to-day exiles from their firesides, and dare not return to their families, for the only reason that they will not forswear their principles. Now, whilst it remains true that the Union men of Texas constitute a very small proportion of the white population, and whilst it is true that they are being killed by rebels, it is impossible to escape the conclusion that they are killed for their Unionism. In other words, if they were rebels they would not be killed.

And when we come to examine the persecutions suffered by the freed people, the mass of testimony is so overwhelming that no man of candor can for a moment question the statement that they are, in very many parts of the State, wantonly maltreated and slain simply because they are free, and claim to exercise the rights of freemen. Some months ago, in Panola county, a party of whites rode up to a cabin, where in some freed people were dancing, and deliberately fired upon them, killing four, one a woman and seriously wounding several others. In 1867, in Dewitt county, a white man met a black man riding, and asked him what he was going to do with the whip he held in his hand, and on being answered nothing, shot the freedman, killing him instantly. In the county of Fort Bend, last year, a white man was riding through town, and on seeing a Negro man standing on the steps of the office of the Freedmen's Bureau, he drew his revolver and shot him dead. The criminal had never seen or spoken to the freedman before. In Newton county, 1867, a white man met a colored man driving a team; the former made the freedman get out of his wagon, and then shot him seven times in cold blood. In Fort Bend County, same year, the freed people were holding a fair to procure funds to finish their church and while they were singing a hymn, two white men rode by and fired their pistols into the church. In October, 1867, a white man was traveling in Grayson county, and med a freedman; after passing him a few yards, he turned and fired upon him hitting him in the back. The freedman died in a few hours; he had not spoken a word to the murderer-had never seen him before. But a few days ago a party of white men assaulted the family of an unoffending freedman in Falls County, killing and dangerously wounding another freedman. In the same county, a few weeks ago, two armed white men, in open day, went to the house of a colored man, and without any provocation murdered him. Soon after this, a white man in the same neighborhood rode up to two freedmen, and without any known cause, shot one of them dead and fired at the other. Last week, the colored registrar of Milam County was called to his door at night and shot; and so the bloody story runs.

We mention some minor outrages. In April last a party of white men visited the cabins of two quiet, industrious freedmen, in Freestone county, captured one of them and took him to the woods to murder him; he, however, escaped, being fired at several times, and receiving one wound. In that and adjoining counties of whom are in this city to-day, fugitives from rebel violence. In the county of Marion, bands of armed whites are traversing the county, forcibly robbing the freedmen of their arms, and committing other outrages upon them. Last week a colored woman was whipped in Parker county by a white man; and some time ago, in another county, a white man cut off the ears of a freedwoman. It is openly proclaimed by many of the perpetrators of these wrongs that their object is to compel the Negroes to give up loyal leagues, and to get satisfaction out of them for supporting Yankees.

We could extend the account. We have selected these cases at random, to exhibit the feeling of hatred cherished by a certain class of ex-rebels against Union men and freedman; and we deem them sufficient to sustain our allegation that there is a settled determination on the part of many to suppress the growth of loyalty, and, if possible, to expel or exterminate the white and colored Unionists in the State.

It has also come to our knowledge that there are organizations of disloyal, desperate men in several sections of the State, leagued together for the purpose of murdering prominent Unionists. This fact is set forth in the notices sent to leading republicans in different portions of the State. It is not only believed by many good citizens, but it is claimed and openly asserted by rebels in many localities, that such organizations do exist. The fact is stated, too, by several witnesses. It reveals itself likewise in the outrages systematically perpetrated on loyal whites and freedmen in the localities where these organizations are reported as existing. Some weeks ago, a discreet officer of the United States army was sent with instructions to investigate certain murders in Bell and Coryell counties, and he found tangible evidence of such an organization there. He found it in the murder of six or seven loyalists, several of whom had fought under the Union flag during the rebellion, and had to the last refused to desert their colors. He found it, too, in the terror and dread among the loyalists of that action, and in the precipitate flight of many from the State for safety. In the instances investigated by him, the murderers went in a body at night, in April last, and murdered in cold blood several loyal, law-abiding citizens, rousing them from their beds and shooting them. They then gave out that their victims were horse thieves; but a thorough examination exploded that falsehood. In his official report, the said officer uses this language: "From all that I could learn, it is very evident that the rebels of Bell county have determined to kill or drive away every loyal Union man from the county. This they are doing every day; and after they get rid of the men they seize their stock, or whatever they can lay their hands on; so that, instead of killing horse thieves, hey prove to be thieves and murderers themselves." Again, he says: "There appears to be a regularly organized band in Bell county for the oppression and extermination of the Union element." He also gives the names of some of this organization, and says "they are all rebels and disfranchised."

We have evidence of similar organizations in other parts of the State. Only a few weeks ago, since the meeting of this convention, some arrests were made by the military authorities in Freestone County. The arresting party came upon the criminals by surprised, at midnight, and secured t here of them; and by daylight he whole country was swarming with armed desperadoes from three different counties, who pursued the officer and soldiers, and, numbering about 200, rescued the prisoners. The officer who had charged of the expedition testifies: "It is my opinion that there is an organization of lawless men in that section. One of the men whom I let go stated this plainly to me that they were bound to help one another. And from all that transpired I am satisfied that they have their signals, their runners and system of action."

We have intimated that bad men do not fear the civil courts of Texas. Why should they? During the years 1865, 1866, and 1867, as shown by the State Department, there were 249 indictments for murder found in the district courts of the State, and only five convictions, about two per cent, of the whole. And it is a fact known to all, that for the 900 murders known to have been committed since the conclusion of the war, there has been but one capital execution according to the forms of law; and that was the execution of a freedman in the county of Harris. These figures of themselves demonstrate the insecurity of human life in Texas. The criminal laws of the State are not executed.

In some districts the combinations of lawless men are too strong for the civil authorities, and openly defy them. This is the case in 25 to 30 counties. In some instances the county officers are themselves involved in these acts of violence, or connive at them or willfully neglect to make arrests. The sheriff of one county, for example, is one of a band of murderers; the sheriff of another is at the head of certain desperadoes who have committed numerous outrages, including murder, on the loyal whites and blacks of the county. We have information of numerous cases where the officers of the law most criminally refuse to make arrests for violations of law; and, "no arrest" is the almost universal appendage to reports of lawlessness in our possession, although the criminals are generally known to the community. Not unfrequently they are aided in their escape and harbored or concealed by citizens claiming respectability.

But all of these obstacles to the punishment of criminals are not sufficient to explain the inadequacy of civil government in Texas. We are compelled to introduce here that animosity towards the government and its friends, so prevalent everywhere, as a factor in bringing about such a state of anarchy. It is our solemn conviction that the courts, especially juries, as a rule will not convict ex-rebels for offences committed against Union men and freedmen; neither will they award judgments in favor of Union men and freedmen as against rebels. This is explicitly affirmed in nearly all the testimony before us. In one case, wherein a white man had committed an offence against a freedman, the offender was brought to trial, found guilty, and, because he could not give bond, released; and when the agent of the Freedmen's Bureau notified the magistrate that the law authorized committal in default of bail, the reply was "You would not send a white man to jail for a nigger." In another case a freedman sued a white man; the judge ruled in favor of the freedman, but the jury, contrary to the law and the evidence, decided against him. The case was reversed by the bureau. In another instance a white man brutally assaulted a freedman with intent to kill; he was arrested by the agent of the bureau, turned over to the civil authorities, found guilty, and *fined one cent!* Such cases are frequent. In another county a freedman was tried for assault with intent to kill a white man, and the jury convicted him when the facts proved on trial, as shown in the proceedings of the case, that the freedman was the assaulted and injured party. He was pardoned by Governor Pease. A white boy, 13 years old, was waylaid and shot, and severely wounded, by a man named Johnson, in Hopkins County. Johnson was arrested by the sheriff, a loyal man, brought before Judge Mayberry, of the 8th judicial district, found guilty of a simple assault, and fined $10. The sheriff of Hunt county, a Union man, was resisted and shot whilst arresting a criminal; the said criminal was tried before the said Mayberry, bailed in a bond of $600, and is now at large. In another county a rebel murdered a boy not 14 yeas old; he was tried, and acquitted on the grounds that he had lost an arm in the Confederate service. In another case, a loyal man was assaulted with intent to kill by a rebel, and, after being fired at once, shot and killed his adversary. He was promptly arrested, and compelled to give bond for $50,000. Another loyal man was assaulted with deadly weapons three times by a party of rebels; he made oath to the facts before the proper authorities, but to this day, the said authorities have refused to arrest the criminals, though well known to the sheriff.

The result of all this discrimination against Union men and freedmen is, that they have despaired of securing their rights by law. They feel that the courts are only employed as engines for their oppression, and they would rather suffer their wrongs than seek legal redress, only to be mocked at for so attempting.

In other instances, where the officers of the law are disposed to do their duty, they are not sustained by the citizens. The people are sometimes afraid to aid in the enforcement of the laws, and they not unfrequently, on account of their sympathy with the criminals, positively refuse to do so. In a certain county a loyal sheriff called upon the citizens to assist him in arresting some criminals in town, and the citizens refused, saying, "Call on your nigger friends." Several officers have resigned their places because they cannot get the support of the people in the execution of the laws; many of the important offices in the State are now vacant, because men either fear to accept them, or feel that they could not have the co-operation of the citizens; and we know of efforts being made to intimidate fearless and efficient officers from the discharge of their duties.

A very noteworthy fact developed by our investigations is the increase of crime within the last seven months. Witnesses from various parts of the state testify of increased bitterness against the government and its supporters, and of the multiplication of crime during the last winter and spring; and official data confirm their testimony. This fact, we know, is persistently denied by conservatives, and they claim further that, if true, it is to be charged against the present provisional State government. They tell us that the offices of the State are in the hands of radicals, or military appointees, and that therefore the republican officials of Texas are responsible for this increased lawlessness and disorder. To this we reply—

First. The powers of the provisional State government are very limited, and are exercised in subordination to the authority of the commander of the fifth military district. The State government is without any militia or police whatever. It is dependent entirely on the spirit of the people themselves for the maintenance of order, and is utterly powerless of itself to enforce a single law. Either the citizens themselves must keep the peace, or the military must interfere and compel obedience, or there will be no peace. And we submit that, with such limited powers, and with such a spirit of lawlessness as dominates in Texas, and without the efficient co-operation of the military power, no government under the sun could preserve the peace of society.

Second. It is not true that the offices of the State are held by republicans. Governor Pease qualified as governor of Texas on the 8th of August 1867. There were at that time 2,377 elective offices held by persons elected in 1866. Some time after this, some changes, removals and appointments were made by the military. These all, to the 24th instant, amount to 796. of them 247 were made to fill vacancies, leaving 549 removals and appointments; and 394 of the appointees refused or failed to qualify – many of them declining for fear of assassination; in which cases the old incumbents continue to act. So that there are 1,975 of the elective offices in Texas in the occupancy of those elected in 1866 and only 402 in the possession of military appointees. There are 182 notaries public, appointed by Governor Throckmorton, still in office, and there are only 27 who have been appointed by Governor Pease. It thus appears that only one-fifth of the officers in Texas to day are loyal men. And yet some have the effrontery to hold this one-fifth responsible for the acts of the whole. But, certainly, if any responsibility at all rests upon the State government, it legitimately rests upon the large majority of conservatives who hold the power of the State, and who, as we have seen, too frequently use that power for the protection of criminals. And –

Third. The only period of time in which the present administration of Texas could justly be said to have been republican was marked by the greatest amount of tranquility. That period was between the 8th of August, the date of Governor Pease's qualification, and the 29th of November, the date of General Hancock's assuming command of the district- about three months of 1867. In the three months of September, October, and November, 1867, there were 27 murders committed in Texas, as reported by the Freedmen's Bureau; that is to say, there were nine murders per month. Whilst in the other nine months of the same year, there were 160 murders committed in Texas, as reported by the same authority, that is to say, there were about 18 murders per month, double the former number.

These simple statements are amply sufficient to refute the slander so frequently repeated by conservatives, and to vindicate the present civil administration of Texas from all complicity in the increased lawlessness in the State.

But it is not difficult to fix the responsibility of this increase of crime. Previous to the succession of General Hancock to the command of the fifth military district there was some depose of respect for life in Texas. The numerous arrests of criminals by the military authorities, and the prospect of trial by military commissions, inspired bad men with a salutary fear. But on the publication of General Orders No. 30, from headquarters fifth military district, dated November 29, 1867, a very different and a very turbulent spirit manifested itself through the State. That order was understood to proclaim the supremacy of civil law and the suspension of the military power in the treatment of crime; and hence criminals, who, as has been demonstrated, entertain very little fear of the civil courts, interpreted the said order as a license for the perpetration of all manner of villainies. This was evidenced at the time by words, and by the tone of the rebel press, and more forcibly ever since by unrestrained violence.

During the three months of Governor Pease's administration, aided and sustained by Generals Sheridan and Mower, and previous to the advent of General Hancock, the murders in Texas, as already seen, averaged 9 per month. The number during the other months of the same year averaged 18 per month. And, confining our estimates to the records of the office of the Freedmen's Bureau, the number since the 1st of December, 1867, has averaged 31 per month. During the first month of Hancock's administration, December, there were 30 murders reported by the bureau. In other words, according to the lowest calculation, the peace administration of Generals Hancock and Buchanan has to account for twice the number or murders committed under the Sheridan-Throckmorton administration, and three times the number committed under the Sheridan-Pease administration.

Moreover, fuller reports show that since the policy of general Hancock was inaugurated, sustained as it is by President Johnson, the homicides in Texas have averaged 55 per month; and for the last five months they have averaged 60 per month. And it is for the commander of the fifth military district to answer to the public for at least two-thirds of the 330 or more homicides committed in Texas since the 1st of December, 1867. Charged by law to keep the peace and afford protection to life and property, and having the army of the United States to assist him in so doing, *he has failed.* He has persistently refused to try criminals, rejected the prayers of the executive of the State and the commanding general of the district of Texas for adequate tribunals, and turned a deaf ear to the cry of the tried and persecuted loyalists. And, knowing whererof we affirm, and in the face of the civilized world, we do solemnly lay to his charge the death of hundreds of the loyal citizens of Texas-a responsibility that should load his name with infamy, and hand his very memory to coming years as a curse and an execration.

The obligations of the government and of the citizen are mutual and correlative. If true allegiance is rendered by the latter, ample protection is due from the former. And for and in the name of the loyal whites and blacks in Texas, we do avow that we have been true and unwavering in our fidelity to the United States government. In the face of persecution, in the face of social proscription, in the face of the halter, and in the face of every imaginable peril, we have stood firm in our devotion. If there be a people on earth who can rightfully claim the protection of government, the loyalists of Texas certainly have that right; especially, now that it is in the power of the government to extend it, do they claim protection from the vengeance of those who still pursue them for their allegiance. But, let the responsibility rest where it may, we say it deliberately, *that protection has not been granted us.*

The committee recommend the adoption of the following resolution:

That the president of the convention be requested to forward a copy of this report to the President of the Senate and Speaker of the House of Representatives, to the end that Congress may afford such relief as in their wisdom we may be entitled to.

CALDWELL, *Chairman.*
WHITEMORE,
SUMNER,
EVANS,
BLEDSOE,
COLE,
BELL,
Committee.

Hon. E.J. Davis,
    President of the Convention.

APPENDIX 4

BUREAU AGENT REPORTS THE DEATH OF BEN GRIFFITH

Bureau agent Charles Rand describes the events surrounding the death of Ben Griffith in the following report made from Clarksville (Red River County) on July 21, 1868. Rand's involvement in the killing of Griffith would make him a target of the various outlaw gangs operating in the region as well as members of Griffith's family who resided in Arkansas. Rand would eventually be forced to leave Clarksville under the cover of darkness, escaping to the safety of the military post in Marshall (Harrison County).

Lieut. Chas. (Charles) A. VernouA.A.A. Genl

    I have the honor to report that last evening after sun down a desperado named Ben Griffith entered our town armed with three six shooters and a double barreled gun. He was known by several of the citizens to whom he spoke informing them that his party (names of Baker, Bickerstaff and English) were just at the edge of the town and he was waiting for them to come up. He kept his gun cocked and the butt on his thigh said that they had been below and killed two Yankees and five negroes and burned a train of Commissary shots Stores and that they move to assemble twenty five in all and proceed west and destroy a train that was on its way to the new forts. He dismounted keeping his guns ready for action and entered a grocery kept by one Whilaitt filled a canteen with whiskey, and mounted saying if anybody wanted him to come on they would find him on the Boston road. After he left a freedman came in and said he had been robbed of his pistol and the man that just passed was the one. I immediately ordered the Sheriff to summons a posse and arrest the man only three responded I saddled my horse and we started Two of them kept up and the third could not get his mule into a run. We over took him a mile from town and came upon him just as he was in the act of shooting a freedboy whom he met in the road. He had his gun down within a few feet of the boys head. We dismounted and ran up within 40 yards of him and shouted "Halt". He turned his head and put spurs to his horse. I ordered the men to fire which they did simultaneously and he gave a spring from his saddle and when he reached the ground he was dead.

    I had him directly interred as he had sufficient funds to pay for it.

    The gang have sworn that I shall not live, and as our town is divided in sentiment (see Capt Roberts) I do not know who my friends are. I do not want to retreat; but to stay alone with not a soldier within 60 miles and every second man a sympathizer with the desperadoes is to say the least very unpleasant.

    I have his horse and equipment-gun and pistol. What shall I do with them?

    Please give me a decided order in relation to _____.

            Very Resl Your Obt Sevt [Very Respectfully, Your Obedient Servant]

            Charles RandS. A. Com. [Sub-Assistant Commissioner]

    I do not know who or what he was until after his death only that he had reportedly robbed the freedman

                                            Charles F. Rand

APPENDIX 5

Brevet Major General John J. Reynolds sent the following commands to Captain Adna R. Chaffee on September 1, 1868. As the correspondence indicates, Reynolds ordered Captain Chaffee to Sulphur Springs (HopkinsCounty) in an effort to breakup the operations of various guerrilla bands in the area. Though Captain Chaffee and his fellow officer, Lieutenant Thomas Tolman, suffered several significant set backs, they eventually managed (with civilian help) to restore order in NortheastTexas.

The Commanding officer of Fort Griffin has been directed to detach you with your company and one subaltern for special duty. But Maj. Gen Commanding directs that you move with all possible dispatch to Fort Richardson. The Commanding Officer of which has been directed to reinforce you with sufficient number of men to make a force of one hundred men, he has also been directed to detail two subalterns to accompany the detachment with this force under your command and you will proceed to Sulphur Springs, Texas, and from that point as a rendezvous you will take the field and continue generally in it until the bands of desperadoes commanded by Bickerstaff, Lee, English, Baker or their confederates are broken up or driven from the country.

You will in your discretion divide your command into smaller parties for special services, and you will give orders that no lives be taken unless actual armed resistance is offered by members of these bands.

Arrest as far as possible the men composing these bands of outlaws and turn them over for safe keeping as directed in G.O. No. 13 from H'd Qr's Dist' of Texas to the most convenient post commander. You will see that this detachment moves as light as possible, and you are authorized in your discretion to decide what shall be carried.

Enclosed herewith please find list of names in the counties through which you will pass of men who you can call upon for assistance or information.

The Commanding Officer Fort Richardson has been directed to order Adj. Ass't Surg. J. H. Gunn to accompany the detachment.

You will use every precaution to see that private property is not destroyed by the troops.

All post commanders have been directed to render you every assistance in the way of furnishing you funds and supplies.

The Chief Quartermaster of this District has been directed to turn over to you three hundred dollars for the purchase of forage. This amount will be in checks of $250 that size being more convenient and readily converted into cash.

You will take subsistence funds sufficient from the two forts (Griffin and Richardson) to keep you supplied with fresh beef for sixty days.

You will make frequent and full reports, keeping this H'd Qr's thoroughly informed of your movements.

By Command of
Bv't Major Gen. Reynolds

Bibliography

I. Primary Sources

A. Manuscript Collections and Courthouse Records

James Gee Library, Texas A&M University--Commerce
    L. L. Bowman Papers
    David Pickering-Judy Falls Collection
    Alfred Boyte Howell Collection
    Titus County tax rolls, 1859, 1866, 1867
Confederate Research Center, Hill College, Hillsboro, Texas
    "Eleventh Texas Cavalry," unpublished manuscript
    "Record of Events for the Eleventh Texas Cavalry, October 1861-February 1864," unpublished manuscript
Regional History Center, Victoria College/University of Houston at Victoria Library, Victoria, Texas
    Barry A. Crouch Collection
    Bernard Weisiger Collection
Greenville W. Walworth Harrison Public Library, Greenville, Texas
    W. Walworth Harrison Collection
    Taylor-Smallwood-Howell Collection
Library of Congress, Manuscript Division, Washington, D.C.
    Zachariah Chandler Papers
    Salmon P. Chase Papers
    U. S. Grant Papers
    Andrew Johnson Papers
    Philip Sheridan Papers
National Archives, Washington, D.C.
    Fifth Military District. Papers, 1867-1870, Record Group 393
    Freedmen's Bureau. Papers, 1865-1870, Record Group 105
    Adjutant General. Papers, 1865-1870, Record Group 94
    General Courts Martial, 1812-1938, Record Group 153. From the office of the Judge Advocate General
    "Texas Narratives." In *A Folk History of Slavery in the United States from Interviews with Former Slaves*, manuscript copy. Washington: Works Progress Administration, 1941.
    Service Records, Union and Confederate
Texas State Library, Austin, Texas
    Adjutant General Office. Papers, Record Group 401
    "Bickerstaff, Ben." Vertical File
    Confederate Muster Rolls, Eleventh Texas Cavalry, 1861
    Edmund J. Davis. Governor's Papers, Record Group 301

Andrew Jackson Hamilton. Governor's Papers, Record Group 301
Pendleton Murrah. Governor's Papers, Record Group 301
Elisha M. Pease. Governor's Papers, Record Group 301
Secretary of State. Papers, Record Group 94
James W. Throckmorton. Governor's Papers, Record Group 301
Texas Tech Southwest Collection, Lubbock, Texas
    Rister, Carl Coke. Rister Papers
University of Texas Library, Center for American History, Austin, Texas
    Ashbel Smith Papers

B. Printed Government Documents

Gammel, H. P. Comp. *The Laws of Texas*. 10 vols. Austin: Gammel Book Company, 1898.
Pease, Elisha M. *Message of His Excellency Elisha M. Pease, Governor of Texas to the Constitutional Convention, June 3, 1868*. Austin: Austin Daily Republican, 1868.
Reconstruction Convention of Texas. *Journal of the Reconstruction Convention, 1868-1869*. 2 vols. Austin: n.p., 1870.
Reconstruction Convention of Texas. *Report of the Special Committee on Lawlessness and Violence in Texas*. Austin: n.p., 1868.
Steele, William. *A List of Fugitives from Justice* [in Texas]. Austin: Adjutant General's Office, 1878.
Texas (State of). *Communication from Governor Pease of Texas, Relative to the Troubles in that State*. Washington, D.C.: Government Printing Office, 1868.
Texas Legislature. *Special Laws of the Twelfth Legislature of the State of Texas*. Austin: Twelfth Legislature, 1868-1869.
_____. Senate. *Resolutions of the State of Texas Concerning Peace, Reconstruction and Independence*. Richmond: N.p., 1865.
United States Army, Department of the Gulf. *Report of Operations and General Information on the Condition of Affairs in the Military Div. Of the Southwest and Gulf and Department of the Gulf from May 29, 1865 to November 4, 1866*. New Orleans: n.p., 1867.
Untied States Department of War. *War of the Rebellion: A Compilation of the Official Records of the Union and Confederate Armies*. 128 vols. Washington: Government Printing Office, 1880-1901.
United States House of Representatives. "Conditions of Affairs in Texas." *House Executive Documents, Doc. no. 61*, 39 Cong. 2nd sess. Washington: Government Printing Office, 1866.
_____. *Winfield S. Hancock's Defiance of the Reconstruction Acts: Record from Official Sources Of Hancock's Administration of Civil Affairs in 1867-1868 in Louisiana and Texas: Its Character and Results*. Washington, D.C.: Government Printing Office, 1868.

C. Published Autobiographies, Memoirs, Recollections, and other Documents

Conine, Will. *The Memoirs of Will Conine* [from the] *1860s to 1890s*. Ed. Sharon E. Whitney. Waco: Texian Press, 1999.
Crouch, Barry A. Ed. "View From Within: Letters of Gregory Barrett." *Chronicles of Smith County, Texas* 12 (Winter 1973), 13-28.

Ellis, John M. II. *The Way It was: A Personal Memoir of Family Life in East Texas.* Waco: Texian Press, 1965.
Gillett, James B. *Fugitive Justice: The Notebook of Texas Ranger Sergeant James B. Gillett.* Austin: State House Press, 1997.
McLean, John H. *Reminiscences of Rev. Jno. H. McLean, D. D.* Ed. John H. McLean, Jr. Dallas: Smith and Lamar, n.d. 1983.
Oldham, Williamson Simpson. *Speech of Hon. W. S. Oldham, of Texas, on the Resolutions of the State of Texas, Concerning Peace, Reconstruction and Independence.* Richmond: N.p., 1865.
Roose, Rita B. And Jeanette B. Bland. *Records of Reconstruction Days in Collin County, Texas.* N.p.: Spring Hill Press, 1981.
Sifakis, Stewart. *Compendium of the Confederate Armies: Texas.* New York: Facts on File, 1995.
Stone, Kate. *Brokenburn—The Journal of Kate Stone, 1861-1868.* Ed. John Q. Anderson. Baton Rouge: Louisiana State University Press, 1955.
Wood, William D. *Reminiscences of Reconstruction in Texas, and Reminiscences of Texas and Texans Fifty Years Ago.* N.p.: Privately printed, 1902.

D. Newspapers

Austin Daily Republican. 1868-1869.
Austin Weekly Republican. 1869.
Clarksville Northern Standard. 1847, 1860, 1865.
Clarksville Standard. 1868-1869.
Cleburne Chronicle. 1869.
Cleburne Eagle-News. 1988.
Cleburne Times-Review & Democrat. 2002.
Commerce Journal. 1982.
Corsicana Navarro Express. 1860, 1867-1869.
Dallas Herald. 1863, 1868-1869.
Dallas Morning News. 1986.
Fayetteville Arkansas Observer. 1863.
Flake's Daily Bulletin. 1865-1870.
Flakes Semi-Weekly Bulletin. 1867.
Fort Smith Arkansas New Era. 1869.
Galveston Daily News. 1865, 1868-1869.
Galveston Weekly News. 1860.
Greenville Banner. 1911.
Harrison Flag. 1865-1869.
Houston Telegraph. 1860, 1868-1869.
Houston Tri-Weekly Telegraph. 1865.
McKinney Weekly Express. 1869.
Marshall Texas Republican. 1860, 1867-1869.
Montgomery Alabama State Journal. 1869.
New Orleans Tribune. 1866.
New York Daily Tribune. 1868.
New York Times. 1865-1866, 1868-1869.
Paris Vindicator. 1867-1868.
San Antonio Express. 1865-1869.

Texas State Gazette. 1860.
Traveling Historic Texas. 1992.
Tyler Reporter. 1860.
Waco Semi-Weekly Register. 1870.
Waxahachie Argus. 1869.

E. United States Censuses

1840-1860, manuscript returns
    Hunt County, Texas
    Jackson County, Alabama
    Monroe County, Mississippi
    Morgan County, Illinois
    Titus County, Texas
    Sebastian County, Arkansas

II. Secondary Sources

A. Books

Barr, C. Alwyn. *Black Texans—A History of Negroes in Texas, 1528-1971.* Austin: Jenkins Publishing Company, 1973.
Bartholomew. *Cullen Baker: Premier Texas Gunfighter.* Houston: Frontier Press, 1954.
Baum, Dale. *The Shattering of Texas Unionism: Politics in the Lone Star State During the Civil War Era.* Baton Rouge: Louisiana State University Press, 1998.
Beringer, Richard E., et al. *Why the South Lost the Civil War.* Athens: University of Georgia Press, 1986.
Betts, Vicki. *Smith County, Texas, in the Civil War.* Tyler: Smith County Historical Society, 1978.
Blight, David W. *Race and Reunion: The Civil War in American Memory.* Cambridge: Harvard University Press, 2001.
Bowman, Bob and Doris Bowman. *Historic Murders in Texas: Book 3.* Lufkin: Best of East Texas, 2006.
Bradbury, Mollie Gallop, et al. *The History of Johnson County, Texas.* Dallas: Curtis Media Corporation, 1985.
Buenger, Walter L. *Secession and the Union in Texas.* Austin: University of Texas Press, 1984.
Buenger, Walter L. and Robert Calvert. Eds. *Texas Through Time: Evolving Interpretations.* College Station: Texas A & M University Press, 1991.
Bullard, Lucille B. *Marion County, Texas, 1860-1870.* Jefferson: privately printed, 1965.
Campbell, Randolph. *Gone to Texas: A History of the Lone Star State.* New York: Oxford University Press, 2003.
_____. *Grass Roots Reconstruction in Texas, 1865-1868.* Baton Rouge: Louisiana State University Press, 1997.
_____. *A Southern Community in Crisis: Harrison County, Texas, 1850-1880.* Austin: Texas State Historical Association, 1983.
Carroll, John M. Ed. *Custer in Texas: An Uninterrupted Narrative.* New York: Sol Lewis/Liveright, 1975.
Carter, William G. *Life of General Chaffee.* Chicago: University of Chicago Press, 1917.

Chumbley, Joe W. *Kentucky-Town and Its Baptist Church*. Houston: D. Armstrong, 1975.
Crouch, Barry A. *The Dance of Freedom: Texas African Americans During Reconstruction*. Ed. Larry Madaras. Austin: University of Texas Press, 2007.
_____. *The Freedmen's Bureau and Blacks in Texas*. Austin: University of Texas Press, 1992.
Crouch, Barry A. and Donaly Brice. *Cullen Montgomery Baker: Reconstruction Desperado*. Baton Rouge: Louisiana State University Press, 1997.
Cummins, Light T., and Alvin R. Bailey. Eds. *A Guide to Texas History*. Westport: Greenwood Press, 1988.
Current, Richard B. *Those Terrible Carpetbaggers*. New York: Oxford University Press, 1988.
Davis, Susan L. *The Authentic History: Ku Klux Klan, 1865-1877*. New York: privately printed, 1924.
DeShields, James T. *They Sat in High Places: The Presidents and Governors of Texas*. San Antonio: Naylor, 1940.
Dunning, William A. *Reconstruction, Political and Economic, 1865-1877*. New York: Harper Brothers, 1907.
Eason, Al. *Cullen Baker: Purveyor of Death, and Other Stories*. Overton, Tx.: privately printed, 1981.
Elliot, Claude. *Leathercoat: The Life History of a Texas Patriot*. San Antonio: Standard Printing Company, 1938.
Evans, Clement A., ed. *Louisiana and Arkansas in Confederate Military History*. 10 vols. Reprint; Seccaucus: Blue and Gray Press, 1988.
Evans, Marvin D. Comp. *The Orrs of Miller County, Arkansas*. Fort Worth: privately printed,1951.
Fisher, William H. *The Invisible Empire: A Bibliography of the Ku Klux Klan*. Metuchen and London: Scarecrow Press, 1980.
Foner, Eric. *Reconstruction: America's Unfinished Revolution, 1863-1877*. New York: HarperCollins Publisher, 1988.
Gallagher, Gary W. and Alan T. Nolan, Eds. *The Myth of the Lost Cause and Civil War History*. Bloomington: Indiana University Press, 2001.
Glover, Robert, and Linda Cross, eds. *Tyler and Smith County, Texas: An Historical Survey*. Tyler: American Bicentennial Committee of Tyler-Smith County: 1976.
Harrison, W. Walworth. *History of Greenville and Hunt County, Texas*. Waco: Texian Press, 1976.
Hawkins, David, with others. *The History of Ellis County, Texas*. Waco: Texian Press, 1972.
Hendrickson, Kenneth, E. *The Chief Executives of Texas: From Stephen F. Austin to John B. Connally, Jr*. College Station: Texas A&M University Press, 1995.
Howell, Kenneth Wayne. *An Antebellum History of Henderson County, Texas, 1846-1861*. Austin: Eakin Press, 1999.
Klotter, James C. Ed. *The Human Condition in the Old South*. Wilmington: Scholarly Resources, Inc., 2003.
Levine, Bruce. *Half Slave, Half Free: The Roots of the Civil War*. New York: Hill and Wang, 1992.
Litwack, Leon F. *Been in the Storm So Long: The Aftermath of Slavery*. New York: Knopf, 1979.
Lucas, Mattie Davis and Mita Holsapple Hall. *A History of Grayson County, Texas*. Sherman: Scruggs Printing Company, 1936.

McCaffrey, James M. *This Band of Brothers: Cranbury's Texas Brigade, CSA*. Austin: Eakin Press, 1985.
McCaslin, Richard. *Tainted Breeze: The Great Hanging in Gainesville, Texas, 1862*. Baton Rouge: Louisiana State University Press, 1994.
McPherson, James. *Battle Cry of Freedom: The Civil War Era*. New York: Oxford University Press, 1988.
Mack, H. C. *Texas: Information for Emigrants*. Franklin, Tennessee: Haynes & Figures Publishers, 1869.
Marten, James. *Texas Divided: Loyalty and Dissent in the Lone Star State, 1856-1874*. Lexington: University of Kentucky Press, 1990.
A Memorial and Biographical History of Johnson and Hill Counties, Texas: Containing the Early History of This Important Section of the Great State of Texas, Together with Glimpses of Its Future Prospects, also Biographical Mention of Many Pioneers and Prominent Citizens of the Present Time, and Full-Page Portraits of Some of the Most Eminent Men of This Section [no author listed]. Chicago: Lewis Publishing Company, 1892.
Monahan, Jay. *Civil War on the Western Border, 1854-1865*. New York: Bonanza Books, 1955.
Moneyhon, Carl H. *Republicanism in Reconstruction Texas*. Austin: University of Texas Press, 1980.
_____. *Texas After the Civil War: The Struggle of Reconstruction*. College Station: Texas A&M Press, 2004.
Nash, Jay Robert. Ed. *Encyclopedia of Western Gunmen and Outlaws*. New York: Da Capo Press, 1994.
Nunn, W. C. *Escape From Reconstruction*. Fort Worth: Texas Christian University Press, 1956.
_____. *Texas Under the Carpetbaggers*. Austin: University of Texas Press, 1962.
O'Neal, Bill. *Encyclopedia of Western Gunfighters*. Norman: University of Oklahoma Press, 1979.
Orr, Thomas. *Life of the Notorious Desperado Cullen Baker, from his Childhood to his Death, with a Full Account of all the Murders He Committed*. Little Rock: Price and Barton, 1870.
Perman, Michael. *Reunion Without Compromise: The South and Reconstruction, 1865-1868*. Cambridge: University Press, 1973.
_____. *The Road to Redemption: Southern Politics, 1869-1879*. Chapel Hill: University of North Carolina Press, 1984.
Phelan, Marcus. *A History of the Expansion of Methodism in Texas, 1867-1902: Being a Continuation of the History of Early Methodism in Texas*. Dallas: Mathis, Van Nort and Company, 1937.
Pickering, David and Judy Falls. *Brush Men & Vigilantes: Civil War Dissent in Texas*. College Station: Texas A&M University Press, 2000.
Potter, David M. *The Division and Stress of Reunion, 1845-1876*. Glenview, Ill.: Scott, Foresman, 1973.
_____. *The Impending Crisis, 1846-1861*. Completed and edited by Don E. Fehrenbacker. New York: Harper & Row, 1976.
Rable, George C. *But There was no Peace: The Rise of Violence in the Politics of Reconstruction*. Athens: University of Georgia Press, 1984.
Ramsdell, Charles W. *Reconstruction in Texas*. New York: Columbia University Press, 1910.
Ray, Gladys. *Murder at the Corners*. San Antonio: Naylor, 1957.

Reynolds, Donald. *Editors Make War: Southern Newspapers in the Secession Crisis.* Nashville: Vanderbilt University Press, 1970.
Richardson, Thomas C. *East Texas: Its History and Its Makers.* 4 vols. New York: Lewis Historical Publishing, 1940.
Richter, William L. *ABC-Clio Companion to American Reconstruction, 1862-1877.* Santa Barbara: ABC-Clio, 1996.
_____. *The Army in Texas During Reconstruction.* College Station: Texas A&M Press, 1987.
_____. *Overreached on All Sides: The Freedmen's Bureau Administrators in Texas, 1865-1868.* College Station: Texas A&M Press, 1991.
Russell, Traylor. *Carpetbaggers, Scalawag & Others.* Waco: Texian Press, 1973.
_____. *The History of Titus County.* 2 vols. Waco: Morrison, 1965.
_____. *Pioneers and Heroes of Titus County.* Waco: Library Binding Company, 1974.
Russell, Traylor and Robert T. Russell. *Some Die Twice.* Waco: Texian Press, 1979.
Sayles, John. *The Constitutions of the State of Texas.* St. Paul: West Publishing, 1872.
Schroeder-Lein, Glena R., and Richard Zuczek. *Andrew Johnson: A Biographical Companion.* Santa Barbara: ABC-CLIO, 2001.
Sefton, James E. *The United States Army During Reconstruction, 1865-1877.* Baton Rouge: Louisiana State University Press, 1967.
Sitton, Thad, and James H. Conrad. *Freedom Colonies: Independent Black Texans in the Time of Jim Crow.* Austin: University of Texas Press, 2005.
Smallwood, James M. *Born in Dixie: The History of Smith County, Texas.* 2 vols. Austin: Eakin Press, 1999.
_____. *Time of Hope, Time of Despair: Black Texans During Reconstruction.* New York and London: Kennikat Press, 1981.
Smallwood, James M., Barry A Crouch, and Larry Peacock. *Murder and Mayhem: The War of Reconstruction in Texas.* College Station: Texas A&M Press, 2003.
Sonnichsen, C. L. *I'll Die before I'll Run: The Story of the Great Feuds of Texas.* New York: Harper & Brothers, 1951.
Stambaugh, Lee and Lillian J. Stambaugh. *A History of Collin County* [Texas]. Austin: Texas State Historical Association, 1958.
Stampp, Kenneth M. Ed. *The Causes of the Civil War.* 3rd Ed. New York: Simon & Schuster, 1991.
Stampp, Kenneth M. *The Era of Reconstruction, 1865-1877.* New York: Knopf: 1965.
Stampp, Kenneth M. and Leon Litwack. Eds. *Reconstruction: An Anthology of Revisionist Writings.* Baton Rouge: Louisiana State University Press, 1969.
St. Clair, Gladys. *A History of Hopkins County.* Waco: Texian Press, 1965.
Stephens, Ray A. and William H. Holmes. *Historical Atlas of Texas.* Norman: University of Oklahoma Press, 1989.
Teel, Robert W. *Cullen Montgomery Baker: Champion of the Lost Cause.* Huntsville, Alabama: privately printed, 1995.
Trelease, Allen. *White Terror: The Ku Klux Klan Conspiracy and Southern Reconstruction.* New York: Harper and Row, 1971.
Tuck, June E. *Civil War Shadows in Hopkins County* [Texas]. Sulphur Springs: Wadsworth Publishing Company, 1993.
Vestal, Yvonne. *The Borderlands and Cullen Baker.* Atlanta, Texas: privately printed, 1978.
Wallace, Ernest. *Charles DeMorse, Pioneer, Statesman, and Father of Texas Journalism.* Reprint. Paris, Texas: Wright Press, 1985.
_____. *Texas in Turmoil: The Saga of Texas, 1849-1875.* Austin: Steck-Vaughn, 1965.

Waller, John L. *Colossal Hamilton of Texas.* El Paso: Texas Western Press, 1968.
Warner, Ezra J. *Generals in Blue.* Baton Rouge: Louisiana State University Press, 1964.
Williams, Patrick G. *Beyond Redemption: Texas Democrats after Reconstruction.* College Station: Texas A&M University Press, 2007.
Wilson, Theodore B. *The Black Codes of the South.* Tuscaloosa: University of Alabama Press, 1965.
Wyatt-Brown, Bertram. *Southern Honor, Ethics and Behavior in the Old South.* New York: Oxford University Press, 1982.

B. Articles and Book Chapters

Acosta, Teresa Palomo. "Juneteenth." *New Handbook of Texas,* 3, 1019-1020.
Anderson. H. Allen. "Adna Romanza Chaffee." *New Handbook of Texas,* 2, 24-25.
Ashcroft, Alan C. "Texas in Defeat: The Early Phase of A. J. Hamilton's Provisional Governorship, June 17, 1865, to February 7, 1866." *Texas Military History* 8 (1970), 123-134.
Atkins, Mark Howard. "Marion County, Texas." *New Handbook of Texas,* 4, 511-512.
Baggett, James Alex. "Birth of the Texas Republican Party," *Southwestern Historical Quarterly* 79 (July 1974), 1-20.
_____. "Gordon Granger." *New Handbook of Texas,* 3, 280.
_____. "Origins of the East Texas Republican Party Leadership." *Journal of Southern History* 40 (August 1974), 441-450.
Baker, T. Lindsay. "Ben Bickerstaff Dead or Alive." *Cleburne Eagle-News,* November 3, 1988.
_____. "The First Juneteenth." *Traveling Historic Texas* (1992), 3.
Baum, Dale. "Chicanery and Intimidation in the 1869 Texas Gubernatorial Race." *Southwestern Historical Quarterly* 97 (July 1993), 37-54.
Biffle, Kent. "Bitter Northeast Texas Feud Dogged Rebel to his Grave." *Dallas Morning News.* August 17, 1986.
Bowman, Bob and Doris Bowman. "A Rebel's Rebellion, 1865." In Bob and Doris Bowman, *Historic Murders of East Texas, Book 3.* Lufkin: Best of East Texas, 2006.
_____. "Two Murders in Jefferson: 1868, 1869." In Bob and Doris Bowman, *Historic Murders of East Texas, Book 3.* Lufkin: Best of East Texas, 2006.
Buenger, Walter L. "Secession." *New Handbook of Texas,* 5, 957-958.
_____. "Secession Revisited: The Texas Experience." *Civil War History* 30 (December 1984), 293-305.
Buenger, Walter L. and Alex Baggett, "Constitutional Union Party." *New Handbook of Texas,* 2, 286-287.
Campbell, Randolph B. "Antebellum Texas: From Union to Disunion, 1846-1861." In Light T. Cummins and Alvin R. Bailey. Eds. *A Guide to the History of Texas.* Westport: Greenwood Press, 1988.
_____."Carpetbagger Rule in Reconstruction Texas, An Enduring Myth." *Southwestern Historical Quarterly* 97 (1994), 587-596.
_____. "George W. Whitmore: East Texas Unionist." *East Texas Historical Journal* 28 (1990), 17-28.
_____. "Grass Roots Reconstruction: The Personnel of County Governments in Texas, 1865-1876." *Journal of Southern History* 58 (February 1992), 99-116.
_____. "Grass Roots Reconstruction: The Personnel of County Governments in Texas, 1865-1876." *Legacies: A History Journal for Dallas and North Central Texas* 5 (1993),

4-12.

_____. "Sam Houston, Unionism, and the Secession Crisis in Texas." In James C. Klotter. Ed. *The Human Condition in the Old South*. Wilmington, Delaware: Scholarly Resources, Inc., 2003.

_____. "Statehood, Civil War, and Reconstruction, 1846-1876." In *Texas Through Time: Evolving Interpretations*. Eds. Walter L. Buenger and Robert A. Calvert. College Station: Texas A & M Press, 1991, 163-196.

Cantrell, Gregg. "Racial Violence and Reconstruction Politics in Texas, 1867-1868." *Southwestern Historical Quarterly* 93 (1990), 333-355.

Carpenter, John A. "Atrocities in the Reconstruction Period." *Journal of Negro History* 47 (1962), 234-247.

Carter, William H. "6th Regiment of Cavalry." In *The Army of the United States*. Washington: Government Printing Office, 1894.

Crouch, Barry A. "'All the Vile Passions': The Texas Black Code of 1866." *Southwestern Historical Quarterly* 97 (1993), 13-34.

_____. "Black Dreams and White Justice [in Texas, 1865-1868]. *Prologue* 6 (1974), 255-265.

_____. "Cullen Montgomery Baker." *Handbook of Texas*, 1, 344.

_____. "The Freedmen's Bureau and the 30th Sub-District of Texas: Smith County and Its Environs During Reconstruction." *Chronicles of Smith County, Texas* 11 (Spring 1972), 15-30.

_____. "A Spirit of Lawlessness: White Violence; Texas Blacks, 1865-1868." *Journal Of Social History* 18 (1984), 217-232.

_____. "'Unmanacling' Texas Reconstruction: A Twenty-Year Perspective." *Southwestern Historical Quarterly* 93 (1989), 275-302.

Dippie, Brian W. "George Armstrong Custer." *New Handbook of Texas*, 2, 284.

Dunn, Roy Sylvan. "The KGC in Texas, 1860-1861." *Southwestern Historical Quarterly* 70 (April 1967), 543-573.

Elliott, Claude. "Constitutional Convention of 1868-1869." *New Handbook of Texas*, 2, 284.

_____. "The Freedmen's Bureau in Texas." *Southwestern Historical Quarterly* 56 (1952), 1-24.

_____. "Union Sentiment in Texas, 1861-1865." *Southwestern Historical Quarterly* 50 (1947), 449-477.

Gartin, R. Scott. "11th Texas Cavalry, Titus County Guards, Company I," Internet: 11texascav.org/regiment/i_co.shtml.

Gerteis, Louis C. "A Border War." *Reviews in American History* 57 (December 1989), 559-565.

Gilbert, Bob and Michelle Gilbert. "Hopkins County." *New Handbook of Texas*, 3, 694-695.

Griffin, Roger A. "Elisha Marshall Pease." *New Handbook of Texas*, 5, 112-113.

Grubbs, V. W. "Hunt County Pioneer: Judge Hardin Hart." *Greenville Banner*, April 12, 1911.

Hale, Douglas. "Rehearsal for Civil War: The Texas Cavalry in the Indian Territory, 1861." *Chronicles of Oklahoma* 68 (Fall 1990), 232-253.

Harper, Cecil, Jr. "Bowie County." *New Handbook of Texas*, 1, 670-673.

_____. "Cass County," *New Handbook of Texas*, 1, 1012-1015.

_____. "Freedmen's Bureau." *New Handbook of Texas*, 2, 1166-1167.

_____. "Grayson County." *New Handbook of Texas*, 3, 298-299.

_____. "Titus County," *New Handbook of Texas*, 6, 507-509.
Harrison, W. Walworth. *A History of Greenville and Hunt County*. Waco: Texian Press, 1976.
Hart, Brian. "Sherman, Texas." *New Handbook of Texas*. Vol. 5, 1021-1023.
Hodge, Floy C. *A History of Fannin County, Featuring Pioneer Families*. Herford: Texas Pioneer Publishers, 1966.
Hornsby, Alton, Jr. "The Freedmen's Bureau Schools in Texas, 1865-1870." *Southwestern Historical Quarterly* 76 (April 1973), 397-417.
Hunter, John W. "The Killing of John Vaden at Fort McKavett." *Frontier Times* 2 (November 1924), 14-18.
Howell, Kenneth Wayne. "When the Rabble Hiss, Well May Patriots Tremble: James Webb Throckmorton and the Secessionist Movement in Texas, 1854-1861." *Southwestern Historical Quarterly* 109 (April 2006), 465-494.
Jackson, Charles C. "Colbert Caldwell." *New Handbook of Texas*, 1, 894.
Jetsel, Pam. "Prominent Pioneer E. M. Heath Dead in 1902." *Cleburne Times-Review & Democrat*, n.d., copy in Taylor-Smallwood-Howell Collection, Archives, Greenville W. Walworth Harrison Public Library, Greenville, Texas.
Jones, Nick. "The Lee-Peacock Feud." *Real West: True Tales from the American Frontier* (January 1979), 8-12.
Jordan, Terry G. "The Imprint of the Upper and Lower South on Mid-Nineteenth-Century Texas." *Annals of the Association of American Geographers*. 57 (December 1967), 680-693.
Kiker, Janice Jernigan. "William Jernigan, Founder of Commerce [Texas]. *Commerce Journal*, October 31, 1982.
Kirby, Mary L. "Upshur County." *New Handbook of Texas*, 6, 664-666.
Kozlowski, Gerald B. "Van Zandt County." *New Handbook of Texas*, 6, 707-710.
Kumler, Donna J. "Grayson County." *New Handbook of Texas*. Vol. 3, 298-299.
Lale, Max. "Stockade Case." *New Handbook of Texas*, 6, 106.
Landrum, Graham and Allan Smith, *Grayson County: An Illustrated History of Grayson County, Texas*. 2d. ed. Fort Worth: Historical Publishers, 1967.
Long, Christopher. "Jefferson, Texas." *New Handbook of Texas*, 3, 924-925.
_____."Ku Klux Klan." *New Handbook of Texas*, 3, 1165-1166.
Lathrop, Barnes F. "Migration into East Texas, 1836-1860." *Southwestern Historical Quarterly* 52 (July 1948), 1-31.
Ledbetter, Billy D. "White Texans' Attitudes toward the Political Equality of Negroes, 1865-1870." *Pylon* 40 (1979), 255-263.
McCaslin, Richard B. "Conditional Confederates: The Eleventh Texas Cavalry West of the Mississippi River." *Military History of the Southwest* 21 (Spring 1991), 91-95.
McKay, S. S. "Constitution of 1869." *New Handbook of Texas*, 2, 289.
McPherson, James M. "Southern Comfort." *New York Times Review of Books* 48 (April 12, 2001), 28, 30-31.
Maher, Edward R. "Sam Houston and Secession." *Southwestern Historical Quarterly* 55 (April 1952), 441-458.
Marten, James. "Andrew Jackson Hamilton." *New Handbook of Texas*, 3, 427-428.
_____. "What is to Become of the Negro? White Reaction to Emancipation in Texas." *Mid-America* 73 (April-July 1991), 115-123.
Minor, David. "Alvarado, Texas." *New Handbook of Texas*, 1, 136.
_____. "Collin County." *New Handbook of Texas*, 2, 214-215.
_____. "James Webb Throckmorton." *New Handbook of Texas*, 6, 485-486.

Moneyhon, Carl. "Black Codes." *New Handbook of Texas*, 1, 562.
_____. "Carpetbaggers." *New Handbook of Texas*, 1, 984.
_____. "Edmund Jackson Davis." *New Handbook of Texas*, 2, 526-527.
_____. "Reconstruction." *New Handbook of Texas* 6, 474-481.
_____. "Union League." *New Handbook of Texas*, 6, 626.
Moore, Richard B. "Radical Reconstruction: The Texas Choice." *East Texas Historical Journal* 16 (Spring 1978), 15-23.
Neal, Diane and Thomas W. Kremm, "'What Shall We Do with the Negroes?': The Freedmen's Bureau in Texas." *East Texas Historical Journal* 27 (1989), 23-33.
Norton, Wesley. "The Methodist Episcopal Church and the Civil Disturbances in North Texas in 1859 and 1860." *Southwestern Historical Quarterly* 68 (January 1965), 317-341.
Oats, Stephen B. "Texas Under the Secessionists." *Southwestern Historical Quarterly* 67 (October 1963), 167-212.
Odintz, Mark. "George Washington Smith." *New Handbook of Texas*, 5, 1098.
Peters, Robert K. "From Wilderness to War." In Robert Glover and Linda Cross, eds., *Tyler and Smith County, Texas: An Historical Survey* (Tyler: American Bicentennial Committee of Tyler-Smith County 1976), 11-32.
Pigott, Kelly. "Fannin County." New Handbook of Texas, 2, 945-946.
Pitre, Merline. "The Evolution of Black Political Participation in Reconstruction Texas." *East Texas Historical Journal* 21 (1988), 36-45.
_____. "George Thompson Ruby." *New Handbook of Texas*, 5, 705-706.
Ramsdell, Charles W. "Presidential Reconstruction in Texas." *Quarterly of the Texas State Historical Association* 11 (April 1908), 288-294.
Reynolds, Donald E. "Smith County and Its Neighbors During the Slave Insurrection Panic of 1860." *Chronicles of Smith County, Texas* 10 (Fall, 1971), 1-8.
Richter, William L. "The Army and the Negro During Reconstruction Texas, 1865-1870." *East Texas Historical Journal* 10 (Spring 1972), 7-13.
_____. "'Devil Take Them All': Military Rule in Texas." *Southern Studies* 25 (April 1986), 5-30.
_____. "'It is best to go in Strong Handed': Army Occupations of Texas, 1865-1866." *Arizona and the West* 27 (Summer 1985), 113-142.
_____. "Oh God, Let Us have Revenge: Ben Griffin and his Family During the Civil War and Reconstruction." *Arkansas Historical Quarterly* 57 (Autumn 1998), 255-286.
_____. "'Outside . . . My Profession': The Army and Civil Affairs in Texas Reconstruction." *Military History of Texas and the Southwest* 9 (1971), 5-21.
_____. "The Revolver Rules the Day: Colonel DeWitt Brown and the Freedmen's Bureau in Paris, Texas." *Southwestern Historical Quarterly* 93 (January 1990), 303-332.
_____. "Spread-Eagle Eccentricities: Military-Civilian Relations in Reconstruction Texas." *Texana* 8 (1970), 311-327.
_____. "Texas Politics and the United States Army, 1866-1867." *Military History of Texas and the Southwest*. 10 (1972), 159-186.
_____. "'This Blood-Thirsty Hole': Opposition to the Freedmen's Bureau in Northeastern Texas, 1867-1868." *Civil War History* 38 (March 1992), 51-77.
_____. "Tyrant and Reformer: General Griffin Reconstructs Texas, 1865-1866." *Prologue: Quarterly of the National Archives* 10 (1978), 225-241.
_____. "'We Must Rubb Out and Begin Anew': The Army and the Republican Party in Texas Reconstruction, 1867-1870." *Civil War History* 19 (1973), 334-352.
_____. "Who was the Real Head of the Texas Freedmen's Bureau: The Role of Brevet

Colonel William H. Sinclair as Acting Assistant Inspector General." *Military History of the Southwest* 20 (Fall 1990), 121-156.

Rister, Carl Coke. "Outlaws and Vigilantes of the Southern Plains, 1865-1885." *Mississippi Valley Historical Review* 19 (March 1933), 537-554.

Russ, William R., Jr. "Radical Disfranchisement in Texas, 1867-1870." *Southwestern Historical Quarterly* 38 (July 1934), 40-52.

Sanders, Justin M. "Anthony Benning Norton." *New Handbook of Texas*, 4, 1049-1050.

Shook, Robert. "Federal Occupation and Administration of Texas, 1865-1870." *Texas Military History* 6 (Spring 1967), 3-45.

_____. "Toward a List of Reconstruction Loyalists." *Southwestern Historical Quarterly* 76 (1973), 315-320.

Smallwood, James M. "Black Education in Reconstruction Texas: The Contributions of the Freedmen's Bureau and Benevolent Societies." *East Texas Historical Journal* 19 (1981), 17-40.

_____. "Black Freedwomen after Emancipation: The Texas Experience." *Prologue: Quarterly of the National Archives* 27 (1995), 303-317.

_____. "Black Texans During Reconstruction: First Freedom." *East Texas Historical Journal* 14 (Spring 1976), 9-23.

_____. "Captain Bob Lee, the Confederacy, Reconstruction, and All That Jazz." *Touchstone* 25 (2006), 91-96.

_____. "Charles E. Culver: A Reconstruction Agent in Texas: The Work of Local Freedmen's Bureau Agents and the Black Community." *Civil War History* 27 (1981), 350-361.

_____. "Disaffection in Confederate Texas: The Great Hanging in Gainesville." *Civil War History* 22 (December 1976), 22 (December 1976), 349-360.

_____. "Early 'Freedom Schools': Black Self-Help and Education in Reconstruction Texas: A Case Study." *Negro History Bulletin* 41 (1978), 790-793.

_____. "The Freedmen's Bureau Reconsidered: Local Agents and the Black Community." *Texana* 11 (1973), 309-320.

_____. "G. T. Ruby: Galveston's Black Carpetbagger in Reconstruction." *Houston Review* 6 (Winter 1983), 24-33.

_____. "Perpetuation of Caste: Black Agricultural Workers in Reconstruction Texas." *Mid-America* 61 (1979), 5-23.

_____. "The Predominate Cause of the Civil War Reconsidered: A Retrospective Essay." *Lincoln Herald* 89 (Winter 1987), 152-160.

_____. "Slave Insurrections." *New Handbook of Texas*, 5, 1080-1081.

_____. "Swamp Fox of the Sulphur: Cullen Baker." *True West* 38 (October 1991), Pt. 1: 20-23, (November 1991), Pt. 2: 38-41.

_____. "When the Klan Rode: White Terror in Reconstruction Texas." *Journal of the West* 25 (October 1986), 4-13.

Sneed, Edgar P. "A Historiography of Reconstruction Texas." *Southwestern Historical Quarterly* 72 (1969), 435-448.

Smyrl, Frank. "Unionism in Texas, 1856-1860." *Southwestern Historical Quarterly* 65 (October 61), 172-190.

Sumers, Dale A. "James P. Newcomb: The Making of a Radical." *Southwestern Historical Quarterly* 72 (April 1969), 449-469.

Sutherland. Daniel E. "Guerrillas: The Real War in Arkansas." *Arkansas Historical Quarterly* 52 (Autumn 1993), 257-285.

Taylor, Ulvan T. "Ben Bickerstaff, the Noted Desperado," *Frontier Times* (October 1924),

9-10.

_____. "Bill Langley and his Wild Career." *Frontier Times* 3 (June 1926), 15-17.

_____. "The Lee-Peacock Feud." *Frontier Times* 3 (May 1926), 1-5.

Wallace, Ernest. "Charles DeMorse." *New Handbook of Texas*, 2, 591-592.

Wood, W. D. "The Ku Klux Klan." *Quarterly of the Texas State Historical Association* 9 (1905-1906), 262-268.

Woods, Randall B. "George T. Ruby: A Black Militant in the White Business Community." *Red River Valley Historical Review* 1 (Autumn 1974), 269-280.

Wooster, Ralph A. "Civil War." *New Handbook of Texas*, 2, 121-126.

C. Theses and Dissertations

Albrecht, Winnell. "The Black Codes in Texas." M.A. thesis, Southwest Texas State University, 1969.

Baenziger, Ann Patton (Malone). "Bold Beginnings: The Radical Program in Texas, 1870-1873." M.A. thesis, Southwest Texas State University, 1970.

Baggett, James Alex. "The Rise and Fall of the Texas Radicals, 1867-1883. Ph.D. diss., North Texas State University, 1972.

Bain, Kenneth Ray. "The Changing Basis of the Republican Party, 1865-1877." M. A. thesis, North Texas State University, 1970.

Barnhill, Barbara Clayton. "The Lone Star Conspiracy: Racial Violence and the Ku Klux Klan Terror in Post-Civil War Texas." M.A. thesis, Oklahoma State University, 1979.

Carrier, John Pressley. "A Political History of Texas During the Reconstruction, 1865-1874." Ph. D. diss., Vanderbilt University, 1971.

Conner, Ben C. "The Rise and Decline of Jefferson, Texas." M.A. thesis, North Texas State University, 1965.

Gray, Ronald N. "Edmund J. Davis: Radical Republican and Governor of Reconstruction Texas." Ph.D. diss., Texas Tech University, 1976.

Griffin, Roger A. "Connecticut Yankee in Texas: A Biography of Elisha Marshall Pease." Ph.D. diss., University of Texas, 1973.

Howell, Kenneth Wayne. "An Antebellum History of Henderson County, Texas, 1846-1861." M. A. thesis, University of Texas A & M—Commerce, 1998.

_____. "James Webb Throckmorton." Ph.D. diss., Texas A & M University, 2005.

Keener, Charles V. "Racial Turmoil in Texas, 1865-1874." M.A. thesis, North Texas State University, 1971.

Kosary, Rebecca A. "Regression to Barbarism in Reconstruction Texas: An Analysis of White Violence against African-Americans from the Texas Freedmen's Bureau Records, 1865-1868." M. A. thesis, Southwest Texas State University, 1999.

Kremm, Thomas W. "Race Relations in Texas, 1865 to 1870." M.A. thesis, University of Houston, 1970.

Orren, G. G. "The History of Hopkins County." M.A. thesis, East Texas State Teachers College, 1938.

Owens, Nora Estelle. "Presidential Reconstruction in Texas: A Case Study." Ph. D. diss., Auburn University, 1983.

Russell. Norman C. "The History of Titus County Since 1860." M.A. thesis, East Texas State University, 1937.

Sandlin, Betty Jeffus. "The Texas Reconstruction Constitutional Convention of 1868-1869." Ph.D. diss., Texas Tech University, 1970.

Shook, Robert. "Federal Occupation and Administration of Texas, 1865-1870." Ph.D. diss., North Texas State University, 1970.
Smallwood, James M. "Black Texans During Reconstruction, 1865-1874." Ph.D. diss., Texas Tech University, 1974.

D. Miscellaneous secondary sources

Confederate Veteran. September, 1911.
Farmer, Randolph W. "Ben Bickerstaff: An Apostle of Racial Hatred and Genocide in North Texas, 1865-1869." Copy in Taylor-Smallwood-Howell Collection. Greenville W. Walworth Harrison Public Library.
Smallwood, James M. "In the Eyes of Freedmen: Reconstruction in Texas." Paper presented to the Texas State Historical Association, 2003. Copy in Taylor-Smallwood-Howell Collection. Greenville W. Walworth Harrison Public Library.
Taylor, Carol. "Ben Bickerstaff." Paper presented to the East Texas Historical Association, September, 2005. Copy in Taylor-Smallwood-Howell Collection. Greenville W. Walworth Harrison Public Library.

INDEX

Abolitionists, 22-23, 48
"Address to the People of Texas," Unionist document, 1861, 26
African American soldiers and troops, 33-34
African Americans, 33-34, 64, 70, 76, 114 (also see blacks, freedmen, freed women, freedpeople, Negroes)
Alabama, 19, 46
Alexandria, Louisiana, 57
Alvarado, Texas, 9-10, 135-136, 141-143, 146-152, 154, 158
American Missionary Association, 54
Amnesty Proclamation of 1865, 49
Amnesty Proclamation of 1872, 78
Amory, Mississippi, 19
Anderson, J. B., 40
Anderson, Wade, 56
Andersonville, Georgia, 33
Andersonville, Georgia, prisoner-of-war camp, 33
Antietam, battle of, 95
Appomattox Courthouse (Virginia), 12
Aquilla Creek, 154
Arkansas, 27-29, 34, 36-38, 42-43, 78, 86, 132, 137, 142, 153
Arkansas Militia, 38
Arkansas Post, 137
Armstrong, M. L., 74, 79, 81-82, 103
Army of Tennessee, 43
Arson-insurrection panic of 1860, in Texas, 22
Aston's Furnace, 138
Atlanta, Texas, 121
Austin Southern Intelligenser (Texas), 136
Austin, Texas, 13-14, 26, 48, 51, 53, 74, 89, 135-136, 153, 157

Babb, James, 111
Baker, Cullen Montgomery, 7, 18, 35-38, 41-42, 44, 47-48, 50-51, 54-55, 58, 60-62, 67-69, 74, 78, 83-90, 92, 95-98, 103–105, 112-115, 121-125, 127-128, 130-135, 139, 144, 153-154, 157, 160
Baker, Elizabeth, 35
Baker, John, 35
Baker, Martha Foster, 132
Balch Cemetery (Alvarado), 150-151
Baltimore, Maryland, 24
Barnes, A. J., 149, 152
Barnes, Lee, 134
Barron, George W., 47
Bateman, William "Wild Bill," 56

Battle of Bentonville (Arkansas), 29
Battle of Caving Banks (Indian Territory), 27
Battle of Chickamauga (Tennessee), 13, 31
Battle of Chustenahalh (Indian Territory), 43
Battle of Chusto-Talasah (Indian Territory), 27
Battle Creek, Indian Territory, 28
Battle of Franklin (Tennessee), 43, 137
Battle of Fredericksburg (Virginia), 95
Battle of Gettysburg (Pennsylvania), 95
Battle of Iuka (Mississippi), 43
Battle of Missionary Ridge (Tennessee), 32-33
Battle of Pea Ridge (Arkansas), 29, 36, 43
Battle of Murfreesboro (Tennessee), 29-30
Battle of Nashville (Tennessee), 43, 137
Battle of Perryville (Kentucky), 29
Battle of Richmond (Kentucky), 29
Battle of Round Mountain (Indian Territory), 27
Battle of Wilson's Creek (Missouri), 13, 36
Bauble Church, 154
Beard, William, 155-156
Belknap, Texas, 22
Bell, Jack, 67
Bell, John, 25
Bentonville, battle of, 29
Bickerstaff, Amanda, 19, 39
Bickerstaff, Benjamin F.: acquiring land, 23; birth of, 19; in the Civil War, 27-34, 43-44, 55, Confederate Military Service Record, 34; as a Civil War criminal, 30-31, 55,; death of, 9-10, 147-152; early life of, 21-22; education of, 22; founds a Klan-like terrorist organization, 62; hideout of, 44; leader of guerrillas, 7, 16, 18; parents of, 19; portrait of, 4; and slave patrols, 23; 15, 20, 24-26, 35-41, 44, 46, 48, 50-51, 54, 56, 58-59, 62, 64-71, 73-75, 79-116, 118-131, 135-154, 157-160
Bickerstaff, Francis Mayfield, 19, 21, 124, 126, 159
Bickerstaff, James B. "Black" 19, 23-29, 39, 46-47, 107
Bickerstaff, Seaborne, 19-22-26, 107, 120, 124, 126, 159
Big Creek Thicket, 46
Big Cypress River, 127
Big Thicket, 46
Bird Creek, Indian Territory, 27

Black Cat Thicket, 46
Black Codes, 16, 52, 57-58, 66
Black community, 53-54, 59, 78, 114, 131
    (also see freedmen, freedwomen,
    freedpeople, Negroes, blacks; African
    Americans)
Black Jack Grove, 22, 46, 69
Black militia (in Hopkins County, Texas),
    64
Black schools, 53-54
Blacks, 16-17, 23, 43-44, 57-59, 62, 64, 67,
    71, 75-77, 80, 84, 98, 102-103, 105,
    107, 112-114,122, 125, 127, 129,
    140, 143, 145-146, 157, 161 (also see
    freedmen, freedwomen, freedpeople,
    Negroes, African Americans)
Bloomberg, Texas, 132
Bluebellies, 126
Bluecoats, 89-90, 93, 100, 119
Boardman (first name unknown), 75
Boggy River, 155
Bois D'arc Creek, 58, 74, 83, 87
Bondsmen, 22, 35, 48 (also see slaves;
    chattels)
Bonham, Texas, 44, 67, 155
Booth, John Wilkes, 15
Boren, Henry, 156-157
Boston (Texas) Road, 84
Boston, Texas, 17, 60, 67
Bounty hunters, 156
Bourland, James, 40
Bowie County, Texas, 27, 49, 59, 64, 67-
    68, 114, 124
Bowman, Bob, 33
Bowman brothers, 75, 82, 89, 122
Bowman, Doris, 33
Bowman, G. G., 75, 120
Bowman, Porter, 119
Bowman, Taylor, 119-120
Bowman, William, 75, 120
Branch, George, 82, 89, 120
Brazil, haven for post-Civil War
    Southerners,15; slavery in, 15
Brazos River, 146
Breckenridge, John C., 24-25
Brigands, 97, 148
Brigham, Jim, 79
Bristol, Texas, 140
Brockville, Texas, 140
Brown, DeWitt, 60, 71, 74, 79, 83, 87,
    102-103, 114
Brown, John, 22
Brownsville, Texas, 50
Brunch, first name unknown, 130
Bunton, Peter, 75
Burks, John C., 30
Burns, James, 125, 128-129

Caddo Indians, 21
Caldwell, Colbert, 51, 78

Caldwell County, Texas, 121
California, 52
Campbell, Charles, 156-157
Camp Chase (Illinois), 137, 146
Camp Reeves (Texas), 26
Canby, E. R. S., 141
Caney Creek, 94
Canton, Texas, 17, 86, 138-139
Carpenter, first name unknown, 125
Carribean Islands, 62
Carruthers, Henry, 75
Cason, U. J., 69
Cass County, Texas, 35, 60, 64, 132
Cass, William, 38
Cathey, William 135-137, 141, 145-147,
    152, 157-159
Caving Banks, battle of, 27
Cleburne Chronicle (Texas), 146
Cleburne, Texas, 145-147, 159
Central America, 62
Certificate of Protection, 102-103
Chaffee, Adna, 95-97, 104, 106, 115-116,
    118-120, 122, 131, 146, 148
Chaffee's Guerrillas, 104, 115
Chance, D., 128-129
Charleston, South Carolina, 24, 56
Chattels, 24 (also see bondsmen, slaves)
Cheatam's Ferry, 127-128
Cherokee removals, 46
Cherokee Trail, 21
Chicago, Illinois, 60
Chickamauga, battle of, 13, 31
Choctaw Bottoms, 46
Choctaw Nation, 103
Chustenahalh, battle of, 43
Chusto-Talasah, battle of, 27
Cincinnati Commercial, 17
Civil Rights Movement, 18, 162
Civil War, 91, 95, 97, 100, 104, 108, 137
Civil War, second phase of, 18 (also see War
    of Reconstruction; Second Civil War);
    slavery as the cause of, 17; chaos in
    aftermath of, 12-13; 7, 15, 17, 21, 23,
    26-36
Clark, A. M., 33
Clarksville, Texas, 39, 66, 71, 73, 84-86,
    88, 97
Clarksville Standard, 88
Clarksville, Texas, Cemetery, 85
Coffeeville, Texas, 127
Coker, Thomas, 111
Colby, John, 159
Collier, John C., 142
Collin County, Texas, 11, 56, 64, 95,139
Colored People, 71 (also see blacks;
    freedmen; freedpeople; freedwomen;
    African Americans)
Comanche Peak, Texas, 135
Comanches, 95
Commerce, Texas, 45

Como, Texas, 32
Confederacy, the, and Confederates, 15, 18, 21, 26-29, 32-34, 36, 48-52, 57, 65-66, 69, 73, 98 126, 137, 140-143, 146, 156, 161
Confederate Army, 27, 29, 32, 34, 36, 57, 98, 137
Confederate Conscription Act, 137
Confederate Trans-Mississippi Department, 39
Congress, of the United States, 18, 48-50, 53, 78
Congressional Reconstruction, 72, 86
Constitution, of the United States, 24, 103, 137
Constitutional Convention, of 1866, 53
Contract Labor Code, 57-58
Convict Lease Code, 58
Cooke County, Texas, 40
Cooper, Douglas C., 27, 46
Cooper, first name unknown, 137
Corinth, Mississippi, 29
Corsicana, Texas, 75, 131, 141, 146
Cotton Gin Port, Mississippi, 19
Cotton Hotel (Sulphur Springs), 93
Coward, Peter, 33–34
Crawfish Springs, Tennessee, 31
Creek Indians, 27-28
Cumby, Texas, 46, 69
Cummins, Benjamin, 130
Curtis, James, 113
Curtis, Samuel, 29
Custer, George Armstrong, 51-52, 62

Daingerfield, Texas, 23, 64, 127
Dallas, Texas, 22
Dallas County, Texas, 136
Davis, Edmond J., 17, 77, 103, 136, 160-161
Davis, Jefferson, 86
Democrats and Democratic Party, 11, 16-17, 24, 46, 49, 57-58, 63, 65, 73, 76-80, 86, 89, 94, 98, 102, 105, 113, 144, 154, 160-161
Democratic National Convention of 1860, 24
DeMorse, Charles, 88
Denning, William, 46
Denton, Texas, 22,
Department of Texas, 13
Des Arc, Arkansas, 29
Desperadoes, 55-56, 58, 65-66, 69-70, 80, 84, 96-97, 113, 124, 127, 134, 139, 145-146, 148-149, 155, 160-161 (and see guerrillas; raiders; outlaws; renegades)
Devil's Triangle, 1, 7
Dickson, John, 94
Dixie (also see South), 15, 37, 49, 55, 132, 161

Dixon, Simpson "Simp," 55, 74
Dohoney, E. L., 11
Douglas, Stephen A., 24
Dustman, Norman, 141
Duty, John "Pomp," 16, 55. 69, 73-74, 84, 90, 97, 111
Dyer, Charles, 84-85
Dysentery (in prisoner-of-war camps), 33

Easley, Joe M., 79-82
East Texas, 12-13, 17-18, 22-23, 40, 58, 64, 77-78, 104, 116, 118, 125, 142
Economic hardships, in 1865, 14-15
El Rancho Hotel (Sulphur Springs), 93
Election of 1860, 25
Ellis County, Texas, 22, 53, 64, 69, 106, 122, 135-136, 140-141
Ellis, William, 75, 120, 130
Emancipation Proclamation, 13, 39, 48
Emmitt, Thomas, 16, 69, 97, 125, 127-128
Empire for Slavery, 62
England, 142
English Brothers (George and Jack), 68, 90, 92, 97
English, George "Indian Bill," 16, 47, 55, 69-71, 73-74, 83-84, 96, 97, 106-108, 122, 139
English, Jack, 68, 105
Enloe, Texas, 46
Europe, 15
Evans, I. D., 144
Everheart, Bill, 155-156
Everheart, Jerry, 152, 155-156
Ewing, William M., 11
Extortion, 145

Fannin County, Texas, 11, 22, 40, 44-45, 59, 64, 67, 83, 95, 139, 155
Farrar, Henry, 16, 55, 90-91, 100, 105-106, 111, 115, 128
Farrow (or Farrar), Charley, 40, 93, 128
Favirs, Charles, 97
Fifth Military District, 72, 76, 160
First Frontier District (of Texas), 57
Flakes Daily Bulletin, 85, 88
Flanagan, James W., 77
Flock, first name unknown, 107
Flowers, first name unknown, 80
Forrest, Nathan Bedford, 62
Fort Arbuckle (Indian Territory), 27
Fort Cobb (Indian Territory), 27
Fort Gibson (Indian Territory), 28
Fort Griffin (Texas), 95
Fort Richardson (Texas), 90, 96
Fort Smith (Arkansas), 36, 152, 153
Fort Smith New Era, 153
Fort Sumter (South Carolina), 56
Fort Washita (Indian Territory), 27
Foster, Belle, 132
Foster, William, 134

Fourteenth Amendment (to the
  Constitution), 72
Fowler, Henry, 114
Fowler, J. H., 105
Frame, J. M., 120
France, first name unknown, 130
Franklin, Battle of, 43, 137
Franklin County, Texas, 21, 46
Franklin, Daniel, 130
Fredericksburg, battle of, 95
Freedmen, 38, 40-41, 43, 45, 56, 58-59,
  62, 65, 67, 75-76, 79-80, 82, 84-85,
  103, 105, 107, 112-114, 121-122,
  126, 128, 130, 135, 139, 141, 143,
  155, 159
Freedmen's Bureau, 14-15, 43, 53-55, 58-
  62, 65-69 71, 74, 76-77, 79, 83-87,
  102-103, 109, 112, 114, 129, 144
Freedmen's Colony, 140
Freedpeople, 14-16, 40, 45, 52-53, 57-58,
  66-69, 71, 75-77, 80, 86, 116, 132,
  140, 142-143 (also see freedmen,
  freedwomen, African Americans,
  Negroes, blacks)
Freedwomen, 67, 80, 129-130,143
Freestone County, Texas, 16, 62, 161
Freestone County, Texas, and terrorist
  groups, 16
Frontier Rangers, 36-37

Gainesville, Texas, 22, 40
Galbraith, Sam G., 11
Galveston Daily News, 39
Galveston, Texas, 13-14, 43, 50-51, 77
Gambier, Ohio, 136
Gano's Brigade, 137
General Order No. 15, 113
General Order No. 40, 76
Gettysburg, battle of, 95
Gibson, C. G., 159
Gillentine, first name unknown, 158
Gilliam, Billy, 159
Gillian, William, 141
Gilmer Road, 127
Gilmer, Texas, 17, 126-127
Gipson, William, 28
Georgia, 33, 132
Goode, Benjamin, 155
Gordon, C. G., 128-129, 144
Graham, Finley, 108, 110-111, 116
Graham, Robert B., 108
Granger, Gordon, 13-14, 39, 43, 50-51
Grant, Ulysses S., 12, 96
Gray, W. B., 11
Gray Rock Dragoons, 26
Gray Rock, Texas, 20, 26, 70, 106, 120,
  124-125, 151, 154
Gray Rock, Texas, Cemetery, 20, 154
Grayson County, Texas, 11, 26-27, 39, 64-
  65, 69, 95-96, 108, 139, 155,159

Great Hanging (in Gainesville, Texas), 40
Great Raft (of the Red River), 19
Green, Jim, 70
Greenville, Texas, 46, 108, 110-111
Greenville Guards, 108
Grey, Edward, 91-92
Griffin, Charles, 73
Griffith, Barbara Riddlesperger, 36
Griffith, Benjamin, 16, 35-38, 47, 55, 62,
  67-68, 84-85
Griffith, John, 36
Griffith, Samuel A., 36
Grimes, Charles "Charlie," 79-80, 93
Grissom, Bill, 40, 93
Grissom, D., 40, 93, 97
Grissom, H. B., 158
Grissom, Jack, 91
Grissom, James, 97
Guerrillas, 7, 16-17, 37-39, 55, 65-66, 69-
  70, 73-75, 79, 81, 85, 87, 95-96, 100-
  101, 104-105, 108, 110-111, 116,
  119, 121-123, 126, 135, 141, 145,
  160 (also see desperadoes; renegades;
  outlaws)
Guerrilla war, 16-17
Guest, Elisha, 16, 40, 46, 54-56, 62, 64-67,
  70-71, 74, 83-84, 90, 94, 97, 111,
  114-115, 122, 139

Haiti, 77
Hamilton, Andrew Jackson, 49-51, 53, 56,
  77-78, 160
Hamilton, Morgan C., 77
Hancock, Winfield Scott, 76
Hardegree, first name unknown, 130
Hardin, John Wesley, 40-41, 131
Harper, Dick, 74
Harris, B., 108-111
Harris, Thomas, 111
Harrison County, Texas, 64, 84
Hart, Hardin, 11, 43-44, 108, 110
Hatcher, Ben, 152, 159
Hayes, first name unknown, 155-156
Heath, E. M., 135-137, 143, 152, 157
Heelstring, Texas, 106, 140
Heffer, Parson, 128
Hell, 17, 95, 127, 131
Hempstead, Texas, 51
Henderson County, Texas, 23, 136
Henderson, John, 55, 84
Hendricks, Jackson, 130
Henry County, Georgia, 132
Hicks, first name unknown, 130
Higgs, A. F., 34
Hill County, Texas, 64, 69, 106, 120, 122,
  131, 135, 137, 146-147, 154, 161
Hill, John P., 27
Hillsboro, 120, 135
Hobbs Thicket, 46
Hoffman, William, 34

Honey Grove, Texas, 22, 67, 155
Hood, John Bell, 43
Hood's Texas Brigade, 137
Hopkins County, Texas, 11, 22, 44-45, 56, 64-66, 69-70, 74, 79-84, 87-90,93-95, 98, 103, 105-106, 114, 111, 115, 117, 121-123, 129, 131, 135, 139, 141
Horton, H., 125
House of Representatives, of the United States, 49
Houston, Lum, 40, 93, 97
Houston, Sam, 24-26, 56-57, 136
Houston, Texas, 51, 97
Howard, Oliver Otis, 53
Howell, Alfred, 46
Hoyl, Colonel, 143
Hunnicutt, M. P., 149
Hunt County, Texas, 11, 42-43, 45, 64, 79, 83, 95, 108, 122, 139146, 155, 158
Hurdle, A. J., 64

Illinois, 24, 32-33, 60, 137, 146
Immel, Edgar, 158
Independent Rangers, 36
Indian Frontier (of Texas), 14, 84
Indian Nations, 57, 155
Indian Territory, 26-28, 43, 137
Indians, 18, 21, 27-28
Iuka, Mississippi, 43

Jackson County, Alabama, 19
Jackson, Everett, 81
Jacksonville, Illinois, 60
James, Minerva, 8
Jefferson, Texas, 17, 22, 65, 67-68, 89-90, 112-114,118, 121-122, 124, 133
Jefferson Times (Texas), 133
Jernigan, Curtis, 45-46
Jernigan's Thicket, 45
Johnson, Andrew, 15, 49-50, 52, 72, 76, 86, 105
Johnson County, Texas, 9, 123, 132 135-137, 141-143, 147, 157-159
Johnson, Dick, 55, 74
Johnson, Joshua F., 26
Johnson, W. H., 11
Jones, Cornelius, 120
Jones, Henry, 11
Jonesboro, Texas, 139
Jordan Saline (Texas), 86-87, 138
Juneteenth, 13

Kansas, 27-28, 106
Kaufman County, Texas, 23, 64, 136
Kelley, John, 67-68
Kentucky, 24, 29-30, 32
Kentucky-Town, Texas, 155
Kenyon College, 136
Kinchin, Lum, 107
King, Ben, 140

Kirby, Matthew "Dummy," 47, 67, 123, 131, 134-135
Kirby-Smith, Edmund, 39, 57
Kirkman, Joel, 60
Kirkman, William, 60-62, 68, 114-115
Knights of the Golden Circle, 62
Knights of the Rising Sun (terrorist group)16, 63, 112-113
Knights of the White Camellia (terrorist group), 16, 63
Know-Nothing Party, 136
Kollock, Matthew H., 33-34
Ku Klux Klan and Klansmen (terrorist groups), 7, 16, 55, 62-65, 67, 69, 71, 73-74, 80-81, 90, 94, 97-99, 103, 105, 111-113, 116-118, 122, 127,156, 158
Ku Klux Klan Clubs, 98, 116-117
Ku Klux Rangers (terrorist group), 16, 63-64

Ladonia, Texas, 155
Lafayette County, Georgia, 132
Lamar County, Texas, 11, 30, 45-46, 52, 55, 58, 64, 66, 71, 74, 83, 87, 94, 102-103, 105, 129-130, 139, 155
Larenburg, Lieutenant, 99
Latimer, Albert H., 59, 66
Lauderdale County, Mississippi, 36
Lee, Charles, 102
Lee, Daniel, 42
Lee, Polly Davis, 42
Lee, Melinda, 43
Lee, Robert E., 12
Lee, Robert Jehu "Bob," war crimes of, 43; 7, 16, 18, 40-48, 50-51, 54-55, 62, 65, 71, 74, 78, 83, 87-90, 92, 94-98, 100, 102, 1-4-106, 108, 111, 116, 122-124, 130,139, 144, 146, 154, 156-157, 160
Lee, William, 43
Leonard, Texas, 45-46
Limestone County, Alabama, 46
Limestone County, Texas, and terrorist groups, 16; 62, 161
Lincoln, Abraham, 13, 15, 24-25, 39, 48-51, 56
Linden, Arkansas, 36
Line Ferry, 132, 134
Little, John 138
Lockhart, James, 97
Lollar, L. A., 11
Longley, "Wild Bill," 67
Lost Cause (of the Confederacy), and outlaw gangs/guerrillas, 16; 7, 37, 40, 52, 55, 69, 79, 102, 114, 124, 132, 140, 142
Loudon, Tennessee, 29
Louisiana, 17, 34, 37-38, 51, 57, 72-73, 77, 103, 106, 125-126, 142. 159
Louisville, Kentucky, 32

Lower South, 24-25
Loyal League (also see Union League), 51, 57
Loyal Union Association, 51

McCain, first name unknown, 127
McClanahan, John P., 33-34
McCulloch, Ben, 29
McIntosh, James, 28-29
McKinney, Collin, 56
McKinney Messenger (Texas), 83
McKinney, Texas, 83
Mack, H. C., 123
Madison County, Texas, 161
Malloy, Adam G., 71, 121
"Man Eater" (Bob Lee), 156-157
Mansfield, Texas, 78
Marion County, Texas, 64-65, 89, 112-113, 120-121
"Marshall Boys," 83
Marshall, John, Sr., 16, 111, 124, 130
Marshall Republican (Texas), 88
Marshall, Texas, 14, 17, 22-23, 65, 84, 86, 88-89, 96, 118, 125
Maryland, 24, 34, 95
"Massacre of the Saline," 37
Matthews, "Doc," 30
Maxey, Rice, 11
Maximilian (Emperor of Mexico), 14
Mayfield family, the, 142
Measles, 33
Memphis, Tennessee, 43
Merideth, Stephen, 141
Methodist Episcopal Church (North), 22
Mexican-American War, 13
Mexico, 13-15, 49, 94, 103, 126
Milford, Texas, 22
Miller County, Arkansas, 132
Miller, John, 92
Milliken, Samuel, 147-149, 154
Mills, Roger Q., 63
Mills, Stephen, 149
Miner, E. W., 11
Mississippi, 19, 25, 29, 36, 43
Mississippi River, 25, 36, 43
Missionary Ridge, Battle of, 32-33
Missouri, 13, 29, 34, 36, 130
Monroe County, Mississippi, 19
Moore, Robert, 148-149, 152
Moore, W. R., 86
Mountain Boomers, 37
Mount Pleasant, Texas, 47, 68-71, 97, 124, 126
Mount Vernon, Ohio, 136, 146
Mount Vernon, Texas, 23, 47
Murfreesboro, Battle of, 29-30
Musgrove, Edward, 117
Mustang Thicket, 46
Myers brothers (David and John), 152
Myers, David, 149
Myers, John, 149
Mystic Red, 22

Nashville, battle of, 43, 137
Nashville Pike (Tennessee), 30
Nashville, Tennessee, 43, 137
Navarro County, Texas, 23, 64, 69, 75-76, 121, 131, 141, 143, 146
Navasota, Texas, 51
Negro domination, 77
Negroes, 52, 56, 59, 71, 77, 84, 131; (also see freedmen, freedpeople, freedwomen, blacks, African Americans)
Nelson, C. S., 139
Nelson, John, 94
Newcomb, James, 77
New Deal Era, 162
New England, 77
New Orleans, Louisiana, 25, 50-51, 62, 72-73, 77, 103
New Orleans Tribune (Louisiana), 62, 77
New Rebellion, 58, 87-88, 97, 139
New York Times (New York), 139-140
New York, 13, 49, 58, 77, 139-140
"Nigger killers," 56, 127
Norman, J. F., 32-33
North, the, and Northerners, 22-24, 27, 49, 51, 53
North Carolina, 30
North Texans, 27
North Texas Frontier, 27
Northeast Texas, 7, 9, 11, 13, 18, 20, 22-23, 27, 35, 39-42, 45, 47, 51-52, 55, 59-60, 64-73, 76-77, 79, 86, 88-90, 92, 95-97, 100, 104-106, 108, 111, 115, 188, 135-136, 139, 152, 154, 157, 159-160
Northern conspiracy, 22
Northern Division of Texas (during the Civil War), 27
Norton, Anthony Banning, 17, 136-138, 146-149, 152, 154, 159

Oakwood Cemetery (Jefferson, Texas), 133
Ohio, 95, 136, 146
Old Scratch, 148
Old South, 16, 21
Opothleyhola (Creek Indian leader), 27-28
Oquilla Creek, 131, 146
Orr, Belle Foster, 134
Orr, Thomas, 121, 131-132, 134-135, 154
Orr, William, 132
Outlaws (and outlaw gangs) 11, 15-16, 18, 71, 76, 85, 87, 98, 106, 122, 140, 144-145 (also see desperadoes; guerrillas; renegades; raiders)

"Pale Faces," (terrorist organization), 63
Pandemonium, 17, 60, 67
Panola County, Texas, 59

Paris, Texas, 11, 23, 58, 66, 71, 74, 87-88, 103, 130, 139
Paris Vindicator (Texas), 88
Paschal County, Texas, 127
Pateet, first name unknown, 141
Patterson, Bernard, 30, 55
Patterson, James, 55
Peacock, Louis, 105, 157
Pea Ridge, battle of, 29, 36, 43
Pease, Elisha M., 56-57, 73, 77, 137-138, 141, 144, 147, 152
Pease, Walter B., 96-97, 106, 108, 110-111, 115-118, 120, 123-126, 128-130, 144
Pearson, Sergeant, 70
Peculiar Institution (slavery), 24
Peninsular Campaign (Civil War), 95
Penn, Bill, 154-156
Pennell, Texas, 94
Pennsylvania, 95
Peoria, Texas, 131, 146
Perry County, Arkansas, 36-37
Perryville, battle of, 29
Petty, Mary Jane, 33
Pierce, Lee, 64
Pilot Grove, Texas, 95-96, 99, 101, 104-105, 156-157
Pilot Point, Texas, 22
Pine Bluffs, Texas, 19
Pine and Palm (newspaper), 77
Plains Indians, 18, 118
Planters, 14
Pneumonia (in prisoner-of-war camps), 33
Poindexter, Ned, 70
Point Lookout, Maryland, 34
Popular Sovereignty, 24
Porter, Julia, 120, 122, 129
Potts, Mrs. L. E., 52, 54-55
Powell, John W., 142-143, 145, 149-150
Presidential Reconstruction, 15, 50
Prisoner-of-War camps, 33-34, 137, 146
Pulaski, Tennessee, 62
Purdom, Major, 143

Quahadi Comanches, 95
Quitman, Texas, 17, 23, 65, 120

Raiders, 7, 67, 91, 93-94, 101, 104. 109, 111, 114, 120
Rainey, 74
Rames, Lee, 47, 67, 74, 97
Rames, Seth, 47, 74, 97, 121
Rand, Charles, 65, 71, 84-86, 144
Panola County, Texas, 64,
Reconstruction, 7, 15, 17, 50, 72, 86
Reconstruction, as continuation of the Civil War, 7, 72
Reconstruction Acts, 72
Red Hand, the (terrorist group), 16, 63
Red River, 19, 27, 45-46, 55, 67-69

Red River County, Texas, 11, 39, 54, 59, 64-66, 69, 73-74, 83-85, 102, 105, 122, 139, 155
Red River District (of Texas), 19
Redeemers, 18, 78, 161
Renegades, 59, 80-82, 86, 97, 99, 102, 105-107, 114-116, 126-128, 135, 144, 146, 160 (also see guerrillas; desperadoes; raiders; outlaws)
Republic of Texas, 19-20
Republicans (and Republican Party) 23-25, 48-50, 53, 56, 65, 72-73, 77-78, 80-81, 87-89, 98, 102, 105, 112, 125, 136, 144, 160-161
Reynolds, C. A., 33
Reynolds, Elijah "Lige," 103-104
Reynolds, J. J., 88-90, 95-98, 103-104, 113, 118-119, 144
Richland Creek, 140
Richmond, Arkansas, 38
Richmond, Kentucky, 29
Riley, Gordon, 69
Ripley Creek, 107
Rio Grande, 103
Roberts, Oran M., 26
Robin Hood, 68
Robinson, Lieutenant, 101
Rock Creek, 91
Rock Island Barracks Prison (Illinois), 32-33
Rockford, Illinois, 60
Roger's Shoeshop (Alvarado, Texas), 149
Rollins, L. R., 60, 67
Roosevelt, Franklin D., 162
Round Mountain (battle of in Indian Territory), 27
Rosecrans, William, 30
Ruby, George T., 77-78
Runnels, Hardin R., 38
Rusk, Texas, 23

Sabine County, Arkansas, 37
Sabine River, 51, 119, 122-123
Salmon, James, 121
San Antonio, Texas, 14, 103
Sanders Creek, 102, 122
Sands, J. H., 101-102, 106
Sartin, Amanda, 65
Sartin, Zara, 65
Schreyer, Gustavus, 101, 106, 120, 125-126, 144
Scott, H. E., 130
Scurry, 33
Seawall, first name unknown, 128
Sebastian County, Arkansas, 36
Secession, 25-26, 38, 57
Secession Convention of Texas, 56
Second Arkansas Mounted Rifles, 28
Second Civil War, 47, 83, 88, 111, 116, 140, 160 (also see War of

Reconstruction; New Rebellion)
Sevierville, Tennessee, 32
Sharecroppers, 67, 84, 122, 145 (also see sharecropping)
Sharecropping, and poverty, 16; 54, 57-58, 64
Sheridan, Philip, 17, 72-73, 76, 78, 95
Sherman, Texas, 27, 99
Shreveport, Louisiana, 34, 125-126, 159
Simpson, Phillip, 56,
Sinclair, William H., 67
Sixth Cavalry Regiment, 68
Slave Codes, 16, 22
Slave patrols, 22-23
Slave rebellion, 22
Slavery, 7, 15, 17, 22-25, 37, 52, 62
Slavery controversy, 22
Slaves, 22-23 (also see bondsmen; chattels)
Slow Civil War, 161
Smallpox, 33
Smith County, Texas, 12, 22, 140
Smith, Dick, 139
Smith, George W., 113, 118
Smith, J. F., 32,
Smith, Joseph, 11
Sneed, H. H., 152
Snow Hill, Texas, 69-70
South, the, 15-18, 21, 23-25, 49, 62, 152-153, 161-162
South Carolina, 24-25, 56
Southern Aristocracy, and President Andrew Johnson, 15
Southern Democrats, 24
Southern Rangers, 36
Southerners, white, 15, 19, 21, 24-26, 35, 72, 77
Spencer, Herman, 80
Springhill, Texas, 120, 140
Starr family, 81-82
Starr, Luke, 81-82
Starr, "Mrs.," 81-82
Starr, Samuel Henry, 68-71, 96, 144
Steelhammar, Captain, 138
Stephens, Abb, 97
Stokes, C. W., 120, 130
Stone, Kate, 13
Stricken, Charles, 141
String fellow, James W., 106
Sulphur Fork, of the Red River, 38, 45-46, 67-69, 82
Sulphur River, 38, 45-46, 67-69, 82, 89-90, 132
Sulphur Springs, Texas, 23, 32, 45, 58, 65-66, 69, 79-80, 82-84, 91-9-101, 103, 106, 108, 110, 115-116, 118-120, 122, 124, 125, 127-130, 141, 144
"Swamp Fox of the Sulphur River" (Cullen Montgomery Baker), 47

Tarrant, Texas (also called Old Tarrant), 90, 106
Taylor, Colonel, 89
Taylor, R. H., 11
Taylor, William "Bill," 56
Ten Percent Plan, 15, 48-49
Tennessee, 13, 16, 22, 35, 29-31, 33, 35, 43, 49, 62, 78, 86, 137
Terror, 65-66, 71, 130
Terrorists and terrorist groups, 11, 16-17, 18, 39, 54-55, 62-67, 70, 73-74, 78, 83-85, 87, 96-97, 105, 113-114, 117, 119, 144, 156, 159-161
Test Oath of 1862, 73
Teutonic Brotherhood (terrorist organizations), 39
Texarkana, Texas, 132
Texas Constitutional Convention of 1868-1869, 78
Texas Homestead Law (barred blacks), 57
Texas House of Representatives, 160
Texas: Information for Emigrants, 123
Texas Legislature, 136
Texas Militia, 26
Texas Rangers, 161
Texas Senate, 49, 57, 78, 160
Texas State Police, 161
Texas Supreme Court, 26, 78
Texas Troubles, 123
Thickets, 38, 45
Thirteenth Amendment, of the U. S. Constitution, 15, 50, 53
Thomas, Buck, 80
Thompson, Josiah, 9-10, 56, 65, 97, 135, 138, 141-142, 145-146, 148-150, 152-153, 157-158
Throckmorton, James Webb, 56-57, 65, 73, 76
Tidwell Thicket, 46
Titus, Albert E., 62
Titus County Guards, 26
Titus County, Texas, 11, 21-23, 25-27, 34-35, 38-39, 45-47, 59, 62, 64, 66, 69-71, 74, 83-84, 92, 106, 108, 124, 139, 144, 148, 152, 159
Tolman, Thomas, 90-101, 104, 116, 118, 122-123, 126-129, 131, 144, 148
Tombigbee River, 19
Topeka, Kansas, 106
Traitors, 50
Trans-Mississippi, 137
Traylor, Henry, 97
Trelease, Allen, 62
Trinity River, 118, 120
Tuck, June, 47
Tuck, P. A., 82
Tulsa, Oklahoma, 27
Tyler, Texas, 12-14, 17, 22, 65

Union, the, 24-26, 50
Union Army, 30
Union League, 51, 57, 77, 80, 112 (also see Loyal League)
Union soldiers, 16
Unionist Convention in Northeast Texas, 1865, 11
Unionists (and Unionism), 10-11, 13-14, 16-18, 21, 24-26, 40, 46, 49-52, 55-58, 62-67, 69, 71, 73-77, 79-82, 86-89, 98, 102-106, 108, 112, 117, 131-132, 136, 139, 146, 156, 158, 160
United States Army, 158
Union soldiers, 107
Union troops, 103
United States Colored Infantry, 33
United States Constitution, 15
United States troops, 27
Uphur County, Texas, 64, 83-84, 127
Upper South, 24

Vaden, John, 91-94, 103-104
Vagrancy Code, 58
Van Buren, Arkansas, 28
Vandiver, A. G., 120, 130
Van Dorn, Earl, 29
Van Horne, William, 108-110, 126, 128-129
Van Zandt County, Texas, 22, 64, 69, 80, 87, 92, 136, 138-139, 146
Verdigris River (Indian Territory), 28
Vernou, Charles, 58, 88, 96, 99-101, 106
Victress, the (steamboat), 19-20
Virginia, 12, 95

Waco, Texas, 106, 145, 152, 159
Waco Semi-Weekly Register (Texas), 145
Walker County, Texas, 161
Walker, Dick, 114
War of Reconstruction, 18, 40, 65, 71, 87, 95, 160 (also see New Rebellion; Second Civil War)
Washington, D.C., 48-49, 105
Waxahachie, Texas, 22, 140-141, 152-153
Wayne County, New York, 13
Waxahachie Argus (Texas), 153
Weakly County, Tennessee, 35
Weatherford, Texas, 159
Weaver, Charlie, 40, 93, 97
Weaver, Horatio, 40, 65
Weaver, Joseph, 82, 121
Weaver, Ralph, 40
Weaver, Rash, 93, 97
West, the, 24
West Point Military Academy, 13
West Texas, 18, 84, 90
West Texas Indian frontier, 90
Weston, William, 97
Wheeler, Joseph, 31

Whig Party, 136
White Brotherhood (terrorist organization), 62
White Caps (terrorist organization), 62
White Oak Creek, 44-46, 66, 69, 97, 128
White Rock, Texas, 155
White supremacy, 63, 161
Wilcox, Jeremiah, 68
Wildcat Thicket, 42, 45-46, 105, 156-157
Wiles Plantation, 126-127
Wiley, Moses, 68
Wilkinson, Thomas, 97
Williams, Peter, 140-141
Willis, Samuel, 38
Wilson's Creek, battle of, 13, 36
Wings, first name unknown, 108-109, 111, 119, 122-123
Winnsboro, Texas, 120
Winters, Joe, 97
Withers, Will, 123, 128
Wood County, Texas, 22, 64, 122, 146
Wortham, Colonel, 98
Wortham, William "Billy," 97-98
Wright, Anderson, 113
Wright, G. W., 11
Wright, M. H., 11
Wright, T. G.,

Yankees, 14, 16, 30, 33, 43, 45, 58, 62-63, 70-71, 84, 91, 101, 112-113, 120, 127
Yellow Fever, 68
Yeoman farmers, 14, 21, 23, 42, 84
Young, Thomas, 36
Young, William C., 27-28

www.ingramcontent.com/pod-product-compliance
Lightning Source LLC
Chambersburg PA
CBHW030517080526
44586CB00011B/223